Deckerson Thomas is a chartered public finance accountant and a fourth-generation descendant of slavery, born in the West African state of Sierra Leone.

Deckerson's direct lineage to slavery and his quest to establish its profound and lasting emotional and psychological effects motivated him to research and produce this pioneering and epic historical and contemporary account. The arduous journey of Africans from slavery through colonialism and present-day imperialism has never been portrayed so succinctly. He has painstakingly laid out this narrative and brilliantly highlighted the continuum from the dark days of servitude to the present from an African perspective.

To the memory of my dear mother,
Florence Elfrida Thomas

Deckerson Thomas

OR PORTO

Shadow on the Horizon

AUSTIN MACAULEY PUBLISHERS™

LONDON • CAMBRIDGE • NEW YORK • SHARJAH

A CIP catalogue record for this title is available from the British Library.

ISBN 9781528903110 (Paperback)
ISBN 9781528903127 (Hardback)
ISBN 9781528903134 (Kindle e-book)
ISBN 9781528957397 (ePub e-book)

www.austinmacauley.com

First Published (2019)
Austin Macauley Publishers Ltd
25 Canada Square
Canary Wharf
London
E14 5LQ

Table of Contents

Preface

The effect of servitude on Africans is generally trivialised in modern times especially by those who, by sheer fate or fortune, accrued enormous economic and financial gains from activities relating to and involving the trade in and exploitation of Africans.

The continued reinforcement of the pejoratively-discriminative colour coding of Africans, within social and intellectual context, contributes to the general ignorance and apathy towards the latent trauma that slavery and the prolonged subjugation of colonisation have had on Africans.

I was born into a family descended from slavery, in Freetown Sierra Leone, the legendary hotspot for the capture of humans and the staging post for what resulted in the widespread colonisation of a continent.

Whilst growing up in the mountain village of Regent, a historical settlement of liberated slaves in Sierra Leone, I was often referred to as "Krio Boy" like other progenies of liberated slaves. This label seems overtly innocuous but is a significant identification of a group of people perceived as foreign to the country, who were treated with suspicion and guile. That characterisation followed me through to adulthood when the effect became apparent and sometimes perplexing. The Creoles were intrinsically despised by other ethnic groups, who regarded themselves more native to Sierra Leone than the Creoles. This assumption through no fault of theirs was due to complexities that this book will attempt to explore.

Although the Creoles themselves were not entirely cohesive, they however harboured a reciprocal disregard and dislike for the other tribal groups whom they considered uncivilised and with lifestyles they felt were below their own. Civilisation to the Creoles was essentially the practice of Christianity and its antecedent British culture. They often blame the indigenous population for many of the ills in society. There has always been a mutual distrust between the Creoles and other ethnic groups since the formative years of the resettlement of liberated slaves in Freetown, the present capital city of Sierra Leone. Over time, the unavoidable influence of the British helped to promote the rancour between the Creoles and the other tribal groups with whom they shared a common space. The tension became intense and remained so for prolonged periods, especially during the political struggles in the late 1950s, to succeed the departing British colonial autocrats. The Creoles, however, never stood a chance against the overwhelming tide of hostility from the rest of the country but were, however, resolute and learnt to live with their fate. Despite the almost unbridgeable schism that exists amongst the other main ethnic groups, the Creoles remain a common enemy to all.

Regent village was a community built by liberated slaves and their descendants. Their dwellings were designed and constructed to replicate and reflect the architecture and culture of slavers and plantation owners they were familiar with in Europe and the Americas. The Regent settlement was deliberately and strategically located along a valley overshadowed by very steep hills and mountains. The abundance of fresh water and arable land suitable for vegetable gardening and upland farming were alluring essentials to sustain the settlers. The sedate environment and culture of the people hardly changed over the years. The Creoles were conservative and practiced Christianity avidly. The very religion that was used by British colonialists to pacify them during their resistance against domination and exploitation.

During my adolescence, I spent endless hours listening to the views and opinions of my parents which were generally liberal compared with the extreme convictions and ideologies of many others. As time went on, it became clear that despite the hostility shown towards them by other ethnic groups, there was something much stronger that held them precariously together than the superficial differences that threatened their very existence. My parents and their peers spent inordinate hours, often extoling the virtues of notable Creole firebrands for their heroics in confronting the autocracy and atrocities of colonialism. Names like Wallace Johnson, Galba Bright, Coffee Nicol, Malamah Thomas, Ajayi Crowther and many others who carried names bestowed on them by their slave masters. Those were eminent Creoles who in diverse ways made a difference during the harsh days of colonialism. These heroes featured repeatedly in many passionate debates and arguments they had. Their discussions were almost always about their perceptions of how the British usurped their political rights in favour of the other ethnic groups within the country.

As I grew into adulthood, I began to question some of their postulations and moral judgments of especially the male figures within and out of my family circle. I came to realise that although they had strong feelings against the males within the other ethnic groups, they were particularly partial towards the irresistible beauty of women from especially the Mendes, with whom many of the Creoles fathered children. A reciprocation of such overtures by males from other ethnic groups was considered abhorrent by the chauvinism that pervaded the society of the Creoles. Despite their hubris, the Creoles were generally petrified of the Temnes, another ethnic group with which they maintained a relatively tenuous relationship.

Ironically, despite the hardship and suffering inflicted upon them by the British, the Creoles somehow managed to cultivate a rather strange affinity for them. Conversely, they failed abjectly to recognise the many attributes they shared with the other ethnic groups. Rather, with the effluxion of time, they became preoccupied with trivialities and were consumed with envy for the political power the other groups wielded.

The Creoles comprise a relatively small ethnic group peculiar to Sierra Leone. Families are therefore easily traceable. My late mother often introduced us to families close to ours and encouraged us to maintain relationships as best as we could whilst we go through life. However, it was quite noticeable that she hardly struggled to breeze through the genealogy of her family, whenever she felt the need for self-reassurance. She would mention the same names repeatedly and was truly agonising to watch her desperately try to construct a family tree with hardly any root, that, for all intent and purposes, could stretch beyond her own parents and immediate relatives.

My close friends were mainly Temnes, Mendes and a few Konos. Though my associations were genuine and seemingly filial, perhaps instinctively making up for the deficiencies within my own family and community, there were often signs of suspicion and the occasional hostility towards me. Whatever odd feelings were manifested towards me or my peers were nothing like the tension that existed between my mutual friends. Being from the main rival Temne and Mende tribes, they were diametrically opposed to each other. This was a chasm founded on centuries of hate and distrust. A similar and familiar status quo that exists in many other parts of the continent. In some other African states, the relationships between competing tribes is much more incendiary and explosive compared to the passive incubation of hate cleverly disguised by my country folks in Sierra Leone. These near irreconcilable differences between ethnic groups still pervade Africa mostly with adverse consequences. The historical influences and hallmark of slavery and colonisation in all of these debilitating situations, though not obvious to all to fathom, are still potent and destructive.

The complexities of growing up as a "Krio Boy" aroused my curiosity and motivated me to examine the social, cultural and destructive political differences that continue to drive us apart.

Introduction

Or Porto is a narrative relating to the enduring impact of slavery on the West African country of Sierra Leone in particular and as a microcosm of the widespread oppression and exploitation of Africa as a whole. Since the dreadful and appalling years of slavery right through to modern neo-colonialism, a continuum passes us by with hardly a ripple.

Sierra Leone is peculiar within the context of slavery and colonisation in Africa. Its distinctiveness is derived from being the original experimental staging post for the return of *liberated* slaves resulting from the strategic change in the trade of Africans by Europeans. The use of what is now the capital Freetown as a base for the colonial administrative headquarters for West Africa, also adds to its uniqueness and historical importance.

There is a plethora of historical accounts and narratives on especially the Trans-Atlantic trade in Africans, into the horrors of the barbaric and callous servitude of slavery by Europeans.

Disappointingly, most of these accounts are presented by the perpetrators or interested parties to such a hideous crime against the African race. As is now widely reported, an estimated fifteen million Africans were taken from the continent against their will through force and to a large extent, by trickery and deception. The popular but less credible narratives inform those seeking the reality behind this abhorrent act, that Africans were sold over to British and other European slavers by their fellow Africans.

This despicable act widely regarded as a trade carried on for hundreds of years from the fifteenth to the early nineteenth centuries. The estimate of fifteen million Africans captured and transported to various locations in the world might, however, be conservative, and this is based on captured individuals who survived the arduous oceanic journeys to the slave markets and subsequently the plantations. A quarter of Africans taken, perished through inadequate nutrition and the insanitary and inhumane conditions in which they were tethered and transported. The mortal remains of those who failed to make the Trans-Atlantic journey were merely thrown overboard the laden vessels to be consumed by sharks and other carnivorous aquatic creatures.

Africa was severely de-populated by this collective and co-ordinated brutality against the inhabitants of the continent. To contextualise this mass extraction of people demographically, the total number of individuals taken equates to about a third of the present day population of the United Kingdom. This immense loss of human resources has had significant long-term negative socio-economic and political impact on the continent and its people, up to the present.

Conversely, whilst Africa was lamenting this loss, an immeasurable contribution was being made by those who were taken, towards building the infrastructure and developing the economies across Europe and the Americas. Albeit by force, intimidation and coercion. They laboured through interminable physical force with blood, sweat, tears and pitifully without recompense. The price for their indefatigable toil was most often a slow and painful certain death.

Africans taken into the bondage of slavery were subjected to the most horrendous treatment by Europeans known to mankind. The motivation for degrading and the widespread oppression of the African race was primarily economic but became seriously ideological over time. The perceived invincibility of the oppressors inevitably morphed into the concept of white supremacy. The widespread belief by Europeans during those dark days and to a large extent the present, that the colour or complexion of the skin of a person can define or determine their intelligence, capability and prospects, reflects the frailty of the mentality of those promoting such a pernicious ideology.

Seeing how terrified, emaciated and supine Africans became in the hostile environment of servitude, motivated and most certainly led Europeans to develop extreme prejudices against people of that race. Such prejudices had percolated Caucasian societies and cultures and underpin the interaction and engagement with Africans ever since, resulting in the pejorative classification of Africans as *"Black People"*.

Slavery is fundamentally the purported ownership of human beings, acquired through various forms, including pecuniary exchanges for the purpose of exploitation by force, intimidation and coercion for economic outcomes and does not reward or benefit the enslaved.

The notion that members of one race can own people from another race, outrageous though this may seem, is most certainly what gave rise to the concept of the supremacy of Caucasians over Africans. A concept that is based superficially on complexion and skin colour. Ownership of human beings was generally considered to be a right and not illegal within Europe during the years of intensive slave activities. The title of owner undoubtedly empowered Europeans to do whatever they wished to Africans and in accordance with their individual judgement and personal convictions. They, therefore, did whatever they deemed appropriate in their dealings with enslaved Africans, who were mere chattels. Even animals owned by some of the European slave dealers were treated humanely than Africans. Africans were objects found, acquired and transacted in slave markets within Europe generally in the years of this abhorrent activity, just as one would any piece of item with an intrinsic value. Only in this situation, Africans are real human beings.

African servants were ubiquitous in royal courts and homes of the gentry who could afford the cost and maintenance of ownership.

King James VI of British Royal lineage, whose sexual preference was thought to be partial to men, had African boys in his royal household to satisfy his desires and to entertain his loyal friends. Strangely, on his nuptial to Anne of Denmark, the fourteen-year-old daughter of the Protestant King Frederick II, in Oslo in November 1589, James VI took with him four young Negros (Africans) who he ordered to dance naked in the snow ahead of his royal carriage. This depraved act was supposed to impress his young bride and to demonstrate his prowess and virility. The unfortunate Negros, as Africans were widely termed, contracted pneumonia from that cruel exposure and subsequently died.

In 1665, Samuel Pepys, an English naval administrator and Member of the British Parliament renowned for his diary entries during that time, visited the lavish home of Sir Robert Vyner, Lord Mayor of London to borrow money for and on behalf of King Charles II. Pepys recorded that Sir Robert Vyner had shown him the body of an African boy who had worked as a servant in his elaborate mansion and was said to have contracted, suffered and died from tuberculosis. The corpse of the boy was ordered to be dried in an oven and the dried remains kept in a box, which would be exhibited to visitors for entertainment and a sign of his affluence and power.

One of the most degrading acts against Africans was the frequently held "African and Asian Shows in Europe". These shows were perverse and organised to crudely display African sexuality and physical peculiarities. African men and women in slavery were forced to parade naked in public during those organised human fairs. In the 1800s, naked Africans were extra entertainments common in cabarets and theatres in France and in England. Naked slave men were popular specimens used for painting by students in art academies, to mention but a few of some of the depravities meted out to Africans in servitude within Europe during that time.

Human zoos and Negro villages became popular across Europe displaying Africans to the public. Africans were put in restricted enclosures, whipped and ordered to perform tricks and quite often requiring the African slave women to strip and bear their nakedness to satisfy European curiosities about African physical characteristics. The object of these sideshows was to portray Africans as primitive, stunted, underdeveloped and abnormal.

An African child in a human zoo

This image depicts an African child in a human zoo as a special attraction to crowds of Europeans and being fed over the fence like an animal.

These shows attracted millions of visitors across Europe and went on well into the 1900s manifested by the following poster advertising a human zoo in Germany in 1928.

Europeans who, ironically, came somehow close to regarding Africans as humans, for example:

Bosman van Nyendael, a Dutch East India Company sailor who visited Africa, characterised Negros (Africans) as *"crafty, villainous, fraudulent, very seldom to be trusted and cheating"*. Africans (Negros), by his perception, *"have no integrity, no fidelity, are born and bred villains, have degenerate vices, sloths, idleness, so incredibly careless, stupid, they feast and are merry, dance, drink and they feast at graves. Africans (Negros) are insensible of grief and necessity, they sing till they die and dance into their graves"*. Such warped thinking supported the irrational ideology of white supremacy that continues to oxygenate and promote the practice of prejudice towards Africans worldwide.

The irony of the behaviour of this perceived supremely enlightened and pristine Caucasian race, is their inability to recognise and fathom the extent of ignorance that pervaded their own societies. Europeans during those days, who professed to be educated with an appetite for further edification, seized upon the acceptable widespread lawless behaviour towards Africans and undertook various scientific, brutal and inhumane experiments purported to be researches on Africans who were bought or acquired by various other means from slave markets and farms.

Africans who were acquired from slave markets for the purposes of scientific studies were regarded as mere specimens. They were murdered and dissected in order to explore conjectured anatomical differences peculiar to Africans which were used to support their innate belief that Africans were indeed sub humans. These experiments were carried out by both Europeans and Americans. Between 1771 and 1837 for example, the Dutch carried out extensive experiments on African slaves and accumulated huge collections of body parts and specimens for future observations. Such unethical practices carried on until well into the 21st century. These studies were to determine whether Africans possess the mental capacity and ability to execute rudimentary activities with dexterity supposedly akin to Europeans.

Some of the weird conclusions of these depraved European scientists included that Africans are generally incapable of carrying out the simplest of mental tasks without supervision from their superior white masters. Robert Parks in his essay in 1918 regarding the differences in temperament between Europeans and Africans, postulated:

'*The Anglo-Saxon was a pioneer and a frontiersman, while the Negro is an artist, loving life for its own sake. His metier is expression rather than action. He is so to speak, the lady among the races*'. This in many ways sums up the hubris and bigotry that underpin racial prejudice even to the present day.

By the late thirteen hundred up to the early fourteen hundred, word had gone out to Europeans through Arab traders that there was a potential reservoir of gold along the west coasts of Africa. European interest was cultivated following the apparent ostentatious display of this precious metal by King Mansa Musa of Mali, during his Muslim pilgrimage to Mecca around 1325. The Portuguese who already had trading contacts with North African Arab traders immediately embarked on several sporadic exploratory voyages to establish trade contacts within present day Senegal and Guinea in pursuit of gold.

European interest in slavery was kindled by the physique, strength and energy Africans displayed in conducting commercial, agricultural and social activities within their communities. With this in mind and the thought of making enormous economic gains from producing cheap agricultural commodities like sugar, tobacco and cotton, Europeans developed cunning plans to lure Africans away from the continent for exploitation into what culminated in the greatest cruelty to humanity mankind has ever witnessed.

Sierra Leone became a vital hub for slavery because of its natural harbour, and fresh water was easily available for replenishing slave merchant vessels. Interestingly, although slave trading by Portuguese mariners had been active since the early fourteen hundred, it turned out that Sierra Leone was officially founded by the middle of the century in 1462 by a Portuguese called Pedro da Cintra. The name Sierra Leone emanated from the Portuguese "Sierra Lyoa". Pedro da Cintra was fascinated by the imposing contour and patterns of the chain of mountains along the Freetown peninsular, which conspicuously dominates the skyline when approached by sea. His overwhelming delight and vivid imagination led him to describe the mountains "Sierra Lyoa" meaning "Lion Mountains". Freetown which is presently the capital of the country, was generally regarded as Sierra Leone at the time, as the hinterland remained unexplored by Europeans for a considerable period of time. However, the stage was inadvertently set for the eventual domination of the people by Europeans mainly through the use of force.

Kidnappings of Africans by Portuguese along the west coast intensified with regular cruises along the Freetown estuary. With time, kidnapping proved to be an inefficient method of acquiring significant numbers of individuals for shipment to Europe and subsequently across the Atlantic to the Americas. Portuguese sea captains had to wait for months at a time to get a full cargo of Africans. Something had to change, and decisions were made to reduce the long uneconomic wastage of time. Direct contact with the Africans emerged as a viable alternative with agencies established to facilitate the removal and transportation of captured individuals, through subterfuge. Making such direct contacts with the Africans had its associated risks resulting from potential hostility. Especially when the loss of so many of their kin is eventually linked or ascribed to activities by the impostors.

Africans were only used to losing people to Arab raiders whenever they engaged in hostilities and skirmishes, but for people to disappear with such regularity and without trace, made them very edgy and concerned. Wild animal attacks were commonplace but sporadic. On occasions of animal attacks, trackers will always hunt down culprit animals such as lions and leopards and kill them to prevent a repeat of the menace.

Unsurprisingly, the first Portuguese sailors who braved the open to engage with the Africans created uncontrollable consternation amongst the people and met their swift demise. Although tension had already been created by the numerous and increasing disappearances of their kin, the main cause of their startle and ultimate frenzy was the strangeness of the pale and febrile physical characteristics of the Portuguese. Their impromptu and surprised appearance within the community of Africans was regarded as hostile. The Portuguese were set upon spontaneously through fear and obvious suspicion. Portuguese mariners were, however, unfazed by the ferocious attacks against their pioneering colleagues and proceeded to make further cautious and calculated approaches, bearing simple gifts of copper ware, mirrors and cotton fabrics.

It was, however, believed that during subsequent seemingly submissive and tactful approaches, the vulnerable Portuguese sailors, with their hands held aloft, would shout, "somos do Porto e significa que nenhum dano." (We are from Porto and we mean no harm.) "Somos do Porto," (We are from Porto) they cried repeatedly in fear that they would face a similar fate to that of their predecessors. During the consternation occasioned by their strange spectacle, all the Africans could hear and easily register from the bewildering plea of the Portuguese, was the phonic, Porto…Porto…Porto.

The Portuguese went on to dominate the trade in West Africans for a prolonged period of time. Their originally preferred method of kidnapping and abductions which was deemed to be slow, time consuming and inefficient was gradually abandoned.

Later, during the fourteen hundred, the British also developed an interest in prospecting for gold and extracting Africans from along the west coast. The British were however in no mood to adopt the modus operandi of the Portuguese. With the knowledge that the Africans were extremely strong and pugnacious, the British were armed with gun powder and Muskets during their voyages. Ironically, the initial skirmishes they had along the west coast were to engage and dislodge the Portuguese from along the Freetown peninsular from where they were launching kidnapping raids.

The immense force exerted by British slavers against the Portuguese was violent and unexpected. This resulted in the displacement of the Portuguese from the west coast of Africa. Despite several attempts by the Portuguese to recover their foothold along the rich western coast, repeated failure against the British relegated them further south of the continent.

The British established themselves along the Freetown peninsular and the nearby sparsely-inhabited islands. This dramatic change in the control of the coastal regions facilitated a rapid increase in the number of Africans that were to be taken away into servitude.

The colonisation of Sierra Leone started in about 1791 when the commercial trade in Africans was becoming a burden on the conscience of European slavers and benefactors. Colonisation is a process of subjugating a set of people; in this case, indigenous Africans by the British and other Europeans through force of arms. Colonisation thwarts all forms of evolutionary development, economic initiatives, creativity and social progress of those colonised. It is not a benevolent undertaking and is characterised by extreme violence, exploitation and paternalism. The colony was governed to be totally dependent on Britain. Sierra Leone remained under British colonial rule for one hundred and seventy years. This was in addition to approximately four hundred and twenty years of violent slave raids within the territory by both Britain and Portugal.

The history of Sierra Leone like many other African countries during the slave trade and subsequent colonial domination has been oral and largely undocumented from an African perspective. Africans in captivity were denied any form of education. European history and culture dominated the curriculum wherever any semblance of heavily-controlled formal education existed.

Sierra Leone to a great extent represents the full circle of events from the initial extraction of unsuspecting individuals into bondage and the return of their *liberated* surviving descendants back to Africa.

The impact of slavery in Sierra Leone is still manifested in all spheres of modern life. Slavery created an unbridgeable social chasm between major tribal groups within the country. This bitter rift arose from the patronage of British slavers which resulted in one tribe perceiving to have lost their kin disproportionately to slavery more than the other. The scars of the incessant vicious and deadly raids on these people became legendary and remained unspoken up until present day Sierra Leone. Social tensions are ever present and more so during the heights of political activities when tribes remain steadfastly polar opposites. Suspicion and distrust characterise their relationships. Consensus and negotiations which once formed the foundation of social cohesion and political intercourse between tribal groups were replaced by discord and hate. The situation worsened through the introduction of guns and gun powder by British slavers and colonisers.

The discord was established between the two major tribes of Sierra Leone as a result of the dramatic change in strategy from kidnapping to frequent terrifying mass raids in the hinterland. This division was capitalised on and promoted avidly during colonial governance by the British. However, because both these major tribes and other minor ones continued to be subjugated by the British for nearly two centuries, the enmity between them was somehow suppressed. Any form of belligerence between them was perceived as a threat to the stability of the territory and was put down violently by the British. Colonial rule in Sierra Leone was undoubtedly violent, brutal and exploitative.

Sierra Leoneans orchestrated and launched several uprisings through various movements against the authoritarian and often chaotic and oppressive colonial rule. Protests and demonstrations of dissent were reacted to by British colonialists with uncompromising brutality. On a number of occasions, additional fighting forces were brought in to extirpate potential ideologically-motivated movements against British interests. The haplessness and psychological scars suffered during those dark days are still evident. The subservience of Sierra Leoneans and their overt dependence on anyone bearing physical resemblances to the colonialists continue to dominate their nuances. Unsurprisingly, the saddest aspect of it all is the adoption of the violent methods of colonialism by Sierra Leoneans themselves against each other, in order to settle political and social issues, up to recent times. One can only conclude that the hard lessons of brutality and oppression still run deep within the society.

The colour and skin tone of the race, tenuous as these might seem, have formed the basis to denigrate, despise, discriminate and perpetrate the mental sting of servitude against Africans by Caucasians the world over.

In recent debates on race equality, Africans are cynically told to move on and forget about slavery. The trans-Atlantic slave trade and its associated cruelty, atrocity and depravity inflicted on the African race by Europeans was of a scale and magnitude that humanity will ever experience. The hurt, the pain and psychological distress continue to this day since the first ominous shadow of a slave ship appeared on the horizon off the west coast of Africa.

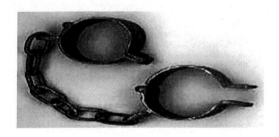

Chapter 1
The Portuguese Slavers

Long before the advent of the European transatlantic slavery, Sub-Saharan Africans lived in societies governed by kings and chiefs, and those who were considered to be of lower status and the proletariat within tribal kingdoms were required to serve the king and his dominion unconditionally at his behest. It was within the powers of the kings in those early days to request male subjects to offer their labour free of any charge to revered guests of the kingdom. This practice is not uncommon in many African societies even in modern times where chiefs and traditional tribal leaders are still held in very high regard. This gesture was in many cases abused by their benefactors, and labourers were often maltreated, overworked, and in many occasions, abuses resulted in severe disability or even death. Sub-Saharan African labourers will serve their new masters they are assigned to unconditionally as they possess delegated authorities from their revered leaders. They will respect them nearly as they would their kings or chiefs directly.

Arab traders who conducted frequent trading businesses within sub-Sahara Africa often enjoyed these grand gestures especially for the transportation of their acquired wares across the hazardous and treacherous Sahara Desert en-route to the north of Africa. Many of these Sub-Saharan African labourers died through exhaustion during the perilous journeys across the desert to northern Africa, as carriers. Those who survived to the end of their respective journeys were often not allowed to make the return journey back home to their kingdoms. The Arab traders will retain their services and through coercion will require labourers to carry out agricultural activities and domestic jobs for them and their families. Other less lucky labourers would be subsequently traded over to wealthy merchants from the Arabian Gulf. These secondary activities where labourers are sold on, were unknown to the sub-Saharan kingdoms and chiefdoms from which the labourers were originally assigned to the Arab traders.

Sub-Saharan African labourers who were not traded onto Middle-Eastern mercantile ventures continue to provide labour to their Arab masters in the north of Africa. Some of the labourers will go on to gain freedom through aging or infirmity and will settle within Arab societies. Those who are set free within northern African communities, almost invariably adopted Islam as their religion, which they practiced piously alongside their former masters and their kindred. Islam, Christianity and other medieval religions recognise and permit the subjugation of individuals of lower caste and especially those considered as foreigners. Individuals who received clemency within the context of Islam would proceed to raising families of their own within Arab communities albeit with curtailed rights and privileges. Over time, some will relent to the allure and pursuit of interested women, proceeded to marry and led ordinary lives. As the population of sub-Saharan African Muslim converts grew within northern Africa, so did their interest and nostalgia for their relatives and kin they had left behind many years earlier. Many of those who harboured such sentiments would venture the life-threatening journey through the desert and join Arab trading caravans southwards in order to re-establish contact with their long-lost relatives.

A feature of pre-transatlantic slavery was the mode of transportation. Mobility within Sub-Saharan Africa was mainly pedestrian. Horses and donkeys were predominantly used to aid transportation in the north of Africa by Arab migrants from the Arabian Gulf. Transportation as a socio-economic activity was physical and irksome. Another popular form of transportation for especially wealthy Africans, was the "Hammock". The hammock was constructed by connecting two beautifully-carved parallel wooden planks elaborately linked with hand-woven strings. The strings are usually made from fermented sisal plants or palm tree fronds. The strings are neatly and tightly woven in order to support the weight of an adult. The hammock is usually carried by at least four healthy strong men with the passenger sitting comfortably aloft, rocking inconsistently with the walking motions of the carriers. Hammocks were constructed in various forms. Some were elaborately adorned with colourfully-woven local country cloth and a covered box wherein the passenger rides, sheltered from the elements. Those built ostentatiously were much heavier and mainly used by chiefs and tribal heads. Carriers were often servants of the king, tribal heads or the wealthy in society. Carriers were in some cases volunteers but mostly hired labour.

Guests of royal households from other tribal clans including Arabs who were perceived to be rich traders were more than often accorded the privilege of a hammock ride within the chiefdoms. There was never a shortage of willing carriers despite the arduous and painful journeys they were required to undertake. Carriers, courtiers and other servants in royal households especially were so dedicated and committed that, out of abject ignorance, were even prepared to be buried alive with the king they serve, when the king dies. Such were the loyalty of Africans to their local administration and community as a whole. This loyalty, friendliness and hospitality were uncommon in other contemporary societies foreign to African cultures. Arab traders always welcomed the service and did not fail to take advantage of and thoroughly exploit the generosity and zealousness of their helpers.

Islam was widespread and generally practiced in the north of Africa but not particularly in sub-Sahara Africa. This was due to the proximity of the northern regions to and historical interaction with the Arabian Gulf. Sub-Saharan Africans who chose to settle and work for their Arab masters in the north, quite often adopted Islam as a religion. Those who were brave enough to reject exploitation and managed to extricate themselves from Arab bondage and survive the ordeal would head southwards without succumbing to Islamic proselytization.

Liberated Sub-Saharan Africans who adopted Islam and raised families within North Africa, returned home with their families and brought with them a wave of Islamic evangelism. This trend continued throughout western Africa including Sierra Leone. The spread of Islam along the coastal regions of Sierra Leone was easy due to the vibrant trading activities conducted by the local inhabitants. They were mainly Temnes, Lokkos and further inland were the Limbas. The Temnes were the dominant tribe along the coast and were accustomed to traversing the water ways with great dexterity in order to carry on trading with local merchants in Kafu-Bullom, one of the few inhabited islands along the Freetown estuary. Trade was mainly in agricultural produce such as kola nuts, grains, spices and salt, dried and smoked fish. Gold was also a major trading commodity amongst traders.

It is believed that the attraction by Europeans to Africa and what became the misfortune of the continent was inadvertently created by an unfortunate historical event which involved the then King of Mali, King Mansa Musa. During the year 1325, King Mansa Musa who was converted to Islam, adopted and practiced the religion piously, decided to make a religious pilgrimage to Mecca, the Muslim holy land. King Mansa Musa who was reputed to be a shrewd leader, planned this trip meticulously to be one that befits his regal stature, reputation and opulence. His entourage was massive including a large number of servants, courtiers and advisers. The grandeur of his lifestyle could not have gone unnoticed by the upper class and bourgeois in the Arabian Gulf. The quantity of gold that the King took with him to trade during his pilgrimage was enormous and the value of the stock remained unknown. News of King Mansa Musa's flamboyance circulated quickly amongst the rich and famous and before long attracted the attention and interest of European speculators and prospectors.

The Portuguese were recorded to be the first to embark on the perilous journey through the Sahara Desert along the well-trodden trade routes by Arab traders. Portuguese merchants traded in various items such as wine, cloth, copper ware and to some extent horses. The prospect of acquiring large quantities of gold following the extravagance of King Mansa Musa was alluring. Their trading adventures also drew more and more Arab traders to the west coast who immediately became hostile towards Portuguese speculators, in order to prevent competition. Europeans, especially Portuguese merchants were already involved in trade and commerce within the Arabian Gulf region but not within Africa and certainly not in sub-Sahara Africa.

Trading along the Sahara route by Portuguese traders did not go well as planned with continuous skirmishes and raids on their convoys by competing Arabs. Loses incurred were significant especially with the potential for fatality amongst their ranks. However, the drive and lust for gold was overpowering and no amount of setback was going to distract the Portuguese from their ultimate objective. Engaging Arab traders as agents or intermediaries between them and sub-Saharan African traders was not an option the Portuguese contemplated.

After years of turbulent competition with the Arabs, the Portuguese traders developed an alternative strategy to enable them circumvent the perils of the hazardous Sahara trade route. The solution was to deal directly with sub-Saharan African traders. The only way this was going to be achieved was by sea. Portuguese merchants and seafarers commenced sailing towards the west coast of Africa with great anticipation and expectations. Wares from Europe continued to exchange for gold, ivory and spices. The booming trade continued for nearly a century until the idea of commercial sugar plantations became a reality in Madeira in Portugal. The demand for Africans who were known to be adept at tilling the soil and were accomplished farmers was compelling. An opportunity for the exploitation of sub-Saharan African farm workers was created through the potential in commercial sugar plantations in Portugal.

The interest in gold, however, did not wane, if anything, it increased their desire to make direct contacts in Mali. Sierra Leone become well known to the Portuguese very quickly following the adventures of Pedro Da Cintra, who in the mid-1400s made his discovery of the coastal settlement official in Portugal. Portuguese merchants who made it their primary objective to acquire Africans to work in sugar plantations began to mobilise and gravitated towards this new found land of Sierra Leone in pursuit of the potential wealth that could be generated by exploiting the physical energy of Africans. They set off on their voyages on the belief that Africans were there for the taking. This optimism was based on the knowledge and reality of Arab subjugation of sub-Saharan labourers in the north and also the number of the labourers who were held in bondage in the Arabian Gulf. The population of sub-Saharan labourers in the Arabian Gulf was much smaller than what the eager Portuguese anticipated to capture in order to meet their economic forecasts and ambitions. They were hoping for larger haulages. Most of the African labourers in the Arabian Gulf were domestic servants and porters and not plantation workers. Additionally, sub-Saharan Africans were detailed to serve in the caravans of Arab traders by their kings and tribal leaders and were not corralled as the Portuguese planned.

A few Portuguese merchants made exploratory voyages to Sierra Leone amongst other landing sites along the west coast. However, contrary to popular belief that there would be an abundance of feral Africans roaming the coasts available for capture, the situation they found could not be more different. They cruised the west coast extensively for prolonged periods without success. Along the waters of Sierra Leone, they encountered traders and fishermen from the Temne tribe who lived along the coast. The Temnes sailed the rivers and the estuary with exquisite navigational dexterity in small dug-out canoes that were fashioned from huge tree trunks. The process of carving out canoes is very labour intensive. Large trees are felled and with specialised local equipment, the canoes are dug out and shaped. Since canoes were usually small and depending on the size of the tree, multiple ones could be made out of a very large tree trunk. Paddles are used to propel the canoes, and these are carved out from smaller tree stems or branches. A standard-sized canoe can carry up to four people and their wares or haul of fish and nets.

The flurry of activities along the coast was unexpected by the Portuguese merchants who kept their distance and maintained a low profile so as not to arouse unnecessary attention from the locals. It became obvious that their ventures were not going to be a stroll in the park as they originally thought and that the need to device new strategies were evident. Whatever methods the Portuguese planned to adopt, one thing was certain, time was not a factor that was within their control. It was going to take a lot longer to get a single individual let alone a boat full of Africans.

The plan hatched by the merchants was to resort to kidnapping any African they could get their hands on. To execute this, they had to stay out of sight, well away from the estuary and launch surprise attacks on fishermen around the coastal waters. The Portuguese merchants would then retain the hijacked canoes to facilitate ferrying future human cargoes from the mainland to their sailing boats. Canoes were more manoeuvrable and could be steered through the rivers discreetly and to hide in the undergrowth of mangroves along the coast. Attacks on canoes were carried out predominantly at dusk and occasionally at night when fishermen were less active or resting. Their canoes were commandeered and the occupants snatched and taken away. Canoes seized were also used by the Portuguese to sail towards land where they lay wait for unsuspecting Africans who would come down to the rivers to swim or take a bath.

Africans, especially farm workers and those who undertook manual work, were found at the banks of rivers at dusk taking relishing baths and performing ablution for evening Muslim prayers. The Portuguese sailors camouflaged themselves and would crawl stealthily out from the undergrowth and wrestled their quarries to the ground restrained them and prevented them from screaming for help. Women and children were easy to capture but young adult males were preferable as they had the stamina to firstly endure the long sea journey to Portugal with minimal food rations. Besides, a team of fit young adult men could put in long hours of hard labour in the plantations.

The process of capture was very slow and time consuming, as raids could only be conducted in the safety of darkness or the fading natural light of dusk. If an adult male was to be captured, only one could be successfully jumped at a time, by a few Portuguese sailors. The raids were certainly not free of injuries. Restraining and transporting a well-built young African or an adult male could be life threating for the Portuguese, who often sustain severe injuries during their pursuit. In order to have a commercial load of human cargo, captains of merchant vessels had to sit it out and wait for months at a time to have a boat full of captives. Kidnappings carried on for several years with increasing ferocity, but the yield was diminishing and waiting times became longer and unprofitable.

The disappearances of so many people did not go unnoticed within settlements along the coasts. The harder the Portuguese assailants tried, the more vigilant the people became. Kidnapping was not a sustainable method and was bound to cause concern amongst the people, but because the Portuguese did not regard Africans as rational beings, their thinking was myopic and their methods devoid of sophistication. Each failed attempt to take a potential captive made their heists less viable and rather precarious. Hysterical escapees would return to their locality and inform their compatriots of their brush with what they quickly regarded as dangerous and mysterious phenomena. Rumours of strange pale-looking human-like monsters lurking in undergrowth made the rounds quickly within settlements. Some of the stories were about strange-looking mermaids emerging from streams and rivers attacking especially men. The mermaid legend has endured and continued even to modern times. People were extremely scared and lost their confidence to go down to river banks on their own and without protection.

The mysterious disappearances of people also became a cause for concern amongst chiefs and tribal leaders. After several meetings and consultations, decisions were made that only groups of women and children should go down to the river banks. No individual other than men should take the risk. Men were allowed to continue to take their bath on their own if they chose so to do. The flaw in that decision was that men were in fact the primary target of the assailants. Whilst the number of women disappearances reduced, the number of children and men continued although without significant increase. It was also widely believed that the loss of so many people was due to the anger of the gods who had allowed evil spirits to afflict them with grief and sorrow for improprieties and other misdemeanours within their communities. Traditional ceremonies and rituals were performed and animal sacrifices were frequently made in order to appease the evil spirits that may be angry with them and mete out such terror on the people. Meanwhile the kidnappings continued unabated.

Roundtrips of voyages by the Portuguese were taking longer and longer as the wary people maintained their alertness and vigilance despite their ever-growing suspicion and superstition. Captives who are taken early on arrival of vessels along the coast, remained shackled in the vessels for as long as the wait for a full load lasted. Captives were fed meagre rations of oats and scraps from the crew. By the time the vessels returned to Portugal, their human cargos were emaciated and that depended on if they survived the journey at all. The horror of new captives taken onto the waiting vessels would have been palpable to find their kin who had been reported missing and thought to have been snatched mysteriously by mermaids, in the squalid and deplorable conditions within the hold of the slave vessels.

Despite the trickling flow of kidnapped Africans to Portugal, the sugar plantations continued to expand and flourished through the harsh exploitations of Africans already in servitude. The production of sugar cheaply at competitive rates was the pull factor for enslaving West Africans. The continued raids on West Africans however proved to be successful albeit inefficient as mortality amongst the captives was high during transportation. There was increasing pressure on the Portuguese sea farers engaged in this unfolding nightmare for Africans to improve the number of landings of people kidnapped. This obviously should mean a corollary increase in the stock of human cargo deliveries to the plantations. The agitation of plantation owners wanting to increase their output of sugar and inherent profit, was evident. The appetite for increased productivity and profits created a further demand and supply system for African labour. This cycle eventually attracted the attention and interests of other Europeans who figured out the potential pecuniary returns from cultivating sugar at plantation sizes with low cost African labourers.

The rising demand from the plantation owners and the increasing security measures implemented along the West African coasts precipitated the Portuguese sailors to change their approach from the extremely slow process of kidnapping to a much more aggressive and direct approach.

The increasing disappearances of people, especially young men from local communities prompted chiefs and tribal leaders to bolster the security of everyone using the streams and rivers for bathing and other domestic chores. Dedicated groups of volunteers, mostly men, were organised as escorts and sentries along river fronts and pathways. The increased security measures taken did not eliminate the problem of losing their kin but reduced the occurrences, or so they thought. One of the weakness in the measures taken was that the security guards who were invariably men had to maintain a respectful distance from the river fronts when women and children were bathing. This, therefore, permitted the opportunity for daring snatches to be made by the Portuguese sailors, before help could be summoned by the startled and hysterical bathers. Often all the bathers would be taken away without the sentries knowing, as they would often lay snoozing after a hard day's work on their farms. The sailors bravely started moving inland in order to capture workers from farms and dwellings that are close to the coast. Children and young adults who became isolated from the security of numbers were very vulnerable. Those brazen kidnappings by the desperate sailors unsettled coastal settlements tremendously. The Temnes along the coasts of Sierra Leone were ardent Muslims and, therefore, continued to solicit strength and solace from their deity. Superstition was rife especially with the increasing loss of fishermen and traders who plied the waterways to trade with islands nearby. Being devout Muslims, the Temnes began to feel that they had fallen out of favour with Allah. The frequency of animal sacrifices made increased with intense prayers and supplications for Allah's forgiveness, guidance and protection.

The Portuguese sailors decided on a radical change to the kidnapping approach. They thought that by making direct contacts with tribal heads might increase their chances of taking more Africans at much-reduced waiting times with less casualties. The plan was to offer cheap gifts to the chiefs and tribal heads in order to gain their trust and favours. Attractive though the idea seemed, the plan was fraught with unpredictable dangers for the sailors.

Merchants wasted no time in stocking up their boats with cheap cloths, some basic tools for farming and wine. It was believed that the first group of merchants and sailors who braved the open to attempt to engage with the Africans that they intend to capture were swiftly slain by the skittish people in the defence and protection of their communities.

The strangeness of the appearance of the sailors, with their obvious lack of familiar pigmentation, caused consternation amongst the people, who felt that the suspected monsters and mermaids had taken a human form in order to infiltrate their community. That, they thought would spell disaster and a bad omen for the people. However, the hostility of the Temnes did not deter further sailors coming ashore nor did kidnappings subside. The pressure on the Portuguese sailors to increase deliveries was immense, but the prospect of great financial rewards compelled and motivated them into making themselves visible to the Temnes, despite the risk of losing their own lives in the process.

The sailors continued to land in reasonable numbers and persisted in their bid to travel ashore. On encountering the people, they would throw their hands wildly in the air in nervous submission to the fierce aggression of the Temnes and ironically shouting: "somos do Porto e significa que nenhum dano." (We are from Porto and we mean no harm.) "Somos do Porto," (We are from Porto). They repeated this refrain in desperation and fear in order to elicit some compassion and co-operation from the frightened people. A compassion that they were not prepared or intended to return to the Africans. During the frenzy and consternation occasioned by the strange spectacle of their performances and exaggerated submissive prostrations by the Portuguese, the anger of the Temnes dissipated slowly and gradually turned into curiosity. The ease with which these once feared aliens succumbed to the ferocity of the irate warriors overwhelmed the locals. Especially when in previous encounters, the resistance mounted by the warriors had resulted in the wholesale slaughter of the daring sailors. The persistence, apparent frailty and defencelessness of the Portuguese sailors concentrated the minds and interest of the people. Despite the striking similarity to their captors according to the descriptions given by those who escaped being kidnapped, doubts were being expressed about the strength and ability of the Portuguese to carry these appalling acts. The Portuguese eventually developed the idea of using Africans who they had already kidnapped as baits to increase the intensity of their engagement with tribal leaders and chiefs. The slight change in approach did work as the reappearance of individuals who were thought to have been abducted and lost forever, not only surprised the Temnes but reinforced their interest and curiosity in the enigmatic Portuguese sailors.

After sustained but difficult dialogue between tribal leaders, the Portuguese merchants and their sailors, arrangements were reached on several counts. Captives who were used in negotiations were under severe duress to act in the interest of their benefactors. It was agreed that the Portuguese were to halt the kidnapping of their kin. The gifts offered by the Portuguese were cautiously received, but due to their religious beliefs and practices, the Temnes took strong exceptions to being offered alcoholic beverages. In return for the gifts received from the Portuguese merchants and their undertaking not to capture anymore people from the Temne enclaves, the tribal leaders promised to take them to another tribe from which the Portuguese can continue their heists. The Portuguese merchants were no doubt pleased with the breakthrough and were optimistic for a bumper return of increased captives.

The offers made by the tribal leaders were based purely on the principle of self-preservation. After the agony and trauma of losing so many of their own to what they felt were mysterious assailants, they were prepared to pass the scourge of kidnappings to another tribe in order to secure theirs. The obvious target initially was the Limba tribe and to some extent the Lokko tribe who settled inland further north of the settlements of the Temnes.

The Limba tribe settled north of the Temnes along the major Scarcies River. They are extremely physically-strong and energetic people. They easily rank as the strongest ethnic group even in modern day Sierra Leone, followed closely by the Koranko Tribe. They are however very placid, hardworking but not as religious as the Temnes. Unlike the Temnes, Limbas were not as astute in trading and not generally known to be adventurous. The Limbas and Lokkos have a propensity to imbibe copious quantities of alcohol that the Temnes considered abhorrent in religious terms. The Limbas possess superior dexterity in producing alcoholic beverages themselves. Whilst the Lokkos are proficient in distilling gin from corn, the Limbas are excellent in tapping the ubiquitous palm tree for Palm Wine. Tapping palm trees to extract wine is dexterous and require special talent. A skill that comes to the Limbas naturally. Like the Limba tribe itself, palm trees did not proliferate their land as it does in other tribal enclaves. Therefore, extracting the fluid of life from a living tree, repeatedly on a rotational basis, without killing the tree, is an admirable ability only this tribe possesses. The consumption of alcohol was a usual pastime for these two tribes which made it easy for them to be plied with Portuguese wine, making them even more vulnerable and easy to lure into captivity.

The Temnes were quite aware of the characteristics of these two tribes, hence their spritely move to redirect the Portuguese in their direction. The Portuguese gift of wine came in very handy in winning over their co-operation. The Temnes being traders and business-minded acted as facilitators for the Portuguese merchants. Despite their religious belief, the Temnes can be tenacious in the pursuit of their business objectives. This is a credential that is well known by all the other tribes. The Temnes fully co-operated with the Portuguese sailors with unrestrained enthusiasm. Where force was required, they spared no compassion. They intimidated and drove the Limbas into submission. The Limbas and Lokkos were terrified of the Temnes and were willing and ready to volunteer their services to them without question. Failure to co-operate will incur their wrath.

The alliance between the Temnes and the Portuguese traders continued for several years. Whilst this symbiotic relationship brought enormous benefits in gifts but most importantly it spared their kin from being kidnapped. During the years of cooperation between the Temnes and Portuguese merchants, the Portuguese were able to increase their human cargo to the delight of the sugar plantation owners in Portugal. Unfortunately, the Limbas and Lokkos were not as lucky, as during these periods of intense capture and forced removal, thousands of them were taken away into servitude causing social and economic problems within their communities. These two tribes were the first to suffer significant reductions in their numbers. Through sheer resilience and the instinct to survive, they subsequently developed a non-bellicose approach to avoid capture. Their industry and genius were remarkable and equally admirable. The Limbas especially started speaking the language of the Temnes and some even migrated into their settlements and integrated into their communities along the coast in order to seek protection. The Lokkos, on the other hand, made desperate attempts to forge relationships with the other major tribe closest to them in the hinterland.

Portuguese merchants were able to increase their human cargo through the corporation of the Temnes, but the more they delivered, the more the plantation owners demanded in order to expand and compensate for natural wastage. The need to produce cheaper products for home and Europe wide consumption was ever increasing. The rise in demand for Africans was putting additional pressure on existing sea farers, and kidnapping ventures became an attraction for potential Portuguese adventurers. However, the most significant interest came from other Europeans who immediately developed lofty ideas about the capture and exploitation of Africans. The potential profits and financial rewards were alluring, and morality was not a virtue to be gained in the circumstance.

The emerging threat of competition from other Europeans was immediately noticed by the Portuguese pioneers. The interest manifested by the British in the soaring business ventures of dealing in Africans by the Portuguese was calculated and real. The British had a variety of purposes and undertakings for which cheap African labour could be thoroughly exploited and utilised. Portuguese merchants and sailors in reacting to the threat of competition from the British, responded by increasing the frequency of their voyages to Sierra Leone and other West African coastal settlements. The frequency of the Portuguese visits increased tremendously, and their Temne associates became very familiar with the sight of Portuguese in their midst. The Temnes did not know the names of individual sailors neither did the sailors cared to know theirs. The Temnes called all the Portuguese sailors "Or Porto", derived from the repeated phonic of "Porto". The Temnes in their uncanny familiarity with the Portuguese, resorted to addressing all fair-skinned Europeans they encountered as Or Porto. This mistake was much to their peril. An error that generations will pay dearly for in centuries to come, for there were ominous shadows on the horizon.

Chapter 2
British Slave Raids

By the early to the mid-sixteenth century, the Portuguese were well established in the batter trade for Sub-Saharan Africans. The exchange was not in the least legal or fair, and why would it be? Humans were traded off for inferior exotic European wares. The value the Temnes attached to this appalling transaction was psychological and certainly not intrinsic. The mere fact that they managed to stem the disappearances of members of their tribe and also able to successfully deflect the onslaught of the Portuguese onto the Limba and Lokko tribes generated much more utility out of the transactions than anything pecuniary. Although their collaboration with the Portuguese merchants appeared to be effective and worked well in their interest, the longevity of the alliance was not guaranteed.

The British had been constructors and suppliers of boats and ships to Portuguese merchants for more than half a century, during their monopoly of human activities along West Africa. As the demand for bigger vessels increased, so did the curiosity and interest of the British in this insidious practice, with its perceived lucrative rewards. British adventurers and speculators obtained Royal Warrants, a form of approval from their head of state and government to carry out reconnaissance of the slaving fields of West Africa. With those dubious documents in hand, they headed straight towards and into the human trade fest and savagery that was being meted out against West Africans. This move by the British was destined to put them in direct competition and collision with the Portuguese who had been raiding the west coast unchallenged ever since the discovery of the potential human reservoir. The nightmare of Africans and Sierra Leoneans in particular was about to become even more real. The abuse and barbarism against the African race, at a scale humanity will ever witness, was about to unfold.

Despite the stout resistance demonstrated by the Portuguese merchants and sailors to defend the west coast against the determined aggressive participation by the British, their efforts proved futile. The British introduced extreme and unprecedented violence into an already barbaric and despicable activity. The Portuguese suffered a bloody defeated and were driven further south of the continent towards Angola, where they re-establish and continued their devious activities to capture Africans into bondage. The approach adopted by the British was completely unlike that of the Portuguese. The Temnes soon realised that their ingenious collaborative strategy, developed and implemented with Portuguese acquiescence, had no mileage with the planned enduring raids of the British merchants. The Portuguese business practices and the manner in which cheap African labour was exploited to produce affordable agricultural produce for European markets stimulated the elaborate British model. A model that was developed to perpetrate and maximise the exploitation of Africans.

Portuguese detainees introduced British merchants to Sierra Leone and other coastal settlements from where they had been kidnapping Africans for years. The Temnes had a rude and unexpected shock when on their usual welcoming greetings of "Or Porto", they were confronted by musket-toting impudent and impatient British merchants. The lack of reciprocal enthusiasm from the few subdued Portuguese sailors in the midst of the British immediately gave the plot away. The Temnes were initially tentative in dealing with the new benefactors who were barking commands at the Portuguese detainees, their now erstwhile cohorts. However, as time went by, the Temnes quickly learnt to cooperate unconditionally when the results of the use of muskets by the British became obvious. Muskets were to be the new tool and a regular feature in the modus operandi of the British. The message was loud and clear that the new "Or Portos" were not and did not intend to settle for the odd Limbas and Lokkos captured in little skirmishes. They wanted more, and the population of the Limbas and Lokkos put together did not meet their expectations and would not warrant the elaborate scheme they had planned. It became apparent to the Temnes that they could no longer protect their own and quickly found their young women, men and children once again being taken away, in the dramatic turn of events, by force of arms. The demand for cheap labour to work on farms and other hazardous labour-intensive projects in Britain escalated astronomically. By the latter part of the fifteen hundred, the feasibility of transatlantic avenues for extensive agricultural activities became a reality.

The extraction of humans from the region by the Portuguese and the subsequent involvement by the British caused an increased distraction for the Temnes who found it extremely difficult to fish and trade with nearby islands. Normal regular economic activities were severely disrupted. The strength and stability of their communities were seriously threatened by the European insurgencies. Survival became strenuous and perilous. There was widespread panic amongst the people, afraid of being captured or being killed resisting capture. Food was scarce, and agriculture which was not the speciality of the Temnes could scarcely be carried out under the threat of kidnappings and abductions. The chiefs and tribal heads once again had to come up with an ingenuous plan to save their communities which were now in turmoil and rapidly depleting. The focus of the Temnes turned to a much larger tribal group in the east and south to theirs. The Mendes are a much larger ethnic group to theirs but were well organised.

The Mendes are the other main tribe in Sierra Leone and have been a rival group to the Temnes ever since their ancestors moved southwards from northern Africa. The Mendes are a cohesive people with a tighter social bond than the Temnes. Unlike the Temnes, they are not predominantly Muslims. The Mendes are gifted with agricultural and farming skills which were their main social and commercial activities. They also carried out small scale fishing and were extremely skilled hunters. Amongst the various agricultural produce cultivated, rice was the main crop produced by this group of hardworking people. The scale and quality of the cultivation of rice by the Mendes was significant not only for the consumption of their community but to facilitate trade with other tribes within and out of their environs. Rice planting to harvesting required a great deal of social co-operation, planning and organisation. These are qualities that characterise the Mendes. The Mendes are naturally endowed with the most beautiful vocal range in singing amongst all the tribes in Sierra Leone. This talent is usually displayed magnificently whilst working the fields as entertainment and mostly during harvest celebrations. Although the Mendes were fierce warriors, they were also great entertainers and very hospitable.

Rice cultivation is a skill that is always associated with the Mendes, and this unique ability was what was going to be the bane of their simple existence during the appalling kidnapping and capture of Africans into servitude by Europeans.

Ever since the arrival and settlement of the Mendes, in Sierra Leone, rivalry between them and the Temnes had always been strong, and the Temnes had always triumphed over them. Although the Mendes were warriors themselves, they were unable to match the ferocity of the Temnes who long before the advent of mass kidnappings and capture of their kin, had been a superior fighting force against other tribes. The Mendes usually carried huge stocks of rice for consumption and trade which generally attracted the interest of their rivals, who were not always prepared to pay for the exchange through trade. Sporadic attacks and pillaging raids were made on the Mendes by the Temnes, especially during lean periods. Such aggression had always been a source of great tension between these two tribes. Conflicts were frequent and often settled through diplomatic tribal exchanges, discussions and negotiations. Over time, the Mendes mastered the art of dealing with persistent aggression through diplomatic manoeuvrings and displayed their eloquence and relatively superior intelligence to the Temnes, who had scarce patience and flare for such procedures. The Mendes will engage tenaciously in talks for weeks or months as necessity dictates, in order to achieve their aims. They never forgive nor forget issues they perceive to have suffered from unjustly and will avenge such setbacks whenever the opportunity arises.

The Mendes are a gregarious tribal group and feel very comfortable and confident amongst themselves. They possess little trust in others which is not surprising after their historical experiences with their arch rivals. They do not particularly find adventure in nomadic escapades which made them less astute in business ventures, a quality the Temnes possess and used effectively in dealing with Arab traders for centuries. Their inclination to spend their entire lives amongst their own and within the environment they are accustomed to, made them good settlers and why their population grew larger and faster than all the other tribes.

The introduction of guns and gun powder by British merchants along the west coasts brought unseen violence amongst these once placid communities. A thunderous explosion from a musket followed by huge plums of gun powder smoke caused instantaneous death, fear and chaos. These were scenes often repeated and experienced by the Temnes, when those who resisted capture met their fateful end. Physical resistance by the Temnes during the initial encounter with the British was swiftly suppressed, and the British proceeded to establish an export routine along the estuary. Port Lokko was established and became a major sea port from where huge numbers of Lokkos, Limbas and Temnes were transported by small boats to waiting vessels stationed out at sea. Seeing the avaricious appetite of the British for Africans by the Temnes, their survival instinct was triggered once again. The time had come for their rivals to surfer a similar fate to theirs and that of the Lokkos and Limbas whose population was being depleted rapidly.

The Temnes surreptitiously introduced British merchants to the Mendes through food raids as trading and fishing activities were severely disrupted by the fear and trauma of kidnappings and capture. The British were very pleased to find such a flourishing community of people completely oblivious to their menacing exploits in other areas within their wider environs.

The Mendes were astonished and taken aback by the appearance of the strange-looking men amongst the ranks of the Temnes. They swiftly launched fierce attacks to repel the impostors, albeit nervously. The Mendes soon discovered that the game had drastically and dramatically changed. There was no longer going to be the usual combative encounter that will last for days followed by diplomacy. Several explosions erupted from the muskets of the British; the air was clouded by gun powder smoke, and a few of the intrepid warriors lay dead in an instant. The rules had changed; the fighters were left in total shock and pandemonium ensued. With the help of the Temne raiders, a few of the Mende warriors were captured and the frightened people corralled and taken away to the land of the Temnes for export.

The symbiotic relationship between the Temnes and the British accrued much more benefits to the latter than the former. The Temnes were given respite from capture and subsequently became employees of the British merchants, assisting in marshalling countless numbers of Mendes for transportation. The British were reluctant to use their muskets against, what they regarded to be, the fine specimen of the Mendes. But the presence of the muskets in raids made it easier for the Temnes to plunder food and livestock from their quarries. On the other hand, excessive use of their arsenal well into the dense hinterland and miles away from any possibility of replenishment was a risk they were not prepared to take in the face of perceptible danger. The British had discovered a reservoir of Africans, and their exploitation will last for centuries. The indiscriminate nightly raids on their settlements, the trauma of capture and restrain brought the Mendes instinctively closer. The knowledge that their arch enemies were collaborating with the aliens incubated an unremitting animosity against the Temnes. The opportunity for dialogue and negotiations had all but disappeared with the smoke of gun powder. Lawlessness became the new order and replaced the tranquillity that characterised their peaceful and simple existence.

The discovery of the Mendes was quite pleasing to the British merchants and adventurers. However, the continued raids and capture of the Mendes was not without its logistical problems. Long treks into the hinterland had to be undertaken, and return journeys lasted weeks or even months at a time. The problem was compounded when the victims captured had to be matched through thick tropical forests in single file caravans, overseen by a few British sailors and their local Temne orderlies. Quite often, some of the captives, especially males, will fancy their chances and run into the thick undergrowth and disappear without trace. Such loses were considered costly by the British who valued captured Africans based on opportunity cost than anything else. Each African captured must be taken alive at all cost to Britain and against all odds. On arrival in Britain, the situation changes dramatically and market value is attached to each human for auction like cattle.

The rate of escaping individuals increased with every venture as the number of Mendes captured increased and treks became longer. This was not a problem envisaged initially by the British or the Portuguese earlier when kidnappings and capture were predominantly carried out along the coasts. The operation was pretty straight forward and mostly uneventful but the numbers taken were low and took longer to fill up waiting vessels.

The Mendes attracted a lot of interest from the British particularly because of their rice cultivating skills. The new found treasure in Sierra Leone coincided with the grandiose plans of the British to exploit the fertile and sparsely-inhabited lands of the Caribbean and the Americas. Most of the Temnes, Limbas and Lokkos captured by the Portuguese spent the rest of their productive lives in sugar plantations in Portugal whilst those captured by the British initially, worked mostly in all spheres of the British economy where brute strength was required. Wherever African slaves found themselves, hard labour and toil were their sunrise and sunset. Their lives were worth but a tuppence.

This was not going to be any different for the Mendes, only that things were going to get worse as a result of profitability, wealth creation and avarice.

Word spread quickly amongst the merchants that whilst sailors embarked on the treacherous journeys into the heartland to capture

Africans, they lose a significant number of them on their way back to load the cargo holds of the slave vessels. Measures were promptly taken to prevent runaways. A new line of business became mainstream in Britain for blacksmiths and metal workers who started producing several forms of crude-metal restraints ranging from neck brackets and locks to leg and ankle irons. Several thousand miles of chain links were forged. Chains were used to link slaves to each other. These restraints were used regularly on the Mendes which reduced the incidences of loss through escapes. The restraints, once put in place, were only removed in the event of death during the long sea voyages, when the corpse of the dead African would be thrown overboard the merchant vessel.

The pain and suffering the Mendes went through was unimaginable. Capture often involves violently rounding up people who were mostly taken unawares during dawn raids or groups of people ambushed and captured whilst working in their farms. Captives would be kept chained without food or water, until the sailors are satisfied they have had enough for the return journey to Britain. The captured people had to carry foodstuff and other wares looted from their stores, to take back to the vessels and partly as rewards for the Temne orderlies. Trekking for miles in the tropical heat across dense jungle terrain whilst shackled and tethered to each other was not a stroll in the park. This was only the beginning of an ordeal that will last for months until they reach their final destinations across the Atlantic where the nature of their strife changes drastically.

After trekking several gruelling miles through the jungle to the Port of Lokko, the Temnes would prepare meals for each set of captives and give them clean water to drink before they were taken in small canoes downstream towards the large waiting merchant vessels. For the captives, this was their last relatively decent meal, for the condition and treatment that awaited them in the vessels were beyond the imagination of any rational human being. Captives would endure sub-human conditions for months during the treacherous sea journeys to either the slave markets in Britain or the Americas.

With the assistance of the Temnes, the captured Mendes would be processed swiftly and efficiently at the port. This would involve sorting the captives into small groups of women and children for the canoe trip to the merchant vessels. The men were organised in much smaller groups in order to prevent any rebellious behaviour aboard the small canoes. If for any reason the men decided to put up a last stand whilst being transported to the main vessels and in the process tipped the canoes over, they were left to drawn shackled and tethered. An attempt to rescue tethered men would be suicidal and was not even contemplated by the British sailors. The only distress such incidences caused to the sailors was the ordeal of reporting the loss of the valuable human cargo.

Raids on Mende enclaves continued for centuries and so was their resistance to capture. The Mendes were not pushovers, and as time went on, they became accustomed to the terror of the British muskets. Like the Temnes, they took security measures and ambushed their assailants as often as the opportunity arose. British sailors lost a lot in their ranks during raids, not to mention the casualties amongst their Temne aids and helpers who were ordered to lead attacks and had to wrestle their quarries into submission in order to take them alive.

Kidnappings and capture of the Temnes, Lokkos and Limbas caused a significant disruption to their way of life. Once organised communities conducting trade and business as usual became extremely pensive, frightened and less productive. A culture of dependence was created by the British who they continued to serve not by choice but for their basic survival. Even their survival was not guaranteed as new merchants and sailors who entered the competition to capture as many Africans as possible, would often launch surprise raids on their already terrified and depleted communities.

This mindless barbarism was to continue for another two centuries affecting not only the Mendes, Temnes, Lokkos and Limbas of Sierra Leone but other tribes across the continent. Millions of Africans would make the dreadful and perilous sea journeys, some never made it to the end, but one thing was certain, they would all suffer a similar horrendous fate.

Chapter 3
Expansion into the Hinterland

During the fifteenth through to the seventeenth century, Europeans made the most of the opportunity they had to exploit the African race in order to build their own cities, boost their economies and improve the lives and general wellbeing of their communities. They successfully created and built a secure foundation on which the present and future generations will continue to thrive. But the methods used to achieve these goals were so despicable; their behaviours and treatment of Africans were almost beyond human comprehension.

The trade in Africans was a nearly free source of human labour that became so popular, it lasted some four hundred years uninterrupted. This exploitation carried on with unbridled impunity. Europeans were killing each other on the high seas for control and domination of this unsavoury business. The British were a major player in this trade and displayed their prowess in diverse ways but mainly by force of arms.

Opportunities for the British to cultivate a variety of agricultural produce cheaply in commercial scales within the Caribbean and North America were attractive and boundless. This fuelled the appetite and increasing demand for human labour in the absence of mechanisation that is common in modern times. Africans, sadly, were picked on to be the human equivalent of tractors and combined harvesters.

The explosion in demand for Africans was so significant, the coastline of West Africa became littered with merchant vessels of different shapes, sizes and capacity. Each one awaiting to be filled with captured African human cargo. The demand for Africans by the British was so huge, they had to rethink their strategy in order to improve the efficiency of roundtrips in order to increase throughput. They consolidated their control and domination of the waters from the Gambia down to Nigeria.

Port Lokko was one of the few ports set up along the west coast for the purpose of shipping Sierra Leoneans and other Africans into the bondage of slavery. The processing of mainly Mendes during that era, along the Port for transportation to the waiting merchant vessels, was slow and plagued with unforeseen dangers. The potential for the Temnes who were not particularly trusted by the British sailors, to collude with the Mendes and stage deadly rebellions was a danger that was ever present. The distrust between them was mutual as the Temnes were always on their guard anticipating that the avaricious British slavers could turn on them at any time without warning.

A change to the way captives were processed before departure to slave markets, and ultimately the plantations was very necessary. The change in the processing methods was, on the one hand, to reduce the number of captives held within Port Lokko and the surrounding environment at any one time and secondly, to identify and sort the cargo according to the merchant owners. Identification of cargo become problematic as voyages were sponsored by various investors. The sizes of the consignment of human cargo was ever increasing, making the process very intricate and challenging. Adjusting stocks for loses in particular, as a result of deaths or incapacity, was no longer easy as investors expected full inventories of live and physically-fit humans. Losses resulting from deaths during the long sea voyages were made up for in subsequent consignments. The pressure on the sailors to keep the stock of humans alive till they reach the final port of discharge was enormous. This was a difficult undertaking for the sailors as merchant ships had to be filled most of the time above the stipulated sailing capacity of the vessels.

During the peak of the capture of the Temnes, the British who overpowered, defeated and drove the Portuguese away, conducted extensive frequent cruising along the Freetown estuary. Bunce Island was one of the islands raided, and the few Temne inhabitants captured and taken away. The island was to become a major holding and processing site for thousands of people captured and awaiting shipment.

An artist's impression of the fortresses at Bunce Island

Bunce Island is a very small island but is strategically located along the Freetown estuary with waters around it deep enough for big merchant vessels to berth alongside in order to facilitate easy loading of their human cargoes. The occupancy of the island was ordered and sponsored by the British government through the Royal African Company, an organisation that was set up to actively participate in the capture and sale of Africans. The island was occupied, and a fortress was constructed to offer protection from pirates and other Europeans interested in the rich pickings of Africans from the west coast. Appropriate facilities were constructed including the famous dungeon in which captives were kept in dark, damp and cramped conditions unfit for any life form, let alone humans. The island was cleared of all traces of the Temnes who once lived there and were replaced by living quarters for the slavers. Mendes who were mainly targeted for capture because of their expertise in the cultivation of rice were especially valuable in utilising the limited land space. With Bunce Island in their control, the British who were keen to produce commercial quantities of tobacco, rice and cotton on the fertile lands of the Caribbean and North America, increased their raids and captured hundreds of thousands more Mendes and others from the hinterland.

Bunce Island like other ports set up for the shipment of African captives, was heavily militarised. The Royal African Company, strangely, was originally named the "Company of Royal Adventurers of England Trading with Africa". Royal Charter was granted to the organisation guaranteeing total monopoly for extracting Africans from all the regions on the west coast including Sierra Leone. The granting of monopoly by Royal Charter gives the connotation of trade, which was not quite the case. The Charter fundamentally empowered the Royal African Company to fend off other Europeans who were interested in catching Africans for slave labour and most importantly putting out an uncompromising message of British State sponsorship. The Charter also reflected British thinking and attitude towards Africans generally, by empowering and legitimising this nefarious and despicable act against human beings. A right to capture women and separate them from their children; to capture children and subject them to dehumanising conditions and deprive them of a future; the right to capture men and deny their families sustenance, and the right to uproot and destroy entire villages, communities and towns through force of arms.

Europeans generally regarded Africans as animals who they thought were freaks of nature purely because of their distinct physical characteristics that are dissimilar to theirs. As a result of this very poor thinking and perception, Africans were callously subjected to the most horrendous conditions from which even most animals are afforded legal protection in modern times.

The port and fortresses on Bunce Island provided facilities for large numbers of captives to be processed more efficiently after capture and before shipment. Most importantly, the use of the Island reduced the potential for any form of collaboration between the disgruntled Temne orderlies and the Mende captives. Overtime, the Temne recruits who provided assistance to the British slavers, developed a natural proclivity to sympathise with the Mendes, resulting from witnessing the brutal and inhumane way they were being treated by the British slavers. The worse was, however, to come.

The establishment of ports and fortresses along the west coast by the British and the corollary increase in numbers taken, encouraged more speculators and investors to join in and participate in the business of capturing Africans and selling them to plantation owners. The increased flurry of activities however posed very little competition for the Royal African Company. The backing and support of the British government meant that vessels of wayward speculators could be commandeered and sailors detained by the Company. Many of the vessels that left British ports bound for the slaving fields of West Africa were laden with tons of iron shackles and other restraining equipment, important to the conduct of this depraved activity.

Examples of restraining shackles:

Leg Manacles   **Neck Irons**

The acquisition of free land in America and the Caribbean by Britain, through methods that could hardly be characterised as legitimate, intended for use as plantations, precipitated the significant increase in the capture of lots more Africans. This dramatic elevation in seizures motivated the start of slave markets in the Caribbean and North America. The onslaught on the Mendes was relentless in order to meet the soaring demand. More settlements were attacked by British sailors supported by armed Royal Navy personnel. British slavers became over enthusiastic and undertook more adventurous journeys farther in land and all over the east and southern regions of Sierra Leone.

Despite the increase in gun-toting slavers, the Mendes were not usually shot directly even when resistance by the them in many instances was fierce, life threatening and robust. They were more valuable to the sailors alive than incapacitated by gun shots. Men were reluctantly shot by the British sailors only if their own lives were in so much danger that the use of the firearm was considered absolutely necessary. Most often, a plausible explanation would have to be adduced for killing a healthy and strong potential captive. The Temne workers were not entitled to the privilege, nor allowed to carry guns, for obvious reasons. On many occasions, the Temne workers who usually led groups will be set upon by the Mendes during ambushes. A lot of Temnes lost their lives in such skirmishes as the British sailors would bark orders at their orderlies to try and subdue the belligerent Mendes rather than save their colleagues who were in mortal danger. Such was the policy of the slavers, of self-preservation and total disregard for the safety of those who were under their charge in the pursuit of their cruel and immoral enterprise.

Larger numbers of Mende women, men and children were captured. Only the very old and infirm were spared. The Temne helpers were usually driven to total exhaustion during raids. They carried heavy loads of metal restraints and foodstuff from Port Lokko for long distances, almost across the country deep into the settlements of the Mendes. During ambushes, they were extremely vulnerable as they would already be weak and tired from the perilous journeys they had made. The load of any worker who fell victim to ambushes and other violent encounters were distributed amongst the survivors. Wild animal attacks and frequent snake bites were other perils suffered by the workers. Unlike their slave masters, the Temnes did not have footwear and not all of them were trained or possessed the skills of hunters and trackers. The British sailors did not allow them to carry machetes, bows and arrows on such treks because they were not to be trusted with such offensive and dangerous weapons. Treks would last for weeks, and when they reached closer to the villages and towns of their quarries, they would locate clearings ideal to set up camp. Usually, such clearings would be farms and the huts that the Mende farmers use during the day as shelter from the tropical sun. The slavers would occupy the huts as sleeping quarters where they would bed down for the night after dinner. The Temne workers would take turns at sentry duties in order to fend off animal attacks and very rarely, surprise ambushes staged by the Mendes. The Temne servants would feed on dried meat and fish that they had prepared prior to their trek, to last them for the return journey. The sailors usually have thick biscuits and canned food that they heat on the fire and brew tea whenever they could.

Treks were hazardous for the British sailors too, who suffered from mosquito bites and sun stroke. Some of them did contract malaria and died during long walks in the tropical rain forest. In spite of the dangers of seeking and capturing people from such hostile environments, the financial profits were too much to resist and made it all worthwhile.

The increased flurry of activities by British sailors resulting from setting up of the Bunce Island entrepot system, quite often caused the Temne men a lot of concern and heartache. A huge number of the Temne men were in the charge of British sailors, and because the demand for more captives was unrelenting, Temne men were required to spend prolonged periods away from their own communities. Many of the men would return after months to find that some of their own families had been captured and taken away by rogue sailors who cruised the coast and kidnapped whoever they found. Women and children were much more vulnerable without the men. The Temne men kept losing out whatever clever deals they struck with the British. They were unable to mourn the loss of their families as they knew precisely what had befallen them. They had no option but to continue to join the caravans to capture more people in order to secure their own survival. The Lokkos and Limbas who had lost so many of their kin, moved further north inland away from the Temnes. They were terrified of the Temnes and always suspicious of them. They were completely oblivious to the complexities of the strange activities that threatened their very existence. However, the focus on the Mendes who were many more in numbers than they were, gave them some respite. This situation allowed the smaller communities who were less threatened to re-organise, consolidate themselves and endeavour to make the most of what they could of their beleaguered and unpredictable lives. There was hardly anything good that could be attributed to the act of kidnapping, capturing and subjecting humans to a life of oppression and pain.

During raids on Mende villages and communities the slavers would wake up very early, long before sun rise and organise their Temne workers and servants to prepare to carry out surprise attacks on the Mendes whilst they are still asleep. The groups would make their move on the villages rounding up families as they slept. Pandemonium would ensue, women and children wailing and the men through natural instinct, would put up whatever feeble resistance they could in order to protect their families. The inevitable outcome was for them to be set upon and subdued, tethered and led away to the designated temporary holding site. Babies who are not trampled and killed by the marauders were left screaming for their mothers until the little energy they had dissipated and could scream no more. Slavers were not interested in babies, the very old or the incapacitated. They would leave them behind to starve and eventually die if they could not fend for themselves. The trauma suffered by many of the lactating mothers must have been horrendous. To be snatched and taken away from their babies or watch their babies being trampled to death, must have been horrendous, painful and sickening. These were actions that defied human reasoning.

A few busts from the muskets of the slavers would create extreme fear and made it easier to subdue pugnacious male captives and their dependants. By sun rise, entire villages would have been corralled. In instances where the slavers perceived any potential danger in controlling the captives, the odd individual would be shot dead by the sailors in full view of their compatriots including children. Such desperate and inhuman behaviour by the British sailors was to make an example out of any intransigent captive and a lesson for the rest to comply with orders.

After villages were totally decanted and the Mende captives taken to designated clearings, they are made to sit tightly close to each other in rows in order to reduce individual mobility and the possibility of revolt. Sorting and restraining of the captives were done by arranging them according to their heights, and U-shaped metal put around each captive's necks. A line up of a dozen or so individuals were connected by a long iron bar. The iron bar is slid inside holes at the end of each U-shaped neck iron, and the end of the iron bar padlocked to prevent removal. Younger captives are handcuffed and tethered with linked chains. This process is excruciatingly painful, dehumanising and reduces captives to less than animals. They were devoid of privacy and personal hygiene thereafter. Individuals passed out bodily waste on each other when the need arises. Women who had lost their new-born babies or very young ones, would wail incessantly to the irritation of their captors. The British captors would angrily bark out orders to their Temne servants to whip them mercilessly to keep them quiet. They did not show any sympathy or remorse for their actions which were motivated by pecuniary rewards and pure greed. Once the captives had been hooked up and tethered, they remained in that state of painful discomfort until the slavers and their support staff decided to start the return journey to Port Lokko. No food or water was given to the captives until they reached the Port. With luck, they were allowed liquid intake if they came across streams or rivers on their hazardous and perilous passage through dense foliage in the heat of the blazing tropical sun.

Before the caravan set off on the return journey to Port Lokko, the servants were ordered to pillage whatever food and livestock they could find around the destroyed settlements. Babies and old people were left behind with not a grain of food or a drop to drink and were left to starve and perish. In rare occasions, those neglected and left to perish would be found and rescued by people from nearby villages. These discoveries by those who were yet to experience this mindless cruelty were usually taken aback and served as a warning to them. They would endeavour to take measures to protect themselves like those before them only to be confronted by unimaginable violence and brutality that no amount of precautionary security they could afford would prepare them for.

Abuse of captives was rife and was carried out routinely by the British slavers with impunity. Women were raped repeatedly, and captors with lustful preference for men and boys would abuse young captives when the opportunity presented itself. Women from the Mende tribe are generally beautiful and sensual. They are naturally gifted with attractively smooth well-sculptured bodies. Theirs is a gait of seductive allure that no shackle or restraint could suppress.

After feeding themselves to satisfaction from the stolen food stock, the British slavers would select the best looking women, remove them from the common restraint, strip them to nakedness and have their savage ways with them. Some women would be forced upon repeatedly to exhaustion. These behaviours were not particularly pleasing to the Temne servants who were mostly devout Muslims, but there was nothing they could do to stop the immoral behaviour of their masters. Their survival was in the hands of these strange human beings who had wrecked their lives and made their relationship with the Mandes irreparable through suspicion and hate.

Information was speedily transmitted across Mende communities about the collaboration of the Temnes with their evil cohorts, the British slavers who have brought chaos, destruction, disappearances and death to their towns and villages. These repeated raids on the Mendes left them bitter and angry with the Temnes. Differences between them which were once settled through dialogue and consensus became irreconcilable. The Mendes steadfastly believed that, had it not been for the Temnes, the scourge of slavery, characterised by kidnappings, capture and untold suffering would not have visited them. This postulation may not entirely hold true because, as the demand for Africans grew exponentially, it was only a matter of time before British and other European slavers and merchants had discovered them within the hinterland. The historical raids by the Temnes to secure grains and livestock during lean periods from the Mendes and the knowledge that they were extremely talented farmers were information that helped the British slavers to seek them probably earlier than they otherwise would. However, whatever the issues were, the seeds of bitterness, hatred and discord had been established, and this was to become an enduring legacy between these two major tribes.

The return journey to Port Lokko was an arduous trek that lasted for days, and the journey time was ever increasing the farther raids had to be conducted in the hinterland. Return journeys would start at dawn well before sunrise and before the height of the tropical heat and humidity. The Temne servants who on the first leg of the journey were laden with boxes of shackles and iron bars, would carry bags and baskets full of grains, fruits and vegetables on the return journey. Livestock were kept behind the caravan and herded by servants, mostly young children who could not carry heavy loads.

Despite the whipping and shouting at the captives, the journey to the port did not get easier over time. In fact, it became slower the more captives there were. Shackled captives had to learn quickly and adapt to synchronise the way they walked in order to reduce blisters around their necks and feet. The Mende men were born warriors, and no amount of restraint suppressed their displeasure over the cruelty meted out on them. They did not disguise their urge to put up a fight whenever they felt their aching bodies could take no more beatings. The men would attempt to disrupt the march to the harbour by refusing to co-operate when ordered to move faster. They would stand or protest about the lack of food or drinking water. They would scream obscenities at their captors who were oblivious to their verbal protest. The more they protested, the more punishment they received from the British slavers and their support workers.

The caravan would only stop when the British slavers felt dehydrated and in need of sustenance and some rest. During breaks which happened when the sun was high in the sky and perspiration threatened the survival of the British slavers, the Temne servants were ordered to cook whatever they could for themselves and the captives. Cassava, a tuber and a popular carbohydrate diet, would be cooked and shared sparingly amongst the captives and just about a mouthful of water to quench their thirst and to moisten their patched lips. If breaks were fortuitously taken close to rivers or streams, the captives were allowed to drink more water. The ration barely kept their metabolism active during the long march. The meagre rations were merely to keep them alive until they reached the port. However, their plight was not going to improve either during the perilous sea journeys that awaited them.

The dramatic change in fortunes of the Mendes during the intense and prolonged period of capture was hard to bear. They would go to sleep with their families and woke up into the nightmare and hardship of bondage. They were being treated worse than their livestock. Whilst they were shackled closely together and made to sit around practically naked, they would watch their livestock grazing freely with no care in the world around them. Captives were not allowed to communicate with each other in order to reduce the potential for insubordination and rebelliousness. Stop-overs at nights during the long cross country march was usually challenging for the captives. Such night stop overs were usually a welcome break for the weary and aching bodies of the captives but there was no logistics for sleeping. The British slavers had sleeping bags and tents reserved for their own comfort. The captives were organised in rows on clearings made by the Temne servants. All the captives would have to lie down at the same time and in almost the same angle. No individual could get up in the middle of the night or at any other time to relieve themselves. Those who were shackled with their legs tethered to each other, usually young children and teenagers, had a bit of flexibility.

West Africans in chains ready for shipment

The discomforts and pain the captives suffered during the long trek to the port were incredible. Captives could hardly catch a wink during the night as they lay on the forest floor. They were occasionally bitten or severely stung by the fearsome driver ants of the tropical jungle or sustain snake bites and stings from other poisonous creepy crawlies. Individuals who succumb to such hazards or the perils of this dehumanising and irksome journey were untethered and abandoned in the forest to be scavenged on by wild carnivorous animals. Such loses usually angered the slavers who in response would reduce the number of stopping breaks they took in a bid to exit the jungle as quickly as possible with their bounty intact. Increasing the pace of the captives usually frustrated the captors and motivated the excessive use of whips, inflicting more pain on the already battered and distressed captives.

The torture and cruelty the Mendes suffered in such a massive scale during those jungle treks were beyond belief. People who were once going about their normal civil business and living a life of peace and tranquillity found themselves being treated like felons without warning. This is the price they paid for the skills they possessed. By the time they reached Port Lokko, they would realise that their suffering had only just begun.

On arrival at Port Lokko, whatever was left of the food and livestock stolen days or weeks earlier would be left with the Temne servants for them and their families if they were still around when they returned from their raids. Quite often, like the Mendes, they would return and discovered that a member or their entire family had been captured by other British raiders. Such loses were usually hard for them to bear not knowing what their families would have had to endure. Their experiences and what they had witnessed with the Mendes being taken away did not make their grief any easier. It was absolutely torturous for them to imagine that their kin would have received a similar degree of cruelty in the hands of the British during similar surprise raids.

Temnes who served the British Or Portos were themselves once thriving traders, fishermen or farmers before they became seriously complicit in the abduction and abuse of their fellow Africans. Irrespective of whether they were from other tribes, this dastardly act was weighing heavily on their consciences as ardent Muslims believers. Their relationship with the Or Portos, the generic name for all Europeans amongst the Temnes, was opportunistic to ensure their own survival.

On arrival at Port Lokko, the next stage of sorting was to facilitate the transportation of the Mende captives to Bunce Island. The job to resuscitate the near helpless captives would fall to the Temne workers who were hired and left behind at the port to protect the stock of shackles, extra boxes of gunpowder, implements and other wares. They were usually under the close supervision of a few British sailors who they provided unpaid labour for during the wait for the return of their colleagues and their captives. They would take over the processing in order to relieve some of those who had trekked the round trip. Other duties they performed were to maintain the facilities and help to protect the port area from potential European bandits.

The commandeering of Bunce Island by British merchants, brought with it a policy that would ensure the Temnes who were forced to serve them as helpers, were strictly kept ignorant of what the entire process from capture to shipment was. To guarantee this, some of the strong men from the Temnes were taken to the Island to carry out laborious tasks including building the fortresses, the dungeon and planting vegetables. Their tasks also included pacifying and restraining rambunctious captives and to cook and feed occupants of the dungeon. Men who are abducted from the mainland for these duties were never allowed to make any form of contact with other servants who were stationed on the mainland. The reason for this disconnect was very obvious. The operations on the Island were peculiar, and information on what happened there to the stock of captives held must remain confidential at all cost.

The British were not so worried about the Temne servant's reaction on the mainland as much as they did from rival merchants especially the Portuguese who never ceased to attack the British ports to reclaim what they considered their lost territory. Not only that, the stock of Africans held would be an inviting prospect for the desperate Portuguese. The impact on servants on the mainland, if such information was leaked through to them, could be de-motivating, and they most likely would not want to continue to co-operate with their British benefactors in conducting future raids. Similarly, servants who were involved in the ferrying of the captives to the Island were not allowed to disembark under any circumstance at all. All canoes were to return back to the mainland before dusk. Any canoe found loitering around the Island was shot at and destroyed. Bunce Island was a well-guarded and protected secret.

One of the many British canons used to defend Bunce Island

Sailors on the mainland were replaced by military personnel when the number of captives and processing activities increased significantly. This was to maintain firm control on the servants. Refusal by the Temnes to join raids was absolutely forbidden and not tolerated. Individuals who dared to express their unwillingness were severely punished. Corporal punishment was sanctioned by the administration and was applied, sometimes sadistically by some of the British personnel throughout the entire operation. There was no distinction between captives and servants when it came to dealing with dissent.

Sorting out captives prior to transfer over to Bunce Island was not a very simple task. When abductions were carried out exclusively within the northern regions, treks lasted for a few days at a time and the captives who were mostly Lokkos and Limbas were transported straight to waiting vessels. However, as treks became longer with increasing numbers of captives, the more intricate sorting became.

By the time the Mende captives arrived at Port Lokko, they were usually emaciated after weeks of trekking with little hydration and food. Even the British slavers with all their privileges and facilities felt the strain.

At the Port, the Temne servants were detailed to prepare as much food for the captives as they possibly could from the stock of grains they had pillaged. A few livestock would be slaughtered to add protein to the meagre diet. Captives who fell ill and were considered harmless were unshackled and allowed to bathe on their own and resuscitated by the slavers as best as they could in order to reduce mortality. Every death counted against them. Women who were noticeably pregnant were isolated and kept on the mainland until they had their children and then taken to the island. For the rest of the captives, respite was farfetched. Their neck restraints were removed and both legs shackled and tethered by link chains to restrict mobility. They were then herded in batches down to the river to clean themselves and dry out in the sun. By then, even their loin cloths or whatever protected their modesty would be unfit to salvage. The stench of unclean bodies would pervade the cramped settlement. The gun-toting British salvers would sit along the river banks and fist their eyes lustfully on the captives whilst they clean themselves. Depending on their sexual preferences, they often isolate the odd men, boys or attractive women and raped them severely. These debauched behaviours did not go unnoticed by the Mende men in captivity.

Often the men could hardly bear the painful screams of their women folks being abused. The anger and rage made them forget that they were in bondage. A few of them would attempt to jump unsuspecting slavers, and whenever they were successful, the ranks of the British slavers would sustain an irreplaceable loss. The consequences of such an action was grave but the captives came to realise somehow that in spite of killing their captors, their own lives would still be spared. They will, nonetheless, have to endure the relentless brutality of corporal punishment. During such episodes, the Temne servants who were also becoming exasperated with the inhumane treatment to them and the captives, would pretend not to understand what was going on and would refuse to go to the rescue of their beleaguered masters.

At the port, a huge variety of leg irons, neck irons, handcuffs and miles of link chains stocks were kept for use during raids and transportation of captives to the Island. One of the punishments for men who attacked slavers was to wear a specially-made neck collar. The metal collar was adorned with several spikes that prevented the movement of the head and made it impossible to lie down and sleep. Another measure that was taken by irate slavers was to install face masks on men who were intent on launching spitting and biting attacks on slavers. The slavers had a huge range of paraphernalia to restrain or inflict suffering and hardship on captives. The creativity of British blacksmiths in forging the variety of metal restraints was astounding and reflected the mentality of the British towards Africans.

Illustration of a shackled rebellious slave

After the captives had been rested, refreshed and left practically naked, they were organised in small groups to be canoed to the Island. Transfers were made during the day and by fading light, the last canoe should vacate the moorings of the Island. Whatever went on within the fortress of the island were a closely guarded secret.

Raids on the Mendes living in the hinterland became very significant that other economic activities undertaken by the Temnes and the Lokkos who were drafted into the service of the slavers diminished to a level that threatened the basic existence of their depleting communities. The only viable employment for them was to become servants to the slavers if they were lucky; if not, they were captured and taken away. The continued exposure of the servants especially the Temnes who were considered tougher, to the repeat brutality and cruelty to captives during raids, traumatised them a great deal and was against their Muslim religious principles. Life was unpredictable and unbearable during the slave years. Life for those who served the British slavers and those who were captives was arduous and marginally different. This was a life that lasted for incredibly four hundred years. One where servants could easily become captives without warning and spend the rest of their days in abject misery and deplorable servitude. Generations of Africans were born into a life of hardship, being hunted like animals and brutalised until their demise.

The brutality of the British on Africans was painfully mindless. Violence was thought to be the only means of obtaining the co-operation of their African subjects. Muskets and gun powder became ubiquitous all along the West African coast, and the Temnes knew only too well not to confront an Or Porto carrying one. Over time, the frequency with which they witnessed the extreme cruelty against the Mendes, made the Temnes disaffected, plotted and tried to sabotage the exploitative methods of the Or Portos, whenever the opportunity arose.

Once in a while, Temne servants who were unwilling to participate in this horrendous barbarity became recalcitrant and would put plans together and mutinied against their masters. Uprisings against slavers during return treks back to the port with captives was usually the worse. Captives would join in the melee even though they were restrained and in the pandemonium, some captives would attempt to escape. Often, the Temne mutineers would come out worse, succumbing to several musket shots and survivors rounded up and put in check. Rebellions became very frequent as time went by, and undoubtedly, trust between the slavers and their servants was scant and repeatedly tested. Slavers instituted rotational sentry duties amongst themselves during night stopovers for their own safety. Sentry supervision duties by the slavers was mainly to keep an eye on the servants and to prevent them from mischief. That did not stop the Temnes from manifesting their displeasure at the way they were treated. What frustrated the Temnes most was that the Mendes who should be their natural ally in the circumstance they all found themselves in, did not have an iota of trust in them. A chasm of distrust had been established between them by the slavers. The principle of divide and conquer. The opportunities that the Temnes may have envisaged through collaborating with the British slavers in order to preserve themselves and their kin never materialised. Hardship, cruelty and brutal domination by British slavers became the norm. Hatred and deep loathing for the Or Portos was evident but the musket always prevailed.

Chapter 4
Bunce Island – The Factory

Bunce Island was the less preferable choice by the British to use as the main holding port for processing and the shipping of captured Sierra Leoneans into slavery. There are two larger islands, Tasso and Sherbro Islands along the Freetown estuary on which the British originally set up operations and built fortresses to support their nefarious activities of kidnapping and capturing humans. The occupation of these islands were through the usual force of arms on the authority of a dubious Royal Charter by King Charles II of Britain. The Charter also granted monopoly to a company that the king himself had business interests in to conduct *trade* within and along the West African coast. Trade was merely a pretext to capture human beings to be exploited in plantations and other economic activities in Britain and other places where British interests were unchallenged. The King deployed the British navy in order to support and protect the slave fields, ships and other exploitative activities of the Royal African Company from other marauding Europeans. The Royal Navy's presence along West Africa was to terrorise Africans and also to prevent any other British merchants who attempted to violate the exclusivity granted by the Charter. It is beyond belief and incredible that such a despicable act against Africans was sanctioned at the highest level in the British governance structure. To capture and sell Africans. Proceeds from trading in Africans by the company was shared between the king and other investors of the Company. In contemporary times, this will be regarded as "*Blood money*" or more formally, proceeds from "*Crime*".

The Royal African Company which replaced the original Company of Royal Adventurers of England Trading with Africa, was given additional latitude by a new British Royal Charter in 1668 replacing the old one of 1660. The mandate of the replacement Charter included the establishment of the new company and powers to take over the islands along the Sierra Leone estuary by force of arms. Also, the Company was to construct permanent fortresses (garrisons) for the use of the armed troops. Another significant and important condition of the Charter was that "Martial Law" must be imposed and enforced along the West Coast of Africa by the Royal Navy, necessary to impose order and control. Martial Law on a people who had nothing to do with Britain and were oblivious as to why they would require protection under the prevailing circumstance. The reason for the protection was merely economic, to strengthen and uphold the monopoly to capture Africans and prevent others with similar intentions from doing the same.

The use of brutal military force against any form of resistance mounted by the Temnes, Mendes or others within Sierra Leone was effectively sanctioned by the King. Curiously, the wide ranging conditions of the Charter also included and empowered the Company to set up "Factories". This poses the question of what the primary activity of the factory set up at Bunce Island in particular was about. The Factory was merely a euphemism for the processing of humans captured for shipment into slavery.

On the death of King Charles II, it was not surprising that his brother King James II who succeeded him invigorated the capture of Africans in a bid to increase his share from the proceeds of the Company. It became obvious and quite clear that the business of capture and sale of Africans was evidently lucrative and worth fighting for. Hence, the poor performance of the original Company of Royal Adventurers of England Trading with Africa which preceded the Royal African Company was not to be tolerated.

The Logo of the Royal African Company interestingly was: "*an Elephant and a Castle*". The elephant in the emblem symbolises the value attached to these animals, resulting from the enormous quantities of ivory taken from slaughtered elephants, that once populated the West African Coast. The castle, on the other hand, represented the Royal Navy's active participation and defence of the slaving fields along West Africa. To this day, the Elephant and Castle remains one of the popular historical landmarks in the city of London in Britain, in recognition of the successes of the Royal African Company.

Tasso and Sherbro Islands, although much larger than Bunce Island, were more susceptible to attacks from the Portuguese who once dominated the kidnapping and capture of the Temnes and other tribes living along the coast. When the British forcibly took over especially Sherbro Island, they wiped out all the elephants living on the island for their ivory. This must have been a tremendous haulage that did not escape the attention of the Portuguese, who suddenly became interested in that line of trade too. Not surprising the logo of the company depicted the *Elephant*. The *fortresses and castles* built for security and to display military prowess depicted the other image on the logo of the slaving company. Hence the *"Elephant and Castle"* representing very significant historical activities of Britain along the west coast of Africa. Although the capture of Africans became the primary activity of the Royal African Company, gold, wood and ivory were also plundered indiscriminately as by-products from Sierra Leone like other countries along the west coast.

When captives arrived on Bunce island in little groups by canoes, they are ushered into separate holding pens designated for men, women and children. Men who arrived on the island with the peculiar spiked-neck iron shackle, indicating their temperament, were isolated and taken straight to the dungeon for security reasons and to prevent them from disrupting the activities of further advanced processing of the others.

Entrance to one of the notorious Dungeons on Bunce Island

Since majority of the captives were Mendes, every so often, a few of them were selected to supervise the order and conduct of each group. Those who were appointed to such positions had the freedom to roam the island under the instruction and supervision of the British slavers. An even selected loyal few were allowed to enter the quarters of the merchants to carry out domestic chores. Those who were allowed to enter the quarters of the British slavers were mostly women who would pose little or no threat to their masters. Under no circumstances whatsoever were servants on the island allowed to interact with the Temnes who ferry captives from the mainland by canoe for processing. Supplies for the mainland were carried down to the moorings and left there to be collected by the Temnes on their return trips. Similarly, livestock, fruits and grains were brought over from the mainland and dropped off at the moorings for collection.

Contact was prohibited by the slavers for several reasons. Some of the servants on the island were captives who were captured and processed by the Temnes on the mainland. Attempt to settle grudges could cause instability on the island and disrupt the entire operation. Another important reason for the no contact policy was to protect what was going on within the island from filtering through to the mainland. Once captives had been transferred to the island, Temne servants whose conscience and religious morality were against the way the Mendes were treated, seemed to feel better and literally wash their hands off the process with a sort of relief. It was, therefore, not in the interest of the slavers to let the Temnes know what their Or Portos were up to on the island. These measures adopted did not however eliminate the suspicions of the Temnes. Their first-hand experiences of the actions of the British Or Portos left no doubt in their mind about their capabilities. However, survival and self-preservation were the name of the game, and they played it as best as they could. The security and secrecy of what went on the island were of paramount importance to the administration and merchant slavers.

Since the Royal African Company was owned by the King of England and private merchants by equal shares, the ownership of the stock of captives had to be processed to reflect such ownership. The process of identifying and dividing the stock of captives had to be done prior to shipment. Protection from attacks from their competitors and to maintain order amongst the captives and servants was offered by the British Royal Navy. Therefore, the stock of captured Africans, predominantly Mendes in this instance, had to be split equally and fairly between the King and merchant investors.

The process of sorting the captives initially involved head counting and the captives put into subgroups one belonging henceforth to the King of Britain and the other to the merchants. In one of the out houses was a small station for the resident blacksmith who carried out minor modifications and repairs to shackles, chains and other metal restraints. The blacksmith had a very important role to perform within the grisly and dehumanising operation. Captives who were generally kept stack naked were led individually to the blacksmith who awaited them like a surgeon with implements ready to demonstrate his specialism. Only that, in this instance, the captives unlike the patients of a medical surgeon, would never forget what was going to be inflicted on them, till the end of their days in the plantations.

Captives were kept within the castle in conditions devoid of basic sanitation and human dignity. They huddled together in the evenings and at night to keep themselves warm. The stench of human body and excretions within the enclosures was usually overpowering. It was the duty of the appointed captives who served as workers to feed, provide them with water and ensure some form of cleanliness was maintained amongst them. Captives would repeatedly request the workers to allow them to take a bath. Requests they well knew would not be considered or granted as such a decision would be beyond their remit. The best the workers could do for them, especially when the sun was high in the sky and the heat was unbearable, was to splash them with buckets of cold water, like being hosed down by firefighters.

Workers were ordered to unshackle and take the captives in to the blacksmith for permanent inventory identification called *branding*. This was to append specified markings on captives indicating ownership of each individual. This labelling was to make it easier to account for the proceeds when they are auctioned in the slave markets either in Europe or in the Americas. The markings also symbolised and guaranteed the quality of the human cargo. The screams of men, women and children were disturbing. The pain and suffering were excruciating and unbearable. The act itself was beyond human comprehension.

Captives were pinned to the floor, face up by a couple of workers and the blacksmith would remove a red hot iron from the flames and placed it on the upper torso of the captive. Their skin would sizzle and burn from the hot metal, producing wafts of white smoke. The smell of burning flesh pervaded the air. Unperturbed by the agonising screams of the captives, with a usual slight grin, the blacksmith carried on his menacing duties. The irons were moulded to carry the initials of the owners of the grand operation. One carried the bold letters "**DY**" representing the **D**uke of **Y**ork in England who succeeded his brother to the throne in 1685, becoming King James II. The other iron mould carried the letters "**RAC**" representing the merchants of the **R**oyal **A**frican **C**ompany.

Captives, especially children, would let out ear-piercing screams when the hot iron made contact with their skin writhing in pain under strong restraining hands. Occasionally, captives did suffer cardiac arrests and some would never recover from the shock. The agony and death of captives from this despicable act of branding did not deter the slavers as it was their belief that Africans were born to endure such brutality.

Captives would continue to suffer pain from the branding wounds for weeks until they finally healed, leaving the conspicuous and indelible markings on their naked bodies. These were like batch numbers on manufactured products that slaves carried as tattoos until they died. Hence the naming of Bunce island, "*the factory*".

When the numbers of captives were enough to fill the hold of the slave ships, the captains who usually hung around patiently would load and set sail for the perilous journey across the Atlantic. Often, captives were loaded onto ships still carrying fresh wounds from the branding process. To carry wounds unto slave ships was not a prospect that any of them would ever anticipate. Captives were shackled and crammed together naked in dark, damp, hot and insect-infested holds of ships. This unhygienic conditions often caused branding wounds to become septic resulting in unbearable pain for the captives.

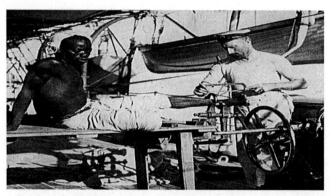

Leg Iron being dangerously sawn off a slave by a British sailor

The sea voyages made by the captives were harrowing. The conditions in the slave ships were appalling. By the end of the terrible journeys across the Atlantic, the African captives were usually left completely emaciated. A lot of the captives who survived the perilous journeys would disembark at the various destinations, in conditions close to death. The physical conditions of the captives were usually so deplorable, the slave merchants would keep the captives at docks, to feed and allow them to regain some weight in order to maximise the sales proceed in the markets.

One such location is the *"Valongo Slave Wharf"* in Rio de Janeiro in Brazil where millions of African captives were discharged, bound for the slave markets. Around the Valongo Wharf, there were mass graves wherein thousands of captives who succumbed to the hazards of the sea voyages were buried. The Valongo Wharf was one of such significant discharging ports during centuries of slaving that the United Nations Educational, Scientific and Cultural Organisation (UNESCO) declared the wharf a world heritage site in 2017. The site, the Organisation indicated, would carry similar official recognition and status in history as Hiroshima where the United States dropped the first Nuclear Bomb and Auschwitz, the site of the Jewish pogrom during the Second World War.

Life on Bunce Island was torturous and ghastly. The extent of abuse on captives was despicable. Captives who were selected to serve their British slavers were traumatised with what they witnessed perennially on the island. Captives who died on the island from, for example infected wounds from branding, were taken out on canoes and dropped in the sea. The reason for not burying them on the island was to prevent contamination of their drinking water which was drawn from a well.

The callousness, insensitivity and cruelty meted out to Sierra Leoneans by British slavers was disturbing. Ironically, the slavers found solace from their hectic factory activities by exploiting the sensual attractiveness of the Mende women who they handpicked to serve as domestic servants. The women would sing melodiously when carrying out their chores. These were mainly songs of melancholy and suffering from their past and most recent experiences. The slavers, however, found them very sexually attractive, within an environment pervaded by human suffering and morbidity.

Female Mende workers were frequently made to entertain their masters with their songs of despair, but because the merchants did not understand the lyrics of the songs, they merely enjoyed the melodies. The women were regularly and repeatedly sexually assaulted by their masters who quite often were inebriated after imbibing copious quantities of gin. Those with a preference for boys would keep teenage Mende boys to be abused on the island until

67

they grow up into manhood. When the slavers felt threaten by them, they too would be branded and put on board ships to be traded in the Americas. Women servants who were repeatedly abused and became pregnant as a result would be allowed to have children. Those too young to conceive, suffered and died from the complications of pregnancy and were interred the same way like others before them, at sea.

Mixed race children born by African women were called *"mulattos"*. Babies born on the island and mainland were kept until they grew older to join the ranks of the slavers. Some of the mulattos grew up to be popular agents of British slavers. They adopted the names of the British slavers, such as Caulker, Tucker and Cleveland. They were as ruthless in the capture of Africans as the British slavers. They did not consider themselves native to Sierra Leone, and why should they, with the domination and abuse of Africans by Europeans so glaring. Most of the mulattos had mothers from the Mende tribe who were initially taken as slaves but were selected by the slavers to work as domestic servants. Mulattos were more often than not conceived through repeated sexual abuse by the slavers, and although the children were allowed to be brought up in the company of their mothers, they usually had some latitude with the slavers. Mixed-race children born in such depraved environment, did not often know their fathers. They usually found favour in the slavers and grew up to adopt their wicked ways. Mulattos were able to speak both the language of their mothers and that of the slavers. They took advantage of their unique position and conspired effectively to capture both Mendes and Temnes.

Mulattos became very effective during the period leading to and after the abolition of the trade in Africans as slaves. The price for Africans in the slave markets soared due to the reduction in supply as only recalcitrant merchants and sailors were determined and prepared to continue the trade through smuggling. The Mulattos were unpopular amongst the natives and paid heavily with their lives in instances where they over-exaggerated their privileged position and pushed their luck too far. They acquired a lot of gold and other precious items from their lucrative endeavours. The reputation of the Mulattos was terrible. After the collapse of capturing people and following the reputation of the ruthless Mulattos, many women from both tribes would abandon mixed-race children at birth to avoid being stigmatised or associated with the outlaws. Some of the women were rejected by their communities and labelled harlots in spite of the abuse they had suffered in the hands of the British slavers that resulted in their pregnancy in the first place.

With the passage of time, the number of workers grew larger in order to cater for the demands of the increasing number of captives held in the entrepot system of Bunce Island. Despite the size of the island, the slavers worked out that it would be safer and more reliable to grow food on the island to sustain the inhabitants. Some of the captives who were well known for their rice cultivation skills and animal husbandry skills were put to work whilst awaiting shipment. Seedlings and livestock stolen on raids were transferred over from the mainland.

The cycle of pillaging, kidnapping and capture continued for over four hundred years. Trekking became longer and the caravans larger over time. Bunce Island became a very important processing site for countless number of captured Sierra Leoneans and many others from neighbouring Guinea and the Gambia. The Mende population and their communities were totally decimated. Abuse and cruelty towards the captives on the island by the British slavers was unrelenting. The agony and suffering by the captives was unimaginable but worse was yet to come. The final steps of the captives from Bunce Island on to the waiting vessels was the beginning of the next phase of extreme hardship during the long journey into the unknown.

Bunce Island is an island were humanity was redefined, a tomb where the souls of many perished and the sweet and melodious voices of the women of the Mende tribe will forever ever linger.

The entire chain from capture to servitude was beset by painful abuse and suffering. After spending time on the notorious Bunce Island, the captives would have been branded like cattle, their legs shackled and tethered to each other and for those who continued to resist, neck iron and muzzles applied in preparation for the longest journey of their miserable life. A journey from freedom, humanity and tranquillity. A journey to evil, barbarism and perpetual drudgery but firstly, a journey to the slave market. A market where they would be penned and auctioned like the livestock they used to keep. A market where they were identified by the branding of the Royal African Company, "**RAC**" and **"DY"**, the Duke of York. A market where they were described as authentic strong *wretches* and *wenches* with skills and abilities uncommon to their owners.

Africans were sold like cattle after enduring the dehumanising and gruelling journeys to European and American slave markets. The following is an illustration of how people kidnapped from

Sierra Leone were advertised for sale. This particular transaction took place in Charleston, South Carolina in the year 1769. A total of ninety-four assorted Sierra Leoneans, including boys and girls whose future turned from optimism to a nightmare of anguish and the perpetual indignity of servitude were being advertised for sale:

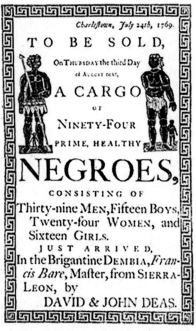

Auction advert for slaves taken from Sierra Leone

The advert referred to "a cargo of ninety-four prime, healthy NEGROES, consisting of thirty-nine men, fifteen boys, twenty-four women and sixteen girls. Just arrived in the Brigantine Dembia, (the vessel) Francis Bare, Master, from Sierra Leon, by David and John Deas (the dealers)".

Whilst nearly all the Mendes taken from the shores of Sierra Leone were transported and marketed in the Americas, most of the Temnes were transported to and marketed in Europe. Mainly Portugal, Spain and Britain. Although the sea journey to Europe was shorter, the experiences were similar.

The operations of the facilities at Bunce Island was subsequently taken over by two British slave merchant companies, Grant, Oswald & Company and John & Alexander Anderson when the abolition movement against the trading of Africans as slaves became too strong for the British government to ignore. The new owners of the Company continued to operate the "*factory*" as a private entity during the struggle for abolition, a period when slave trading became extremely profitable due to the reduction in shipments of human cargo.

The cruelty and brutality on the captives during their transit through Bunce Island continued unabated. The Temnes eventually got wind of what was going on within the walls of the castle on the Island. They detested what the British merchants were doing to the captives, and they finally launched a rebellion against the British slavers. Refusing to provide them with transportation and other logistics. The British Royal Navy ruthlessly put down such rebellions, and those who survived the wrath of the slavers, taken away to be sold. The company operating from Bunce Island was not prepared to encourage any form of rambunctious behaviour from the Temnes that might disrupt their operations and embarrass the British government.

It was quite evident that from the cunning Portuguese and subsequently the militarised operations by British slavers along West Africa and in particular Sierra Leone, the actual trading of Africans as slaves actually took place away from the shores of the continent, in Europe, the Caribbean and the Americas.

The promulgation of Royal Charters empowering British merchants, sailors and armed troops to capture and carry out what could only be characterised as widespread criminality against Africans during such a prolonged period is truly incredible. African communities were perennially under siege. Generations of Africans were born into anarchy, perpetual fear, disappearances and agonising deaths. The life of the Mendes was a living hell because they were particularly sought after as they fetched premium prices in the rice plantations of Carolina and the cotton fields in America. Descendants of the indefatigable Mendes, the Gullahs, still live in South Carolina and Georgia in the United States.

71

Chapter 5
The Human Trade

The trading of Africans by the British in particular, flourished and brought enormous wealth to lots of Britons. The economy boomed during the centuries of dealing in Africans, and ironically, the Bank of England was established amongst other institutions, which subsequently became the reputable banker's bank in Britain. Times were so good that one James Houston, a worker for a firm of 18th century English slave merchants, wrote, *"What a glorious and advantageous (slave) trade this is... It is the hinge on which all the trade of this globe moves."* Undoubtedly, this must have been a wonderful and glorious time to capture and trade Africans. Britain was a major player in this horrendous activity next to the Portuguese and traded a significant proportion of the approximately fifteen million Africans who landed into slavery. When one considers the multiplier effect of the production of the African slaves during their lifetime on plantations in the Caribbean and USA, coupled with the enormous proceeds from by-products of ivory and gold, times had to be *gloriously* good.

What was not so glorious was the destruction of African societies, the indiscriminate slaughter of Africans who resisted capture and confronted British armed forces and lost. Also, most significantly was the dehumanising way Africans were treated which ultimately formed the foundation of the pejorative social status and stereotype of Africans by Europeans. The widespread racism and deplorable discriminatory practices against Africans by Caucasians is no doubt founded on the ideology of supremacy of the Caucasian race to Africans. The result of the prolonged inhumane activity of state-sponsored kidnappings and capture, at such a magnitude that humanity will ever witness, still characterises the way Caucasians engage with and regard Africans.

The ideology of race supremacy based on human skin complexion emanated from dealing in Africans during the slaving era. A pernicious ideology that has to a large extent formed the basis for most prejudices against Africans in modern times. The danger of this belief is that being a latent characteristic innate in so many Caucasians, it exudes and manifest itself in various guises consciously or unconsciously, through the actions and behaviours of those who carry such vile traits. The stability of humanity will always be threatened by such spurious and perfidious thinking and values.

Over four hundred years of capturing Africans into slavery, the resistance by the people never waned.

The determination by successive generations of Africans whether in Africa or in the plantations of the Americas, to extricate themselves from the scourge and horrors of slavery, was staunch. Many lost their lives, severely tortured and suffered immensely in confronting their assailants and de facto masters. Whilst there was a reluctant acceptable practice for British slavers to gun down Africans resisting kidnap and capture in Africa, that was not the case on the plantations. Although plantation owners could kill African slaves at will if they wished, this was not a policy that was pursued because of the value attached to a live slave. Besides, it makes business sense to keep a rowdy but strong productive recalcitrant alive. That does not suggest that the life of an African in or out of slavery was sacred; this was merely a business strategy. Slavers, merchants and a cross section of the British society never regarded Africans as humans; therefore, morality was not a factor they considered regarding the treatment meted out to Africans. To quote a British Navy Captain Yorke who asserted during the eighteenth century discourse on the viability of the slave trade, that "*The West India Planters have the same right of property in their slaves as the farmers of Cambridgeshire have in their ploughs and waggons*". Incredible as this might appear, this was the general perception of Africans by the British public, as mere objects or sub-human that could be owned and cared for like animals. This thinking underpins the bigotry and prejudices experienced by Africans not only in modern Britain but also in other European societies.

The extent of bigotry, discrimination and racism witnessed in modern times is derived from the treatment of Africans in captivity and in the slave markets. The marketing of Africans by British slavers was not dissimilar to the marketing of cattle, horses or farming implements as can be seen from the following sale notices:

TO BE SOLD on board the Ship *Bance Island*, on tuesday the 6th of *May* next, at *Ashley-Ferry*; a choice cargo of about 250 fine healthy

NEGROES,

just arrived from the Windward & Rice Coast. —The utmost care has already been taken, and

This notice was for the sale of 250 Africans, described as "*a choice cargo, fine healthy Negroes just arrived from the Windward & Rice Coast*". Windward is the historical reference to West Africa, and "*Rice Coast*" specifically refers to Sierra Leone. These were predominantly Mende expert rice farmers who were to be sold off the slave ship aptly named "*Bance Island*". The ship was named after the notorious "*factory*" at Bunce Island where countless Sierra Leoneans were processed and branded like cattle prior to shipment to the slave markets. This is an indication of how important the *factory at Bunce Island* was in the slaving business of Britain.

Another notice of sale included the conditions on which the unfortunate Africans were to be sold follows:

Negroes for Sale.

A Cargo of very fine stout Men and Women, in good order and fit for immediate service, just imported from the Windward Coast of Africa, in the Ship Two Brothers.— Conditions are one half *Cash* or *Produce*, the other half payable the first of *January* next, giving Bond and Security if required.

The Sale to be opened at 10 o'Clock each Day, in Mr. Bourdeaux's Yard, at No, 48, on the Bay.
May 19, 1784.   JOHN MITCHELL.

The above notice for the sale of "*A cargo of very fine stout men and women in good order and fit for immediate service, just imported from the Windward Coast of Africa, in the Ship Two Brothers. Conditions are one half cash or produce, the other half payable the first of January next, giving Bond and Security if required. The sale to be opened at 10 O'clock, each day, in Mr Bourdeaux's Yard at No, 48, on the Bay".*

Men and women described as fit for immediate service, sounds like the sale of motor vehicles. The terminology used by the British slavers is indicative of their perception of Africans, not as humans but as chattels. Africans were incredibly exchanged for "*produce*". Most likely, cotton, sugar, tobacco or rice. Their hopes and aspirations as human beings were never to be realised. Their fate and survival depended on the value placed on them and the quantity of cotton or sugar a prospective buyer was prepared to part with in exchange for them. These perceptions and ideologies have been handed down through generations. Hence the unrelenting spate of racism and discrimination within British and other European societies against Africans.

In the United States for example, the struggle between Africans and Caucasians appears paradoxical. African-Americans have been fighting an intense liberation struggle through various forms of affirmative actions for centuries. Some of these actions are not very different from the struggles of the early days in the plantations. Countless number of African-Americans and their leaders have lost their lives in these perennial struggles just as it was centuries ago. The overtly inhumane and unnatural master and servant relationship, as it used to be in the plantations, may have disappeared but has morphed into a more sophisticated ideology which pervades the essence of the American society. The part of America that African-Americans will remain unable to access. An America that believes that, whatever was created on the backs of Africans should remain exclusively with the masters. An America that only sees blood and tears flowing from the bodies and faces of Africans as a manifestation of supremacy and dominance. An America that regards the lynching of Africans as a rite of passage and masculinity. Chants and slogans such as, "*Let us reclaim the dignity of our America*", "*We want our country back*", "*let us make America great again*" and strangely, "*Let us reload*" are all calls to the ideological classes of the "*Masters*" to unite and continue the unrelenting subjugation and social and economic isolation of African-Americans.

The success of African-Americans aspirations and the quest for equality will require a radical transformation and a strategic approach to the movement for change. If the odds against African-Americans are motivated by ideology, then marching, sit-ins and mass protests alone will not achieve the desired outcomes.

In the month of June of the year 2015, nine African-Americans including the pastor who also happened to be a state senator, were shot and killed by a white supremacist inside the oldest African Methodist Episcopal church, the "*Mother Emanuel*" in Charleston, South Carolina. South Carolina happened to be one of the main destinations for Sierra Leoneans taken into slavery. This abominable act was executed in such a brutal and cold-blooded manner for no conceivable reason other than hate fuelled by prejudice. The assassin was a twenty-one-year-old boy who had received a firearm from his parents as a birthday gift. A birthday present that would cost the lives of nine adults, religiously pious Africans who innocently and genuinely welcomed the miscreant into the church during a session of Bible studies, with open arms. Without warning, the bigoted assailant got up during the study session and mindlessly slaughtered each of his defenceless victims without compunction. During the execution of this devout group of nine, who in all their years have endured the scourge of racism and discrimination, the bigot uttered vile racist slurs and in his confidence, remarked that what he was doing had to be done. He was composed enough to reload his deadly weapon twice before completing the gruesome job. Before he walked out of the desecrated edifice of Mother Emanuel, he turned to a petrified survivor and said to her, "*I am going to let you live, so that you can tell the story to others*".

The Mother Emanuel had its origin dating back to 1791 when slaves were prohibited from congregating. Its founders were arrested and detained, but in about 1822, the church was targeted and burnt down following an aborted slave revolt, implicating one of the founders of the church. Thirty-five of those arrested, including one of the founders of the church, were summarily executed. They were accused of inspiring the slave revolt. The church was rebuilt and continued to play an important role in the civil rights movement. After over two hundred years since the trade in Africans was seemingly abolished, the prejudice that motivated slavery is very much alive. Within weeks of the appalling shooting of the nine African-Americans at Mother Emanuel, seven other churches perceived to be African churches were also burnt down.

The extreme prejudice of Caucasian-Americans against African-Americans is despicable and lamentable. The mere mention of gun control and the suggestion to discontinue the display of the peculiar confederate flag by the first African-American president of the United States of America sparked an incredibly-vitriolic reaction from a cross section of the society. Not only did the President become the recipient of the usual racist vitriol, the insensitivity displayed within some sections of the society was appalling. The ideology of race supremacy is pernicious and insidiously destructive. Whilst Caucasian-Americans hold firmly to their beliefs and god-giving rights and privileges including the perpetual subjugation of African-Americans, they invidiously propagate negativity and continue to deprive African-Americans access to conditions that will guarantee them some semblance of humanity, recognition and equality.

The behaviour of Caucasians towards Africans is quite perplexing and to all intent and purposes, goes against human reasoning. The ancestors of African-Americans were brutalised and through their blood, sweat, tears and lives laid the foundation on which the glorious existence of Caucasians now flourish. The natural tendency for any civilisation is to appreciate and be moral to those on whose shoulders the height of economic success was attained. Rather this unusual behaviour appears to be driven by the idea that if Africans were totally annihilated, the consciences of their oppressors would be cleansed.

To influence a change in the bigoted behaviour of the oppressors, requires a commensurate paradigm change in African-American's social, cultural and educational structures and beliefs. The sporadic display of anger and frustration through riots in reaction to atrocities against African-Americans achieves hardly anything. Ideological change happens over time but requires unity, co-operation, dedication and a solid commitment to achieve the desired goals in the face of adversity.

In Sierra Leone, which was one of the original and main sources of humans that sustained the notorious slave trade, there were incessant ambushes and vigorous resistance by the Mendes to protect their families and communities just like other tribes in the country and in other parts of Africa. Although their efforts largely failed against the muskets of British slavers, their resolve and determination contravenes the assertion that chiefs and tribal leaders in Africa were selling their subjects and kin into slavery. When raids were made and the manner in which they were carried out within African communities, most of the leaders were captured and forcibly taken away and their communities left rudderless and in chaos. As they tended to have many beautiful wives, the women were often raped, abused and taken with their children in tow. Chiefs and tribal leaders were themselves battle hardened warriors; their fearlessness and leadership skills were what qualified them for the positions they held in the first place. It is, therefore, inconceivable for men of such stature and status within their enclaves to sell the people whom they had tenaciously defended and in many instances, put their own lives on the line.

The exchange of cloths, rum and sugar for gold, ivory, copper and spices went on with mostly genuine Temne traders who the British merchants would rather not capture or kill. A significant depletion of the Temne population would have had a negative impact on the processing and throughput of the precious items and humans from Sierra Leone.

For centuries, Africans in slavery assiduously fought and protested against the brutality of their bondage. The movement for their emancipation was often vigorously frustrated but never extinguished. There were many major revolts in places like Barbados in 1816, Demerara (Guyana) in 1822, Jamaica 1831-32 and Haiti between 1791-1804. There were also continuous revolts and upheavals on board slave ships. The revolts became increasingly violent, and lots of Africans and few slavers lost their lives during such skirmishes. The economics of slavery was attractive and effective to those who benefited from the lucrative but immoral and despicable trade.

The American independence in 1776 in many ways negatively impacted on the trade of sugar and cotton immensely in Britain, as American plantation owners were free to trade with other Europeans and slave enclaves in the Caribbean. The political dynamics in Britain changed in response to the transformation in America. British slavers lost influence and the clout to frustrate the discontinuation of the outrageous trade in Africans.

A Bill for the abolition of the trade in slaves passed the Houses of the British parliament in 1807. The 1807 Act abolished the trade in Africans as slaves but not slavery itself. Another Bill for the abolition of slavery within the British Empire went through the British parliament in 1833. That Act came into force in 1834 when it received Royal Accent. Ironically, these Acts were enacted to abolish what were in fact illegal and immoral by all conceivable accounts in the first place.

The 1833 Abolition Act sought to put an end to the despicable activity but proposed a gradual reduction in slavery. Initially, slaves who were incredibly six years old and younger were freed. Slaves who were over six years old were to be re-designated apprentices. It was proposed that apprentices were to be discharged from servitude in two stages, in 1838 and 1840, when the final set would be released from bondage. The change in nomenclature which was practically forcing slavers to recognise slaves as human beings instead of properties, was vociferously rejected by slave owners in both sides of the Atlantic. The apprenticeship scheme was eventually abandoned but the rest of the Act remained enforceable with provisions to compensate slavers and plantation owners for the loss of their stock of slaves.

Plantation owners and other slave owners were heavily compensated by the British government for the loss of their "*business assets*" in slaves to an estimated £20m. That was an enormous amount of compensation in those days. This was an indication of how significant the trade of Africans was to the economy of Britain. Amongst those who received compensation for holding Africans as properties was the Bishop of the Church of England in Exeter at that time. An amount of £12,700 for 665 slaves held in the West Indies was paid to him. A member of the British Royalty who owned 2,554 slaves in six plantations was paid over £26,000. Those were huge sums of money paid out by the government. The total compensation of £20m would equate to billions of pounds in current times. There were all sorts of complications regarding the compensation payments akin to business transaction relating to the loss of property. The act of paying out compensations was clearly a demonstration of the fact that the British society regarded Africans purely as business assets rather than human beings. Incredibly, in modern Britain and other European countries, the progenies of slavers and successive generations do not recognise and pitifully fail to understand the impact the trade in Africans as slaves has had on the African race. The effect on Africans is far more than the financial loses their ancestors incurred as a result of this social change. Africans, as victims of this appalling activity, are strangely scoffed at every so often when they attempt to bring the effect and legacy of slavery to the spotlight. Such an attitude is undoubtedly potent bigotry and the continued pejorative manner in which Africans are generally regarded.

Lots of wealthy Britons today have inherited riches built on the blood, sweat and tears of Africans. There are many homes and families in Britain that still possess artefacts and memorabilia belonging to the days Africans were traded as commodities in slave markets.

In reality, both the 1807 and the 1833 Acts did not actually put an end to slavery, as the capture and trade of Sierra Leoneans continued unabated. Nonetheless, the 1833 Act especially motivated some slaves in the Caribbean to commence and others to intensify their fight and movement in the pursuit of freedom from servitude.

Since the trade in slaves did not take place in Africa but in Britain and within its enclaves, the spirit of the 1807 Act was to abolish the trade in slaves which in turn was hoped would diminish or eliminate the demand or pull factor that motivated the capture of Africans. The Acts abolishing the trade in slaves were a complete opposite of the Royal Charters, which were ironically not rescinded. Royal Charters empowered and granted monopoly to British merchants to capture Africans illegally, declaring the west coast of Africa an exclusive kidnapping and capture zone for British merchants and companies trading in slaves. The ultimate act of despotism in the modern world.

There was intense filibustering by the slavers lobby in Britain during the early years, preventing the original Act intended to abolish the evil trade in Africans and to successfully make it illegal to conduct such a trade. Notwithstanding, the negative publicity and revolts by the slaves continued to create awareness and drew moderate public attention to the cruelty and barbarism of the trade and its associated activities.

Merchants, farmers and businesses in Britain who once flourished through the use of unpaid African labour, anticipated that with the eventual passing of the Act, they would be liable to fines and prosecutions if they continued to hold Africans in servitude. Acknowledging the inevitable and the reality of change, they took pre-emptive measures prematurely driving away the African slave labourers from their farms and homes with threats of certain death if they dared to return.

With nowhere to go, hundreds of Africans began sleeping rough along the streets of Britain begging for hand-outs and scraps. The plight of the poor people and the negative publicity it generated, prompted an initiative by the government to transport them back to Africa from whence they came. In 1791, the British government ordered the Royal Navy to round up as many of the poor Africans loitering around the city of London and to transport them back to one of their notorious stomping grounds, Sierra Leone. The Royal Navy arrested about four hundred Africans, men and women, some of whom were domestic servants, took them aboard their ships and set sail for the west coast of Africa. Interestingly, the removal of indigent African slaves from the streets of London, for transportation back to West Africa, serendipitously triggered a change in the strategy of exploiting Africans by Britain.

Chapter 6
The Experiment

When the first naval shipment of abandoned slaves arrived in Sierra Leone, the ruling Temne leader based within the Sierra Leone peninsular, King Tom was approached by the British armed forces and ordered to accept the African returnees into his community. In the ensuing interaction with King Tom, he was coerced into signing a document, the contents of which he was unfamiliar. Nonetheless, under immense pressure, he proceeded to sign what at best could be characterised as a dubious and an illegal transaction calculated to acquire land. The document turned out to be a Treaty that accorded instant rights to the British government to facilitate the return of slaves to and occupy an undeterminable piece of land in-perpetuity. Another intrigue was that the piece and parcel of land that was appropriated by the Treaty was to be under the exclusive ownership and control of the British Crown. The Royal military personnel succeeded in having their way with King Tom who succumbed to their ultimate pressure. The military personnel then proceeded to demarcate a selected area and made it safe as a settlement for the returnees. The returned slaves were then apportioned rations and implements then left behind to fend for themselves under the purported responsibility of King Tom. However, because the returned slaves had lost the resistance to malaria and other tropical deceases over time, during their enslavement in Europe, they found it excruciatingly difficult to cope with the heavy topical rainfall and climatic conditions of Sierra Leone. The entire settlement succumbed to and perished from the virulence of malaria and other tropical illnesses. The death of all of the returned slaves was a slight setback for the project.

Despite the failure in their original attempt to resettle the slaves, the British government was not deterred by the hazards of the potential camp environment. With the Treaty that was signed by King Tom in hand, the British government proceeded to set up a new organisation to manage the land acquisition and to continue the resettlement program. The *Sierra Leone Company* was subsequently formed by the British government to facilitate further organised repatriations of African slaves, who by then were regarded as *"Black Poor"* within British societies. The Africans were no longer referred to as slaves because they were deemed to be without ownership. To empower the company to remove and return more abandoned African slaves from the streets of England, under a seemingly legitimate environment, a bill was passed in the British parliament entitled *"The Sierra Leone Settlement"*. The Treaty that King Tom signed under duress underpinned the bill. The settlement that the original set of returned slaves occupied and its immediate environs were declared British property within the context of the Bill for *the Sierra Leone Settlement,* which passed through parliament in May 1791. Whilst the Royal African Company dealt with the extraction of Sierra Leoneans and other Africans, the Sierra Leone Company symbolised the dawn of a new episode of subjugation and tyranny on the people.

From 1792 onwards, and until after the abolition Act of 1807, African slaves were returned to the settlement in Sierra Leone by the British on the pretext of an experimental project. This experimentation turned out to be a subtle but deliberate change in the strategy of subjugating Africans. Since general opinion on the method of capturing and enslaving Africans was changing, it was considered prudent by the British government to explore other means of achieving the same outcome with minimal social cost.

Attempts were also made to resettle African slaves who had gained liberation from bondage in America and had migrated northward into Canada for their safety. They had moved away from the deep southern states in America, following the American Revolution. These slaves were called *Nova Scotians*, named after the place they settled in Canada, Nova Scotia. A larger number of African slaves from Nova Scotia were transported to Sierra Leone under the purported sponsorship of the British government. With the protection of British armed forces, the Nova Scotians were returned to a slightly different location towards the east of the peninsular in Sierra Leone. Granville Town was the new site away from the location where the *"Black Poor"* slaves from Britain settled originally. The successive groups of African slave returnees from Canada were more adaptable to the conditions in Sierra Leone which were not dissimilar to the harsh conditions in the plantations in America. They swiftly established a settlement connecting to the original site.

Another group of African slaves where returned to the Sierra Leone peninsular after those from Nova Scotia, Canada. A group of rambunctious slaves who had been fighting perennial battles for their freedom as unpaid plantation workers, were also encouraged to return to Sierra Leone from Jamaica. Those were Africans who maintained their resistance and persistent in their rejection of enslavement. They launched sporadic violent revolts against slave masters in the sugar plantations of Jamaica. They had been militants and every so often, a few of them were recaptured and executed for their militancy and disruption of economic activities. Since they were already out of the bondage of slavery and protected by the abolition Acts of the British parliament, they were entitled to be removed from the slave enclave and returned to Africa unconditionally into total freedom. At least that was what they anticipated. On the arrival of the slaves in the Sierra Leone peninsular from Jamaica, they were united with the Nova Scotians who had already been settled there before them. The returnees from Jamaica were called *"Maroons"*. Unlike the earlier settlers from Canada, the Maroons were impertinent and could hardly conform to the docile ways and practices of the Nova Scotians. It was not long before a flash point occurred between the two groups. The Maroons, some of whom were well accustomed to combat, swiftly defeated their co-settlers and drove them away from their settlement which was located closer to the moorings.

The Sierra Leone peninsular was called *"Freetown"* by British abolitionists. As the name implies, all liberated slaves were apparently granted freedom upon arrival on the peninsula in Sierra Leone.

The Maroons originally from Trelawney Town in Jamaica, took over what is now the centre of Freetown, and renamed the settlement, *Maroon Town*. The differences in attitude and behaviour between the various groups of Africans liberated from slavery were remarkably distinct. Although some of the returnees were born to slave parents within the brutality of slavery and not originally from Africa themselves, the harshness of the conditions of servitude and the legacy of resistance together predicated their temperaments. Therefore, the placid subservience of the Nova Scotians could hardly be comprehended by the Maroons, who never allowed themselves to be totally subjugated by the plantation owners without a struggle. The Maroons were aggressive in their approach to

84

conducting affairs, as was their relationships with the plantation owners. They were however yet to experience the wrath of King Jimmy who was not as charitable as his predecessor, King Tom who was forced by the British to sign the Treaty that ceded land to the British to create the Freetown settlements. With the protection of the Sierra Leone Company and the British Royal Navy, the returnees were able to continue the habitation of their new home to the displeasure of their host, now King Jimmy.

Though the returned people were themselves Africans, the diverse temperaments, languages and cultures generally adopted whilst in servitude made the people who were originally from the same stock markedly incompatible. This was an indication and precursor to the problems of integration and interaction that were going to beset Africans for generations to come.

The abolition of slavery in 1807 threw the trading in Africans as slaves into total confusion. A lot of private British merchants refused to comply with the Abolition Act prohibiting the trade in Africans. They continued capturing people and resorted to illegal methods of smuggling captives across the Atlantic to America and the Caribbean. The reason for their dogged determination to continue the trade was based on their grievances including, that the number of African slaves were reducing drastically on the plantations through runaways and death caused by old age. They claimed that they required to replenish lost stock and were determined to do just that. Another factor that motivated the actions of the obdurate British slave merchants to continue the capture of Africans was the soaring prices paid for individuals in the slave markets in America. The price surges were inevitably the result of the significant reduction in the supply of Africans following the seeming abolition movement.

The intransigent and recalcitrant British merchants continued capturing and smuggling Africans for over sixty years after the abolition of the trade in Africans. During this period of utter chaos, Africans would be kidnapped or captured, processed as usual and put on board ships heading for America, only to be intercepted by Royal Navy patrols enforcing the abolition. These patrols were ordered by the British government, comprising men who were desperate to distinguish themselves from their compatriots who continued to play active part in the trade of slaves. They also wanted to present Britain as philanthropic and altruistic in the prevailing circumstances. Perhaps not as clear cut as that. Their real intention was to contain Africans in Africa and to continue the horrors of subjugation outside the conditions and oversight of the Act of the British parliament that abolished the trade in Africans.

Slave merchant ships intercepted were escorted to Freetown, and their human cargoes unloaded and set free irrespective of where they were captured from initially. This operation became problematic, especially with the Maroons who were located around the moorings subsequently named after King Jimmy. The Maroons and the Nova Scotians who had been living within the settlement, could not speak any of the languages of the new arrivals. The new arrivals were called "*Re-captives*". They were so called because the slave ships wherein they were contained and tethered were intercepted on the high seas and redirected to Freetown by the Royal Navy before they reached their destination. A large number of the re-captives were from what is present day Nigeria.

The Maroons especially were aggressive towards the re-captives and did not allow them to settle in their midst. The Nova Scotians were much more amenable, considerate and charitable towards them. Their mild character was attributed to their exposure to Christianity as a religion whilst they were in the plantations in America. The dynamics was quite intriguing. There were three groups of the same people with three different cultures, temperaments and characteristics. The Nova Scotians were hard working, some of them with acquired skills in carpentry and masonry, worked tirelessly to create their environment, replicating the style of accommodations of their slave masters in the plantations in America. Tasks were carried out communally, and they welcomed the re-captives into their settlements despite the communication issues which they did not see as a problem, bearing in mind that their ancestors were taken into slavery and adopted the languages of their captors. On the other hand, the Maroons who had ceased working hard as slaves for a long time and were used to raiding the plantations they used to work in for food, promptly regarded the re-captives as a potential threat. Interestingly, although the re-captives were emaciated and generally traumatised from their ordeal which was quite fresh, they preferred not to engage the Maroons in any form of aggression but rather to re-orientate themselves and decide either to live with the Nova Scotians or move on. Most of them did move on under the assistance and protection of the scant British forces in the port area and around the vicinity of the Maroon Town.

With the passage of time, the number of re-captives continued to increase but the residual increase did not correlate to the numbers landing. Re-captives who were originally captured in Sierra Leone did not settle in Freetown. They navigated their way back to their kin in the hinterland. Some of those from Guinea or Liberia also moved on making perilous journeys through the dense tropical forest back to their origins.

The messages brought back by the re-captives varied and sometimes contrasting depending on their tribal group. The Mendes who were in the majority, returned with grim messages of their experiences on the hands of the slavers and their Temne workers. That did not help relations between the two tribal groups in anyway, in fact the desire by the Mendes to seek revenge could not be stronger. Conversely, Temne re-captives who were deeply suspicious of the Or Portos, reported back to their kin about the sprawling settlements they saw in the Freetown area where they were discharged and set free. They were nervous of what the Or Portos might be up to next by their seemingly permanent presence within the new settlements, which were within a striking distances from theirs. The anxieties and aggressions of the Maroons were also due to suspicion and distrust for the British who they thought were in cahoots with the re-captives. The frequent landings and discharge of re-captives was a development that caused the Maroons a lot of unease.

The Sierra Leone Company continued shipping more Nova Scotians into Freetown, whilst the number of the re-captives rose too. Re-captives who were originally captured from as far afield as Nigeria were not keen to navigate their way back but some from Ghana did return. Those who decided to settle in Freetown, forged relationships with the Nova Scotian groups which was larger than that of the Maroons. In order to establish their own communities and to continue to work the land, they made their way to the south of the main settlements up into the mountains where they found a peaceful and uninhabited arable land space.

The Temnes became increasingly concerned with the developments in the Freetown area. They perceived the Or Portos as acting as if they owned their land as opposed to being temporary occupants, who wished to run the resettlements for African returnees as an experiment. It was quite obvious that the British Or Portos were not interested in what the Temne thinking was, as they continued piling confiscated slave ships along the harbour. The flow of liberated slaves and re-captives did not subside in the least, rather, landings continue to increase. The change in the British strategy of enslaving Africans was rapidly unfolding.

The Temne King Jimmy made formal approaches to the Sierra Leone Company representatives regarding their operations in Freetown, but the British did not show any interest in engaging in any form of dialogue. They referred him to the Treaty King Tom, his predecessor signed. The apparent error by King Tom to inadvertently relinquish ownership to an undeterminable piece of land, albeit through coercion, became clear to him.

By 1808, the exasperated King Jimmy and his kinsmen had launched a series of intense attacks on the settlements killing a lot of the returnees. However, in all of the aggressions, the Temnes came out worse as the Sierra Leone Company was able to recruit the services of the British Royal Navy to repel them with severe consequences. The Temnes suffered heavy losses during those attacks and were left increasingly unhappy with the state of affairs.

The military encounter between the Sierra Leone Company and the Temne leaders caused further distrust and hate between them. The returnees were the once who paid the price. The Temnes resorted to making sporadic attacks on the Freetown settlements. This was their speciality, and they drove the fear of God into the returnees who felt their wrath. Often they would kill the returnees, destroy their houses and pillage their food stocks.

As a result of the persistent hostilities by the Temnes and the carnage that ensued, the Sierra Leone Company increased the security around the settlement to protect the returned slaves. However, despite the security issues, the prosperity of the settlements was matching their expectations and the plan to establish a permanent trading outpost. The new strategy was to dominate Africans on their own soil and exploit them as best as is possible and without the conscience of Britons of moderate political persuasion. The rapid expansion of the settlements continues to cause the Temnes increasing concerns as the Company continued to ignore their advances for negotiations. However, there was nothing to negotiate as the Treaty signed by King Tom on which the British relied on did not specify the area of land that was allowed for use by them to support the purported experiment. The deliberate vagary of the document that King Tom was forced to sign was rather disingenuous and typifies the way in which the British conducted business with Africans. When the veracity of the deal was questioned by the persistent King Jimmy, he was dismissed and threatened with force similar to that exerted on his predecessor. Unlike King Tom, King Jimmy did not hesitate to launch more ferocious attacks on the settlements.

After several violent attacks in the ensuing years, the Sierra Leone Company proceeded to survey and document the land on which the settlements were located, with the intention of expanding their occupation as and when the need arose. The Temnes became increasingly suspicious of this ploy and were in no mood to tolerate it. They persisted with their incessant and sporadic attacks on the settlements inflicting significant damages and more loss of life amongst the returnees.

Around 1794, the Sierra Leone Company commenced the construction of a fort for the purposes of defence and a symbol of their intention to establish permanent residence in Freetown. The fort which was completed in 1805, would house the first British Appointed Governor in charge of the settlements and provide administrative services to facilitate the command and control of the settlers. The present day Tower Hill on which the Houses of Parliament is situated, originally named *Smith's Hill*, was the location of the fort, strategically overlooking the settlements. Before the completion of the fortress, the Temnes launched several attacks on the site and surrounding settlements. As a result of those attacks, the plan for the fortress was altered considerably to accommodate a barrack for a sizeable armed force that will incorporate elements of the British Royal African Corp. This regiment was set up initially by the British Government to provide armed protection for the growing number of British personnel operating along the west coast of Africa and to fend off aggression from other interested and competing European countries. The strategy of the British was quite clear since the displacement of the Portuguese during the early years of kidnappings and capture of Africans. The modus operandi of British operators in Africa is either to trick their way into getting what they want or resort to what they are best at. The use of force. A second frontier was opened to fight against the Temnes and to establish a dominant presence on the peninsula. This was no longer an experiment to resettle African returnees but a rather sinister approach to a longer term venture.

The returned African settlers especially those who chose to remain within the environs of the original settlement were very vulnerable to the aggressions of the Temnes. The Temnes were not going to relent on the fight for their land, but because they were unable to take on their foes, the Or Portos, they vented their anger on the defenceless returnees. Their approach appeared illogical based on the fact that the new arrivals on the peninsula were progenies of their ancestral relatives. To the Temnes, this mattered little as the returnees were perceived to be part of a plot by the Or Portos, to occupy their land. Ironically, that was the same way the Mendes regarded the Temnes centuries earlier when they, in order to save their communities, colluded with the very British to capture untold number of Mendes into servitude.

As if the tensions created by the attacks on the settlements were not enough, disgruntlement and discord started between the returned Africans and the British over the use of the very land that the British had wrested from the Temnes. The returned Africans wanted more land to work but were denied by the British administration. They are only allowed to work on land that the administration allots to them. The settlers had waited endlessly for such allotments because their labour was prioritised by the British and were required to work on the construction and successful completion of the fortress.

On the completion of the fortress it was named "*Fort Thornton*" after the English chairman of the Sierra Leone Company, Henry Thornton, a renowned banker in the City of London, who lived in the city, thousands of miles away from the slaving fields of Sierra Leone. The personnel of the Company, some of whom professed to be Christian evangelists, were keen to convert the returned Africans to Christianity as part of the plan to impose a long-term cultural and ideological change on the Africans. Such psychological reconditioning would guarantee their loyalty, docility and minimise the need for the use of coercive methods to control Africans. Christianity as a religion was already familiar to and practiced by some of the returnees during their days on the plantations. Despite the perverted way Christianity was taught to them, they, however, found morality and virtue in a religion alien to them. The plan of the British was to allot land to groups of settlers, to exert ultimate control and to formulate the basis on which rent could be collected from the them by the administration. The returnees were required to produce commercial quantities of tobacco and spices for shipment to Britain and a proportion of what was exported would be retained as land rent.

Included within the fortress was the secretariat and the first post office along the West Coast. The secretariat was to provide administrative duties for the registration of returned Africans, the control of land allotted to each group and to document changes in demography. The returned settlers were not particularly impressed with this arrangement, but in the interest of peace and their urge to work the land and produce enough to sustain their survival, they conceded and complied unconditionally. A few of the returned

Africans refused to commit to the payment of any form of rent after registration. Their protestations were based on the fact that such a payment would contravene their understanding of the conditions of their return to Sierra Leone. They had fought and extricated themselves from the bondage of slavery and volunteered to return to their homeland in Africa in total freedom and without the emerging constraints. Also, what added to their discontentment was that some of the re-captives who had disappeared into the mountains were not apparently subjected to the conditions that were being imposed upon them because they were living within the official settlement established by the British government. Some of the returnees resorted to direct action but were swiftly subdued by the armed forces. The aim of the secretariat was to continue the survey and the documentation of the area of land up to and including wherever the re-captives were and to bring them under the central command and control of the administration.

However, in order to produce commercial quantities of agricultural produce, the Company had to increase the repatriation of Africans from the Caribbean and America. Fortunately for the British, these were slaves who had had enough of the savagery working on the plantations and wished to be transported back to Africa. The British were eager to oblige in order to increase the numbers within the settlement in Freetown.

What was slowly emerging from the idea to return more African slaves was a sinister manoeuvre to localise slavery in Africa and to disguise the slur that characterised the despicable transatlantic trade in Africans. On the other hand, the transformation brought about by the American independence jeopardised the total control British slavers had on the plantations and stock of African slaves who were running loose. There was however nothing charitable or altruistic about the British intentions espoused in the concept of an experiment for the return and settlement of African slaves.

Whilst the returnees to Freetown was a direct corollary of the change in British strategy towards subjugating Africans, another form of migration of Africans from the deep south in America to Liberia in West Africa was emerging. Following on the British experiment in Freetown, a location was sought by the Americans for the return of African slaves who opted to leave the harshness of servitude and extreme discrimination against them in the southern states of America. Through consultation with the British, the area now called Liberia adjacent to the demarcated area of Sierra Leone was identified and allocated to the Americans for the purpose of returning African slaves. The prospect of self-determination, governance and the escape from mass lynching, arson and indiscriminate violence made Liberia irresistibly alluring to the psychologically-broken African slaves. Unlike the African returnees to Freetown by the British, the American slaves had to pay their way to Liberia. They sold whatever belongings they had to enable them to make the journey to paradise and the home of their forefathers, Liberia. Even in their desperation to extricate themselves from the scourge of servitude, their oppressors still found pleasure in exploiting them. When most of them were desperate to sell whatever meagre property or belongings they owned, in order to fund their sea voyage, the Caucasians were ready to exploit them. In many instances, they were cynically prevented from leaving America en-masse by their former slavers. Their motivation was that a mass emigration of Africans from the cotton fields and other farms would deplete the available source of cheap labour there was to be exploited in order to sustain production. Some of the slavers believed that if the Africans no longer wanted to work for them, then they were worth nothing to them and death should be their ultimate punishment. The intense violence and savagery of slavers and extreme white supremacists like the Ku Klux Klan, stimulated the desires of the beleaguered and hapless Africans to return to their ancestral homeland.

The frequent attacks on the Freetown settlements and the threat to charge rent for the use of land, motivated some of the returned settlers to move away from the settlement up into the nearby hills and mountains to join the informal settlements of the re-captives who had been rejected by the Maroons from their community. Those who felt able to comply with the conditions of *Fort Thornton* came to realise that the task to produce enough to enable them to survive and satisfy their financial commitments to the de facto administration was almost impossible without extra labour. The need to solicit assistance from the Temnes however outrageous was compelling. The cooperation of the Temnes was very unlikely, not with the settlers being perceived by the Temnes as associates of their arch-enemies, the Or Portos. Over time, the settlers managed to forge a rather tenuous relationship with the Temnes who gradually came to understand the plight of the returnees but, not to the extent to collaborate with them in their agrarian endeavours. This was hardly surprising having regard to their intense disapproval of the forcible appropriation of their land by the British Or Portos. Through gentle persistence and persuasions by the returnees, some of the Temnes, maybe through their common genealogical heritage, were magnanimous to allow limited contact especially between the Lokkos and the settlers.

The Lokkos were much more conciliatory and keen to improve their own lives following centuries of hardship and harassment. During those years, they were mercilessly hunted down, kidnapped, captured and taken away into slavery. They gravitated towards Freetown to establish trading contacts with the returnees. The Lokkos suffered immense set-backs from the raids on their communities by British slavers during the slave runs. Whilst some of them spoke the language of the Temnes, they were not culturally astute in business and fighting battles like the Temnes. They preferred to provide their services to anyone who would pay, just like they had been to the Temnes. The Lokkos exchanged cassava and rice for cotton cloths, sugar and gin from the settlers. The Lokkos, through their interaction with the returned African slaves, went on to become proficient in the distillation of a local gin called "Omole". Seedlings and cuttings of plants were brought to Freetown by the Lokkos from the north of the country to complement those brought back from the Caribbean, such as *breadfruit* but mainly to assist the settlers with their farming endeavours.

The constant flow of the Lokkos into Freetown became significant, and the exodus did not escape the notice of the British who detested their interaction with the returnees. The British refused to allow the settlers to accommodate and integrate with the Lokkos within their settlement. They were eventually ordered to leave by the administration. The British were wary of the intentions of the settlers who had demonstrated their dislike for the policies of the administration of the settlements. The British preferred to continue with their repatriation of liberated slaves from the Caribbean, whose loyalty they could guarantee.

Refusal to accommodate the Lokkos within the settlement of the settlers redirected them towards the mountain area surrounding Freetown where they came into contact with renegade returnees and re-captives living in small unprotected informal settlements. Hunting of wild hogs and small scale farming were their main activities. The arrival of the Lokkos was a welcomed addition to their numbers, and with the extra labour, they embarked on expanding their farms.

The Sierra Leone Company brought in more liberated Africans from Canada but the number of re-captives were much higher. The British realised that it was easier to increase the numbers within the settlements by commandeering renegade merchant vessels on the high seas, using their overwhelming military force on the guise of enforcing the abolition. The increase in numbers would also pose a threat to the irascible Temnes who were intent on displacing or destroying the settlements. With each successful landing, the prospect of this became remote.

Smuggling of captured Africans was a compelling and extremely lucrative activity for private British merchants who refused to comply with the order of abolition of trading in humans. The Sierra Leone Company was focused and stealthily pursuing the continued subjugation of liberated Africans brought over from the plantations, especially those from the Caribbean and Canada, as some of them had purportedly embraced Christianity, hence disposed to adopting western civilisation. Returnees from the Caribbean, the Maroons, were generally considered aggressive with a diminished tendency to conform to order and routine. As a result, less of those displaying the propensity for violence were encouraged to return to Sierra Leone by the British.

The anticipated increase in manpower through repatriating liberated Africans from plantations by the Sierra Leone Company was optimistic, slow and costly. The realisation that the residual number of re-captives was increasing more than proportionately to those from the plantations, precipitated a change in approach by the administration. The settlement of the re-captives in the mountains was increasing significantly and that attracted the attention of the administration of the Company. Of more concern to the administration was the lack of knowledge and control of their activities. An extended survey of land in the mountain areas was swiftly ordered by the British government and that was to be expedited by the Sierra Leone Company. The rapid increase in the numbers of re-captives returned to the Freetown experiment was in a way a clear indication of the intransigence of British merchants and slavers who refused to comply with the abolition Acts. The British government was incongruously committed to put an end to the operations at Bunce Island decades after the Abolition movement. The recovery of the huge investments on the Island weighed against the prospect of the emerging settlement strategy. Paradoxically, the sale of "Bunce Island" the factory was ultimately considered instead of total closure, at a time when the clamour for the cessation of the enslavement of Africans was gaining public prominence. In spite of the British government's apparent support for abolishing the trade in Africans, *the factory* at Bunce Island was sold to Grant, Oswald & Company and John & Alexander Anderson, private slave merchants. This private company continued to operate the *factory*. The sale was an irony considering the British government's military activity on the Atlantic, confiscating merchant vessels laden with Africans, destined for the slave markets, in violation of the abolition movement. The sale of the *factory* was also a demonstration of the lack of political will in certain quarters regarding the abolition of enslaving Africans. The illicit operations on Bunce Island should have ceased. Whilst the Royal Navy intercepted other merchant vessels containing Africans bound for the slave market and discharged the human cargo in Freetown, the company operating the *factory* was allowed free rein to continue its business.

The trade in Africans after the Abolition Acts became an acutely-corrupt affair. Merchant vessels should have been ordered to return Africans back to where they were captured. Instead, the Africans were regarded as re-captured by the British and dropped off in Freetown which was destined to become a labour camp to support the British economy.

Re-captives and some of their associate Nova Scotian returnees who reneged from paying rent to the Sierra Leone Company had been cohabiting for years, living freely up in the mountain area. They were more productive than the other settlements under the direct control of the Company, principally due to their *laissez-faire* approach. They had developed a hybrid language of communication between them called *Krio*. The language comprised considerable elements of the *patois* spoken in the plantations of the Caribbean and America, plus Yuroba and Igbo from the predominantly Nigerian re-captives. This alliance morphed into a new group collectively regarded as the Creoles. *Krio* is a language unique to Sierra Leone. It is a language formulated by necessity to unite a disparate group of people who shared a common destiny.

Following the completion of the expedited survey of the mountain area around Freetown, the British settlement administration then approached and instructed the Creoles to move on as the land they had been occupying belonged to the Sierra Leone Company. This order naturally caused resentment amongst the already suspicious settlers, some of whom had refused to pay rent to the British administration years earlier. Violence ensued resulting from noncompliance with the instructions of the administration. The services of the Royal African Corp were recruited yet again to put down the rebellion. Following a period of unrest and disturbance, the Royal African Corp was able to round up the riotous group and corralled them within a new location called the "*Kings Yard*", the first of a few to be set up along the peninsula. The new settlement and its immediate surroundings was subsequently named *Regent*, in honour of the Prince Regent of England at the time, by the Sierra Leone Company. This was a gesture and indication of their appreciation of the services of the British Royal forces in suppressing the rebellious Creoles. Regent was an attractive and productive area because of its topography which included vast marshland in the valleys suited to growing a variety of vegetables. These conditions contributed to the flourish of the Creoles.

The defeated and demoralised Creoles were held within the confines of the Kings Yard but were allowed to continue farming, with severe restrictions and prohibited from employing the Lokkos to work on their farms for reasons obvious to the Company and the armed forces. A contingent of the Royal African Corp was strategically stationed on an adjacent hill top to the Kings Yard, called "*Up Sojer*" by the Creoles. There was a small contingent of Royal forces stationed on the hillside to monitor the activities and conduct of the Creoles whose freedom had been severely curtailed by the administration. The Sierra Leone Company then proceeded to land more returnees who were taken directly to Regent in order to dilute the concentration of the hard-line Creoles. Evangelists working for the Company set out to proselytise the Creoles into Christianity. This was largely successful with the settlement becoming very subdued and grudgingly paid land rent through the self-styled missionaries who they came to trust and revere.

In the pursuit of the conversion of the Creoles to Christianity the evangelists proposed to build a church adjacent to the Kings Yard, to provide a sense of community but most importantly, a symbol of influence and domination. A formal request for assistance with the building of the church was presented to the Governor at the time, Charles McCarthy by the missionaries. Resources were subsequently made available by him for the construction of the church which was ultimately in pursuit of the British strategy of containment and exploitation. On completion, the church which took several years to construct was aptly named "*St Charles Church*" after their benefactor, Governor Charles McCarthy.

St Charles Church Regent Village

The naming of the church resulted in a rather strange and dubious canonisation of Charles McCarthy, a colonel in the British Royal Armed Forces. Colonel Charles McCarthy was involved in many military engagements in the pursuit of British government objectives within and out of Britain. Amongst his many military achievements, particularly in Africa was to wage a bloody and controversial war on the Ashanti people of the Gold Coast (Ghana), where he met his demise in 1823.

Enslaved Africans in Britain and America who were said to be liberated continued to be repatriated to Sierra Leone. The Sierra Leone experiment which was purported to have been motivated by the valour and philanthropy of the British was gradually and truly turning into a labour camp.

By the end of the first year after the promulgation of the Abolition Act, the Sierra Leone Company which was set up years earlier to carry out the experiment to resettle the liberated Africans was considered unprofitable, in 1808. The Company was reportedly costing increasingly more to operate, as the experiment that was supposed to finally set the Africans free on their own land was unravelling. The land on which the resettlement was experimented was deceptively confiscated from the irate Temnes. The liberated Africans who were to be assisted to settle and integrate with their ancestral fellow Africans were somehow prevented from doing so. They were deceived and coerced into paying rent for being accommodated within the settlement. The Sierra Leone Company, as a result of the series of deceptions and trickery, had to employ the services of the British military to engage in the violent repression of not only the Temnes who owned the land, but also the returned Africans who were meant to be set free following their intercepted journey to the slave market.

However, after scarcely operating for nearly two decades, the British government was no longer inclined to continue to subsidise the Sierra Leone Company. Profit was always the ethos behind this elaborate scheme. The Sierra Leone Company was eventually wound up and its operations taken over directly by the British government. This deft move by the British government was a significant and clear departure from the original idea of an experiment.

The 1807 Act abolished the trade in Africans as slaves but not the act of enslaving a person.

Therefore, subjugating Africans on their own land, through coercion and violence, did not technically contravene the abolition Act. Hence the evolving strategy of *colonisation*.

Sierra Leone was officially colonised and governance of the territory assumed by the British government. The unsuspecting people were completely oblivious of such a significant change in their fortunes. A change that was to be replicated across the African continent and further influence the course of African history.

Chapter 7
Colonisation

The abolition of slavery was triggered mainly as a result of the determined resistance of the Africans against the indignity and savagery of slavery. British slavers were callous and insensitive to the pain and suffering of Africans. They violently captured Africans from their homes and snatched them from their beds whilst sleeping; the pain of women separated from their children; the suffering of men being shackled and brutally whipped for attempting to protect their families; the pain of women and boys being repeatedly raped; men, women and children smelling their own burning flesh through the agony of branding; the impenetrable darkness of the dungeons; the nightmare of seeing their kin being thrown overboard slave ships, into the gaping seas and the pain and suffering of the life of servitude on the plantations were all too much to bear. Africans persistently challenged the legality and morality of their detention in slavery and being coerced to work without payment.

The widespread revolts by the enslaved Africans were difficult to ignore by the British public. Opinion across sections of the British public was changing but generally remained supportive of enslaving Africans for the enormous economic gains accrued.

The American independence brought about a change that precipitated the shift in strategy by the British government. The reason to discontinue the trade in Africans in the nature and form it was carried out was imperative. However, not everyone saw things that way, especially the slave merchants who had been thriving from the illicit commercial activities.

Some of the justifications postulated by the arrogant and bigoted slavers who advocated for the continuation of the appalling trade in Africans were:

i.   That it was to the benefit of the Africans to remove them from their homeland into slavery. "*We ought to consider whether the Negroes in a well-regulated plantation, under the protection of a kind master, do not enjoy as great, nay, even greater advantages than when under their own despotic governments".* Remarks by a slave merchant, Michael Renwick Sergeant, from Liverpool in England.

ii.   That *"Africans are unfit for other types of work other than to be flogged to work hard in plantations".* A reflection of the deep-seated prejudice in the British society brought about by slavery.

iii.   That African slaves were in fact treated well by their masters and that the conditions of the slave ships were good and acceptable.

iv.   That taking Africans as slaves was righteous and accepted in the Bible. That almighty God approved of slavery in the days of Abraham in the Old Testament days, they said.

Of all the reasons adduced by the avaricious slavers for resisting abolishing holding Africans as slaves, supported by a cross section of the British public, was that the British economy was heavily reliant on slave trade and slave labour. Also, that the trade was absolutely necessary for the success and creation of wealth. In their anger and desperation, the proponents of slavery cynically predicted a total collapse of the economy and the ruin of Britain in general if the trade was abolished.

It was obvious that the British government's seemingly moral stance taken to abolish the trade in Africans was merely a slick move to transfer and localise the subjugation and exploitation of Africans to their homeland in Africa. This approach was to use the pretext of returning Africans who thought they had been liberated back to Africa and to continue to dominate and control them in order to produce agricultural and other goods cheaply for the British market. The investment in the Sierra Leone Company was therefore not an altruistic gesture but part of the change in strategy to remove the scourge, horror and moral blight of the Trans-Atlantic trade from their consciences and from international scrutiny.

Expropriating land from the Temnes, misleading the returned Africans and demanding the payment of rent from them were not charitable gestures. The willingness to use military force to enforce their policies clearly showed the determination of Britain to establish themselves firmly in the country and Africa in general to promote slavery in its new format.

The advantage of setting up the administration in Sierra Leone was that Africans who continued to resist British authority would suffer their wrath, through torture, hard labour and extra judicial killings without any legal framework, oversight or accountability. All of these heinous acts would be localised and contained secretly within Africa and away from any form of scrutiny. In addition, the inclusion of Christian evangelism within their methods was another benign ploy to pacify Africans through aggressive proselytising and enforced culture change.

The Sierra Leone Company was not a charity and was never intended to be one. The Freetown experiment was not a genuine trial to promote the transition and rehabilitation of traumatised African slaves. It was in fact a pathfinder and an obscure body, beyond any form of scrutiny that was capable of carrying out criminal acts, including passively re-enslaving the supposedly liberated Africans. This stealth was to eliminate the culpability of the British government from the mindless and foreseen brutality by their protégés against Africans.

With the dissolution of the Sierra Leone Company the British government took over direct operation and the administration of the Freetown and surrounding settlements. Order was swiftly restored and stringently enforced with more troops on the ground. The stage was set and the course charted for full scale colonisation of the rest of the hinterland.

Gold, ivory diamonds, spices and agricultural land were the motives for seeking total domination. The final but main factor required to achieve these economic benefits was free labour. Although the trade in slaves was said to have been abolished in 1807, the British government allowed the African Company of Merchants, a British Chartered Company dealing in slaves, to continue operating in the Gold Coast (Ghana) as the Royal African Company until around 1821 when the company was dissolved.

The pretext for the dissolution of the company was that it had failed to suppress the taking of Africans into trans-Atlantic slavery. However, rather curiously, the African Company of Merchants four years earlier signed a Treaty of Friendship, that recognised the Ashanti claim to own and control large swathes of land including areas also claimed by the Fantees another dominant tribe in the Gold Coast. The motive for such a move was rather obvious. By 1821, the British government became impatient and irritable by the lack of returns following the signing of the Treaty with the Ashanti people. In 1823, it was purported by the British government that both the Ashanti and Fantees had serious disagreements over land. In a strange twist of fate, the British government appointed the governor of Freetown, Colonel Charles McCarthy who was also in charge of the administration of the Gold Coast to intervene and settle the discord between the two tribes. Colonel McCarthy proceeded to declare war on the King of Ashanti for land rights. This was the very king of the Ashanti with whom a Treaty of Friendship was entered into years earlier by the African Company of Merchants. Colonel Charles McCarthy, who to the British government had been performing extremely well in Freetown, was allowed the resources to take on the King of Ashanti in battle. He sooner realised that he had bitten more than he could chew. He lost his battle against the Kingdom and met his demise in the hands of the Ashanti King the same year, 1823. He and the British government failed to understand why the African Company of Merchants had to conjure the Treaty of Friendship with the King. A bitter lesson was learnt.

The British government swiftly replaced their fallen governor and intensified their programme of domination and exploitation in Sierra Leone. The Sierra Leone British administrative outpost however continued to oversee the governance of the Gold Coast (Ghana) and The Gambia.

The operation by the British to commandeer ships on the high seas conveying captured Africans to the slave market and redirect them to Freetown in Sierra Leone was purely a numbers game. The more re-captives they could hold within the disputed settlements, the stronger the defence would be and the more the potential returns from the laborious activities of the settlers. Fortunately, most of the returnees from Canada (Nova Scotia) had adopted Christianity and were very pious and generally passive. They were used by the administration to influence the re-captives, especially those in cahoots with the rebellious group who had been protesting their resentment against the payment of rent to the British.

The increase in the population of re-captives became significant, and the administration proceeded to establish more Kings Yards around the Freetown area. The increase in numbers also brought about the reduction in aggression by the Temnes. This was due to the forcible retention of some of the Temne re-captives within the settlements. They were treated relatively well in order to motivate them to open better lines of communications with their kin on the other side. Trade between the settlers and the Temnes started gingerly initially until some regularity was established.

Although some of the tension dissipated through cautious commercial interactions, the Temnes never gave up their claim to the land forcibly appropriated from them by the British. They would continue to bring the matter up whenever the opportunity arose.

The British colonialists were particularly pleased by the Temne engagement in trade with the settlers. The Temnes by nature were traders and would not miss any opportunity to improve their lot, especially after the prolonged disruption of commercial trading during the intense capture of their kin into slavery. Whilst the British were enjoying the respite from the Temne aggression, the Creoles too had some leverage to travel into the north of the country to establish trading posts. The Temnes remained suspicious of the Creole settlers because of their association with the Or Portos but realised that they had much more in common with them than the differences espoused by the Or Portos. The Creoles acted as brokers between the Temnes and the British Crown agents as time went on and in so doing became extremely affluent and influential amongst the Temnes.

Whilst the mercantile endeavours of the Creole settlers and the Temnes were flourishing, the British concentrated in exploring the hinterland with the sole purpose of expanding their control. Using the free passage through the north, they traversed into the eastern and subsequently the southern regions, just like they did centuries earlier to capture the Mendes. The Mendes who had been recovering from the decimation of their communities were not amenable to any encounters with the British. Initial contacts with the Mendes proved extremely costly for the British. Undeterred by the uncooperative stance by the Mendes, the British changed their approach and became pugnacious towards them. The pressure on the Freetown administration was immense from the British Government for them to expedite the expansion of domination and control of the country. As a result, there was no allowance for sentiments and by the time the Mendes realised, the West African Field Force had descended upon them killing and burning down their villages. The aggression was overwhelming and the Mendes capitulated.

Unlike the Temnes, the Mendes were not ones to forgive. That was the second brutality they had suffered from the British and because in that round of aggression, they were not dragged away in chains, they were satisfied to co-operate with the victorious British and to wait for another opportunity to avenge their losses. The Sierra Leone colonial project was by then a powder keg, primed and waiting to explode. The Creoles were quietly seething over the deception on their return and the payment of rent demanded of them. The Temnes were contemptuous over the ownership of land in Freetown, and the Mendes who had suffered the most over time found themselves again under immense pressure from the British.

The colonial establishment was swift to convert their military victory into a religious charm offensive that would lead to economic endeavours. The same model that was applied to the Temnes was implemented on the Mendes. Only that, with the Temnes, they showed no particular interest in the religion of the Or Portos. They had been Muslims before they started kidnapping them centuries past. The British did not press the need to convert the Temnes either, as the tenuous truce between them was holding and was very much appreciated by them.

Re-captives who were Mendes, taken away but recaptured on the high seas and brought to Freetown, were often forced to stay in the Freetown settlements, and those who succumbed would subsequently be converted to Christianity. They were used as emissaries to engage with and pacify their kin. To the Mendes, they were no longer considered one of them but were welcomed nonetheless. What was not known to the Mendes was that some of the Creoles carried the same genes as them and were blood brethren. Over time, trade was established between the settlers and the Mendes. The increasing demand for tobacco and grains kept both the Temne and Mende farmers very active and productive, and the Creole traders dispersed countrywide as it was much easier for them to settle amongst their kind rather than in the company of the British oppressors. However, whilst business was gradually improving between the Temnes and the Creoles, the relationship remained just that. Things were completely different with the Mendes, who before long started having children and setting up families with the Creoles. But things were going to change.

The colonisation of Sierra Leone was a surreptitious continuation of slavery but localised in Africa. The objective was clear, instead of transporting Africans to European and American slave markets to be sold on to work on plantations, there was a greater potential in controlling Africans within their homestead to produce for the British market. The transportation of humans was to be replaced by a variety of goods and other commodities. Colonisation will also create direct access to and exclusive control of enormous mineral resources. Incorporating Christianity within the colonial strategy was a cynical but effective ploy to endear the trust of indigenous Sierra Leoneans. But behind the meek façade was a growing military machine.

Towards the end of the ninetieth century, the Sierra Leone colonial administration had modified their approach and was keen to establish mining and logging operations in the hinterland. To enable these operations, there was an urgent need for the administration to construct roads and later rail networks. Construction work within the colony was labour intensive, as was agriculture. The British were not interested in the priorities of their subjects, who preferred to carry on with their agriculture than to participate in road and rail constructions that would not increase food production. The British sensed that there was going to be widespread refusal to participate in the proposed construction work and also unwillingness to carry out mining operations, without their subjects being ordered so to do.

The initial conflict with chiefs and tribal heads was over the use of land for mining and road construction. The local people were very sensitive to the request for land as the way land was acquired in Freetown by the British was an issue of concern to them. As was expected, the chiefs overtly refused access to their land and were prepared to defend their land if the need arose. The colonial administration was not bothered at all about the use of force to acquire land required and considered necessary to promote their goals. What they were concerned about was obtaining workers to carry out hard manual work in the mines and other construction activities. The idea of taxing the people was paramount on the priorities of the administration. The administration knew that although the Temnes and Mendes were allowing trade to be conducted by the Creoles within their chiefdoms, that itself did not mean or guarantee that they would be ready to offer land for mining or allowing any of their kinfolk to participate in any of the proposed activities. Nor would they be prepared to pay taxes. The only option they had or rather the only way the British knew to conduct business was through force. The confidence in the frequent use of force by the British to achieve their goals was purely due to the fact that they had canons, muskets and gun powder. Although not quite efficient in their use, muskets could cause lots of death instantaneously and most of all create mass fear and hysteria amongst the people.

There was no shortage of military fire power along the west coast. The pretext of stopping the shipment of slaves caused the government of Britain to deploy massive military contingents all along the west coast. Their ultimate purpose was to subjugate the people and commandeer their land for commercial activities and ultimately to support the British economy.

The refusal of chiefs to allow the administration to take control of their land caused the administration to bring ashore huge numbers of troops to execute their grand plan. The plan was to commence sporadic attacks on the chiefdoms and force them to submit to their authority and confiscate their land. This was an operation that was going to last for many years.

One of the earlier attacks on Sherbro Island was against mulatto slavers who were still operating, ruthlessly capturing Mendes and smuggling them to waiting British private merchant ships. About 1876, a slaver called John Caulker and two of his accomplices were arrested and executed by the British for his insistence in conducting raids on the Kpa-Mende people for the purposes of slave dealing. The practice of capturing Africans for the purposes of promoting trade in humans was contra to the revised strategies of the British who were focused on local domination and exploitation. The execution of John Caulker was a clear message to all those who refused to comply with or understand the agenda of the colonial administration.

The original strategy to despatch Christian emissaries to the hinterland to proselytise the mainly Mende people was eventually considered too slow a process to achieve the goals set by the British government. Whilst the change in strategy did not discontinue evangelising, a lot of pressure was applied on missionaries to expedite their processes and approach which were expected to pacify large numbers of the Mendes and reduce potential casualties through colonial security operations and aggression.

The Mendes by nature were welcoming but because of their experiences during the slave raids centuries earlier, they were suspicious of especially the British and the Temnes. In order to assuage their fears, Creole Christian evangelists lead the missions into the hinterland. The approach worked as limited contacts had already been made through trade. What became difficult for the evangelists to achieve was to acquire land at the rate and scale that would satisfy the colonial requirements for exploitation. The evangelists were able to obtain small pieces of land to organise community gatherings and to teach young Mendes artisanal skills. That was as far as they could go as the chiefdoms were sensitive to land occupancy and had re-established and re-organised themselves following the prolonged kidnapping and capturing raids in past years. There were strict chiefdom rules over the allocation and use of land across the hinterland. The chiefdom administrations as the British colonial administration came to realise was on a collision course with them and their priorities.

Land was required for building roads and railway, and free labour was also needed to carry out this irksome work. What was to follow in the pursuit of these objectives by the colonial administration defied human reasoning and made plantation work rather appealing. The hinterland was to face the desperation of avaricious and merciless colonial zealots in a fierce and uneven brutal contest.

Chapter 8
The Colony

As colonial aspirations grew, so did the distrust for the colonialists by the Creoles who, in spite of the extreme pressure, continued to conduct business, commerce and evangelising successfully with the inhabitants of the hinterland.

During the early nineteenth century, and prior to its dissolution, the Sierra Leone Company introduced coins as a currency to facilitate economic and financial transactions amongst the settlers in the conduct of commerce. This was promptly rejected by the settlers as the economics supporting the venture was unsound and unconvincing. The Creole objection to the use of the coins was based on the perceived worthlessness of the copper coins called the *Sierra Leone Dollar*. When the Sierra Leone Company initially issued the dollar to the settlers in exchange for their produce, the Creoles were livid and were not prepared to accept the tokens. Unrest broke out between the settlers and the administration who insisted on taking their wares in exchange for the coins. The stand-off and skirmishes required the services of the Royal African Corp to quell. The unrest was put to an end with several of the settlers killed as was the usual and several of them incarcerated. The coins were withdrawn, but the resentment between the Company and the settlers festered, leaving the settlers thinking that the administration will stop at nothing in order to trick them into departing with their nouveau wealth.

The colonial government did not countenance the resentment of the Creoles towards them. They pursued the acquisition of land and labour in the hinterland avidly irrespective of the warnings of the Creoles who knew that they were going to be the primary targets once hostilities between the colonial administration and the hinterland broke out. One thing that was certain, however, was that the coins were going to be reintroduced by the Company once the entire country was under the total control of Britain.

Facilitating the exchange of goods and services through any form of medium of exchange requires the acceptance by those who are expected to use it. In this case the Creoles who dominated the productive sector of the Freetown economy at the time. The medium has to be perceived to have intrinsic value and must be scarce or supply restricted and controlled in order to create the desire to hold and reserve as a recognised store of wealth. One would imagine that the Company and the colonial administration would possess the expertise to appreciate these characteristics if they were so determined to exert their dominance and control of the people. Towards the end of the eighteenth century, the colonialists re-introduced a new form and design of coins. Only that the second time around, it was imposed across the entire country and extreme force was deployed to facilitate its acceptance and use. Around 1883, a boat carrying a stock of the new currency to the hinterland was ambushed, attacked and sunk. Since the colonialists were the only ones who valued the currency, the immediate thought was that of sabotage or alternatively that the boat and contents were stolen by local miscreants. The reaction of the administration was incredible. Without any one to blame for the loss, the administration ordered the destruction of an entire coastal chiefdom suspected to have masterminded the attack. All the houses were torched killing lots of already-terrorised-and-frightened innocent men, women and children. Force was the only reliable tool the British colonialist had, and they dispensed it with reckless abandon.

Representatives of the colonial administration were dispatched to various chiefdoms within the hinterland to request land and labour to support their business ventures. The administration offered lifetime protection for the chiefdoms against further hostilities in return for their buy-in. These overtures were most often rejected by the chiefs who were not particularly interested in forfeiting their land to the colonialists for any offer, whether it be an assurance for security or otherwise. Especially, not after witnessing or learning about the massacre of their people across their region in other chiefdoms.

The administration not particularly surprised from intelligence that the Creoles had been hinting the chiefs of the intentions of the administration to confiscate land and to divert labour from agriculture to activities that will only derive benefits to the colonialists. They conjectured that the obvious loss of revenue to the Creoles was enough to motivate the dissemination of this information to cause mischief and frustrate their drive for eventual dominance. A few of the Creoles were interrogated, detained and punished severely for what the administration regarded as treachery. Essentially, the Creoles alerted the chiefs that offering free labour plus land amounted to taxation for nothing in return. The chiefs had no reason to disbelieve the Creoles who would give them examples of what they had to endure from the colonialists in the Freetown settlements. The Creoles were successful in surreptitiously passing such information, especially within the Mende chiefdoms where they had a large presence through trade and religion. It was in the interest of the Creoles to sabotage the scheme of the colonialists, as a reduction in agriculture would spell disaster for their trading prospects. By the time the administration realised what was happening, the chiefs had started communicating amongst themselves and planning a co-ordinated response to the demands from the British colonialists.

Without notice, the exasperated governor who had been mustering forces from the Royal African Corp ordered armed expeditionary forces, essentially armed attacks, on the resisting chiefdoms. The plan was to take over the rest of the country, dismantling all forms of chiefdom administration and subject them to direct colonial rule with or without their acquiescence.

Not surprising, the first attacks were launched on chiefdoms in Port Lokko. The Port was extremely vulnerable as it had been used extensively during the kidnapping and capturing raids in past years. Another strategy was that if the Temne chiefs were neutralised quickly, the rest of those in the east and south might easily capitulate. How wrong were they, as the Mendes were all primed and waiting for any potential attack by the Or Portos. The operation was going to last for several years in order to achieve their goals. Over several decades, more than fifty military expeditions were conducted, each lasting for over a year on average, with the sole intention to either forcibly confiscate land or coerce chiefs or tribal heads to sign treaties they did not understand, giving away their land. In some cases, the treaties turned out to cede power to rule the people to the administration's preferred chosen local leaders in regime change. Several of such treaties were signed under circumstances sustained through the use of extreme force and violence.

The resistance that the expeditionary forces encountered were so fierce, fighting would continue for a year or more depending on the size of the chiefdom, in order to pacify them. In many instances, neighbouring chiefdoms despatched help and support to those under attack, strategically to stave off or delay attacks on theirs. The Royal armed forces came to realise what was going on and as usual modified their approach through dubious diplomacy, in order to cause doubt and confusion amongst the chiefdoms.

On entering a chiefdom, the expeditionary forces would attempt to capture the chief who they would instruct to cede power to the colonial administration by signing a Treaty. This request, more often than not, met with obvious refusal upon which the forces resorted to physical violence including flogging chiefs publicly to humiliate them in the presence of their people. Fighting usually ensued and would last for as long as they could sustain the aggression, in order to resist the coup d'état. Some of the atrocities perpetrated by the expeditionary forces, mainly through over exuberance and desperation to prove their superiority, would be to set entire villages alight, killing women, children and the infirm who were unable to escape the conflagration. They would strip and flog captured fighters publicly and often carry out gruesome executions in the presence of terrified women and children in order to force their capitulation. These were tactics the expeditionary troops replicated throughout their campaign of terror and mindless barbarism. Villages were isolated and cut-off from engaging in any form of trade in an attrition until their co-operation was secured.

In the first attack on Port Lokko in 1825, a chief called Alikali who as was expected, refused to cooperate with the British expeditionary force, was deposed violently and replaced by a woman, Fatima Kamara. Probably the first female chief, albeit illegally installed in the post against cultural and traditional customary rules. That was the ultimate humiliation in a predominantly androgenic system. These acts by the British manifested their disdain not only for his rule and authority but for the culture and traditions of Africa. The governor instructed and issued an ultimatum to all kings to refrain from calling themselves or being regarded as "Kings". The reason was that by the end of their military takeover, all the hinterland would owe allegiance to only one king and that was to be the King of England. No other local royalty would, therefore, be tolerated.

During a period of twenty-five years, the colonial administration took over the entire Temne chiefdoms and were deep in the north of the country. There was widespread carnage, destruction and terror amongst the people. Another ploy by the British colonialists to expedite the capitulation of Chiefdoms was to include detainees from tribes in Chiefdoms that had been conquered in their advance attacks. This ploy was to create confusion and deflect the animosity by the locals towards the British troops. This strategy was also used against the Creoles, to smear their reputation within the hinterland and to turn their hosts against them. Whenever members from other tribes were spotted amongst the ranks of the British expeditionary forces, it enraged the tribe under siege and heightened their suspicions and animosity for the tribe they were from. The anger and rage of the chiefdom people distracted them from the assault on their communities mainly orchestrated by the British. This trickery created unbridled tribal hate based on the belief that their brothers in other tribes were conspiring against them by colluding with the British to attack and kill them. The policy to create chasms between chiefdoms and tribes resulting in lasting enmity amongst the people was a characteristic of colonialism. That tactic would be replicated in other regions in order to sustain the exploitation of Africans.

In 1859, this tactic was used against the Susu chiefdom in Kambia in the north of the country. A few Temne detainees were coerced to join the expeditionary force's attack and later were instructed to take over the administration of the Chiefdom from the Susu chief who had been deposed by the forces. The Susus were incensed by the lunacy and launched a ferocious counterattack on the vulnerable Temnes and slayed them without compunction.

The violent reaction of the Susus was immediately capitalised on as a pretext to take over the entire Chiefdom by the British who disingenuously regarded their stance as extreme aggression and called in a gunboat and half a battalion of navy to attacked and razed the entire Chiefdom. Scores of women, children and the old were slaughtered en masse. Creoles who were coerced into such dangerous situations cynically by the British often suffered the same gruesome fate.

A district commissioner was drafted in immediately by the colonialists after the massacre of the people to take over and administer the Chiefdom. This was to prevent the people from reorganising and launching counter or rear guard attacks on the expeditionary troops. The cynical use of opposing tribes in aggressions against Chiefdoms to create confusion and hate succeeded in increasing the division and hate between them. Afflicted tribes were known to tell stories of their enemies colluding with the wicked colonialists to kill them and take over their Chiefdoms.

No sooner a district commissioner was appointed and in post, British merchants and traders were allowed to enter the defeated Chiefdoms to establish trading posts. Timber became one of the sought-after trading items for shipment to Britain. In order to facilitate the export of timber, the merchants required labour to work in the process chain from logging to shipment. Hence the reason for the onslaught for domination of the hinterland. The strategy of the British was unfolding, and a new form of slavery was being brutally enforced, and the first labour camps in Africa were emerging.

Incursions by the British colonialists into Chiefdoms, burning down villages and killing indiscriminately left most of the people homeless, fatherless and indigent. Chiefdoms were operated like concentration camps with people forced into heavy duty logging, lifting, sawing and carrying timber over long distances to the port. The lives of the people become chaotic and unplanned. Scarcity of food resulting from forcibly diverting labour form agricultural activities, in once self-sufficient communities, caused hardship sickness and premature deaths. The further hinterland the British expeditionary forces went, the more difficult it became to transport heavy timber loads. Often the oppressed workers refused to co-operate and attempted to obstruct the flow of trade. Intransigence was not tolerated and viewed dimly by the British colonialists. Those who disobeyed orders were dealt with severely and brutally. The treatment meted out to the poor people was far worse than what slaves in plantations in the Americas suffered. The reason for the inhumane treatment of Africans within their homeland was the absence of direct pecuniary interest in them as chattels. The absence of international scrutiny and accountability did not help either. Market value was no longer a motivation to keep an intransigent African alive as was the case with the Trans-Atlantic slave trade. Under the new system of colonisation, the colonial administration had no obligation to ensure or guarantee the upkeep and survival of Africans. There was always a huge reservoir of Africans to replace those killed through torture and extreme violence. The people were left to forage for food or live on scraps and hand-outs from the merchants and traders. Those who had families tended to have a slightly better life as their wives and children if allowed by the British, would maintain small farms for their subsistence, away from land that the colonialists had commandeered. Often this would be land almost barren that takes the poor people extra effort to cultivate and produce only a little percentage of what they would have on the arable and fertile land that had been confiscated.

In 1861, the colonial governor arrested a Temne chief, Bai Kanta, tortured and threatened him to relinquish title to extensive land close to the Freetown settlements. He resisted until the suffering of his beleaguered people was beyond the reasonable human endurance. The British then coerced him to sign a document that purported to be a compensation to him and his people. It turned out the document was actually a cessation of his control of the chiefdom to the colonialists. The deceit caused further increased outraged amongst his people who went on the rampage. A gunboat supported by a contingent of the Royal Navy swiftly put down the rebellion and destroyed the entire chiefdom. The people were shepherded towards the Port where they were enlisted into the labour force of the colonialists.

Road and rail construction became a priority high on the agenda of the colonialists. These were imperatives for the transportation and movement of goods for shipment to Britain. More and more labour was required for the construction of this infrastructure and to support other economic activities. To move huge stocks of timber around without proper roads became irksome and slow. Where enough labour could not be found in conquered chiefdoms, men and boys from elsewhere were drafted and forced to move to where they were most required by the colonialists. The mass overthrow of chiefs, decimating their communities, their land confiscated and forcibly moving populations around caused enormous upheaval, breakdown in family life and disruptions of their society.

Incursions by the expeditionary forces progressed inward into the heart of the country, and the farther they went, the more intense the fighting and the resistance they encountered. Word spread around quickly about impending attacks, putting targeted chiefdoms on alert and on a war footing. Although their defences always turned out to be inadequate and unable to match the fire power of the colonial forces, they did everything within their ability to protect their families and land. If trouble happened to break out in areas that had been taken over, gun boats were called upon from the Royal Navy and towns were bombarded to submission, burning entire villages and killing huge numbers of women and children. Lots of towns and villages, especially those close to the water ways, were regularly pummelled by gun boats as the expeditionary forces became overstretched due to their rapid advance into the hinterland.

Towards the end of the nineteenth century, the entire northern region of Sierra Leone had been brutally conquered by the British colonialists and lots of treaties were signed through coercion including some incredibly ridiculous ones. Whilst those bellicose activities were going on in the northern regions, Christian evangelism was thriving and the Creoles were carrying on a seemingly booming trade in the south and eastern regions. A cultural change programme was slowly creeping into the regions of the Mendes. Christian schools were being built and community churches established. However, news of the approaching expeditionary forces with objectives that would not find favour within the Mende Chiefdoms started flowing into their communities. The Creoles who were amongst the Mendes were avid in their quest to rouse the Mendes to resist the advances of the colonialists. Unaware to the Creoles that the colonialists had got wind of their subterfuge, their fate became inextricably intertwined with that of their hosts.

Eventually, the drive by the colonialists to bring the entire hinterland under their control reached the eastern and southern regions. Although the Mendes had been expecting the onslaught and were in a war ready state, the resistance that was mounted was not as fierce as was planned. The decision by the Mendes not to put up resistance similar to that of the Temnes and other northern tribes, in order to counter the colonial insurgency, mystified the Creoles in particular. The expeditionary forces were so pleased with the rapidity with which they swept through the east and southern regions, they went on a Treaty signing fest. Most of the Mende chiefs willingly signed over whatever they could to the rule and dominance of the colonialists. Mende chiefs who so much as indicated their unwillingness to cooperate were swiftly arrested and taken to Freetown where a prison had been built by the colonial administration to be incarcerated. Chiefs deposed by the expeditionary forces were replaced by local appointees by the British administration. They would usually be people who were overtly subservient and prepared to take instructions unconditionally from them and promote their agenda.

However, unlike the barbarism and savagery that pervaded the northern chiefdoms through resistance, the Mendes suffered very little from the brutality of the expeditionary forces. British merchants and traders wasted little time to descend on the Mende Chiefdoms. The timber trade escalated significantly and with that came the burden of the Mendes. Men and young boys were forcibly recruited into logging and carrying heavy logs to the rivers. They would be gone for days working under extremely-adverse conditions. On their return journeys to their Chiefdoms, they were made to carry supplies for the British merchants. Mende workers who were deemed lazy by the colonial merchants were often flogged to the brink of death. The chief of Chiefdoms from which perceived weak labourers came were usually approached and reprimanded by the colonialists and would regard the chiefs as suspects, doubting their commitment and allegiance to their colonial masters. There were instances when chiefs were taken out and flogged in public if they failed to adduce cogent reasons for the perceived poor performances of their kinfolks.

The reasons for the easy capitulation of the Mendes were twofold. The Mendes were certainly informed and always up to date with details of the carnage within the northern regions, where fierce resistance were mounted against the British colonial onslaught. They knew that many villages were burnt down by the expeditionary forces, killing innocent men, women, children and the infirm. Perhaps, the instinct of self-preservation prevailed and influenced their resolve. On the other hand, during the long years of the campaign of the colonialists to gain total control of all the regions, the Mendes had been benefiting from the peace and tranquillity Christian evangelism offered. Their children were able to receive schooling from Creole evangelists, and some of them were able to secure paid jobs with the colonialists. Their education was based mainly on British culture, supremacy and dominance within their emerging empire. A process of edification that was at odds with African values. Values that did not extol bigotry, exploitation and abuse of fellow human kind. Virtues that believed in community building and fairness for all. However, what mattered most was their survival under an oppressive and coercive regime. By the time their children grew up to become adults, the Mendes, just like the Creoles, started wrestling with their consciences regarding the virtues of the Christian teachings.

Christianity was used to disguise and, to an extent, justify the immoralities of British behaviour and actions towards Africans. But the thought and allure of pecuniary advantages to be derived from their edification, albeit inadequate, over their less fortunate peers was irresistible. They somehow grew to feel that their prospects were inextricably linked to the avariciousness of their oppressors. They began to see their oppressors as a source of eternal salvation. Self-loathing and the manipulative transfer of guilt from the consciences of the British absurdly influenced their perception of their oppressors. They began to lose their assertiveness and succumbed to the Christian teachings and values they espoused.

Hostility towards the indigenous people by the British was very intense. British propaganda and the modus operandi of the military within the country created a great deal of trepidation even amongst the hardiest of recalcitrant. The British colonialists were generally regarded as "John Bull". The Creoles especially referred to their colonial oppressors as "dem John Bull" in awe and in some strange ways, utter adulation. Literatures and symbols depicting Britain as possessing ultimate and divine authority over Africans were effectively disseminated. This propaganda was to induce cultural change and to dissipate any lingering anger for the pugnacious behaviour of the British. John Bull epitomised Great Britain as an industrial and imperial might to the admiration of their oppressed subjects.

The following political cartoon from Vanity Fair features "John Bull" as a caricature of a Caucasian slaver. The slave in the poster pleading for England to relent on their unwavering support for the slave-holding Confederacy in the United States, amongst unrelenting campaign and movements to stop the barbaric trade in Africans.

John Bull's Consistency.

Britannia as taught to colonial subjects, will continue to rule the waves and Britons will never be enslaved. This symbolises an indomitable Britain as a ruthless overlord. The patriotic Britannia elucidates British attitude towards Africans as slaves and their determination to preserve and perpetuate the subjugation and exploitation of the people. The British drove fear and respect into the Creole psyche. The following is a verse of a song about John Bull that was taught to even the young to prepare them to face the horrors and disdain of the British:

"My son I send you to school
To learn how to spell John Bull
J. O. H. N, John and B.U.L.L, Bull
That is the way to spell John Bull"

The motivation for the change in strategy to colonise Africa was crystal clear from when the government of Britain paid over £20m in compensation to slavers and owners who, through the enactment of the Abolition Act, had to release Africans held as slaves. This was a substantial amount of money that the British government was going to recover by all possible means from the continent through continued exploitation of the African people.

Some of the Creoles who found themselves pioneering the teaching of the ideals of the British who they knew had negatively influenced the course of their own history and fortunes were struggling to come to terms with the outcomes of such edification. Being mindful of the draconian rules of the colonialists, they set about to undermine the evil system of the colonialists covertly. The problem with their mission was that their counter narrative was interpreted and regarded as hypocrisy not only by the Mendes but by some quarters of the Creole community too. The Creoles knew they were playing a dangerous game, but they had to pursue the course for the long-term security of their community. Unlike the colonialists, they had nowhere else to go if all else failed. The way that the British had devastated the hinterland, disrupted local life and brought in British merchants to monopolise trade was of serious concern to the Creoles. They had lost many of their own in the indiscriminate killings of entire villages, and business was ebbing due to the forced transfer of labour to the growing timber trade. Nonetheless, the programme of the colonial administration continued undeterred.

In August 1896, the entire hinterland was declared a "British Protectorate" and put under the absolute rule of the British colonial administration.

In preparation for the total conquer and domination of Sierra Leone, the colonial administration back in January 1890, under the instruction of the British government, set up a police force in Freetown to enforce discipline within the colony and Protectorate. Freetown being the Colony and the hinterland, the Protectorate. The police force was indisputably under the unchallengeable command of British officers who were predominantly ex-military personnel. The composition of the force was drawn from the Creoles but also from the Mendes. The Limbas and Korankos were especially targeted for the police force not because of their intellect but because of their docile character. The Limbas and Korankos were admired by the British for their physique and strength. In present day Sierra Leone, officers in the armed forces are mainly drawn from the Mendes, and the demography of the armed forces remain largely unchanged. The Temnes were never encouraged to sign up for service due to their volatility, high self-esteem and assertiveness. They in turn never aspired to be seen alongside let alone fight with or under the command of the Or Portos.

Chapter 9
The Partition of Africa

The approach and attitude of the British towards the people of the hinterland in Sierra Leone, characterised by extreme violence, wanton destruction of lives and property, was partially motivated by their desperate interest in the continent's generally unexplored resources. Towards the end of the nineteenth century, the competition among Europeans within Africa was so strong, there were often flashpoints between the main colonial protagonists for possession of land and access to mineral and other resources.

Africa was largely considered a disputed territory that was up for grabs, belonging to no one and could be exploited by Europeans if they so choose. Hence the violent destruction and dismantling of all forms of cultural and social cohesion there were in order to justify, enforce and impose ideological change on the people. In the process, they created anarchy and confusion amongst the people of Africa that facilitated the easy exploitation of the continent. Coastal regions around Africa were regarded as colonies, especially areas where trading posts were set up for the wholesale shipment of Africans into slavery, like Port Lokko and Bunce Island in Sierra Leone. In spite of the invidious methods employed by the British to acquire land, Freetown was declared a property of the British Crown and remained unchallenged for centuries. Anywhere away from the coastal colonies were regarded as Protectorates and was fair game for interested Europeans to lunch violent raids, occupy areas if they chose and thoroughly exploit the people with impunity. Africans who attempted to assert themselves were mindlessly brutalised or slaughtered by Europeans. These despicable practices characterised the British autocratic and uncompromising dominance of Sierra Leone for centuries.

Curiously, the history of Africa was meticulously presented by European colonialists carefully excluding the untold number of African children, women and men indiscriminately murdered by various colonial administrations across the continent. The number and scale of sexual and other heinous abuses and crimes committed against Africans were airbrushed or inverted to justify the despicable behaviours of European colonisers. The abuse of women, young boys and girls from both the Temne and Mende tribes in Sierra Leone was common rape by adult British males who never showed any remorse or moral conscience. A lot of mixed-race children were born to single parents who had suffered despicable abuse in the hands of lawless aliens who had invaded their communities.

The following portrait depicts the attitudes of the mindless perversions of colonialists:

Colonial Abuse – A Terrified African girl

In the modern discourse on slavery and colonisation in Africa, only the estimated fifteen million Africans who were shipped and dealt in slave markets is generally focussed on. An attempt to quantify the number of Africans brutally murdered in the killing fields and labour camps by British and other Europeans across the continent during centuries of colonisation will easily equate or even exceed the estimated fifteen million taken into slavery.

King Leopold II of Belgium in collaboration with Britain hatched a plan to take control of the vast territories of Congo, right in the heart of Sub-Sahara Africa. The motive was principally to exploit the enormous wealth in the Congo and also to satisfy Leopold's megalomania. France later got wind of the plan and made a move, occupying a portion of the Congo, Brazzaville. There was tension amongst some of the Europeans who felt cheated out of the potential wealth to be had from the despotic control of the continent. As a result, the renowned scramble for territories within Africa by Europeans began. Britain, Portugal and France were initially the main protagonist in this scramble following their intense participation in the trading of Africans as slaves.

The scramble gave rise to the popular Berlin Conference held in 1884-1886, six years after King Leopold manifested his initiative for the Congo. The Conference agreed and confirmed amongst others:

That the enormous territory of what is present day Democratic Republic of Congo, belonged to King Leopold II. Although the administration of the country was later transferred to the Belgian government as a colony, the *Congo Free-State* as it was named, was controlled by King Loepold II, for many years as his private property.

That, new territories claimed as colonies or protectorates should be made known to other significant European participants in order to prevent conflicts amongst themselves.

That, European counties have exclusive right to pursue legal ownership of land through the principle of "Effective Occupation" as introduced by the Conference.

The principle of effective occupation involved dubiously obtaining Treaties signed by the local people, by whatever means employed. This was practically replicating the methods of Britain in acquiring land in Sierra Leone. It also required colonialists to establish some form of administration and fly their official flag to indicate their sovereign ownership. The Conference allowed European countries who already had coastal colonies to pursue and appropriate land further inland as they wished.

All of these decisions and agreements were arrived at without any reference or regard for Africans who owned and inhabited their ancestral land. Their opinions never actually mattered. They are factored into the equation only when it came to exploiting their physical strength.

Conditions agreed by the Berlin Conference and the desperate scramble for Africa by Europeans actually precipitated the haste and savagery of the British in the pursuit of land within the hinterland of Sierra Leone. Declaring control and ownership of land through chicanery and violence was their forte. A variety of desperate, inhumane and brutal measures were taken by the British within the hinterland to achieve their ultimate goal and to outflank other interested Europeans. Hence the reason for the British government's instructions to the colonial administration in 1890, to obtain as many signed Treaties from chiefs along border regions as they could, forbidding and restricting Sierra Leoneans to enter into any form of agreement with rival European countries, namely France, without first consulting the local British colonial administration. The punitive actions taken and the behaviour of British armed forces against Sierra Leoneans during that period, characterised by avarice and bigotry, were undoubtedly and strangely considered legal and proper by the British and by other Europeans.

The atrocities that King Leopold and the Belgian administration went on to perpetrate in the Congo were well known and the realities were beyond human comprehension.

Partitioning Africa in such erratic, despicable and illogical manner in the pursuit of material wealth was one of the major events that profoundly and negatively impacted on the continent. No regard was given to the suffering of families and communities irrationally separated during the arbitrary drawing of borders and demarcating territories.

The Mendes for example, found some of their kin, the Vai people, in Liberia another colonial outpost. This was as a result of a simple line drawn across their villages where British forces were halted, in the south and east of Sierra Leone. The Kono people, another tribal group in Sierra Leone, suffered a similar fate in the northeast when the border between Sierra Leone and Guinea was established with France. The absurdity of the partitioning and the mindless and uncompassionate separation of families by Europeans was replicated across the continent. These divisions are a major cause of present day conflicts within Africa. The infamous massacre of Tutsi and Hutus in Rwanda in modern times is attributable to the absurdity in the way Rwanda and Burundi were separated as an example, within the continent.

Prior to the intervention of Europeans in Africa seeking slave labour, there were no borders. Africans lived in communes characterised by their ethnicity, languages and cultural practices. Although there were conflicts between tribes, there were recognised administrations within each enclave that guaranteed peaceful cohabitation for most of the time.

The scramble for territories and the subsequent colonisation of African countries was quite traumatic for Africans. The continent went through waves of violence varying in ferocity and intensity causing untold destruction and death. Africans were by no means slouch, and in fact, they mounted tremendous and robust defences of their homeland whenever the opportunity availed itself. But for the introduction of muskets and gunpowder and the complications of battles between the Europeans themselves, the outcomes would have been different.

By the early twentieth century, over ninety percent of the land in Africa was owned by Europeans.

Sierra Leone was practically owned by Britain. The country was then split between Freetown, the Colony and the rest, the Protectorate. Total control of the country gave the colonialists unrestricted access to ivory, timber, gold, bauxite, diamonds, iron ore, and, most of all, cheap labour.

Colonial functionaries display a large haul of Elephant Tusks for export to Britain

Labour was diverted from subsistence agriculture which guaranteed self-sufficiency for Sierra Leoneans to road and rail construction and subsequently mining. Mining became very significant, and the British colonial administration subsequently granted a ninety-nine-year lease in 1935 to De Beers to exploit alluvial diamonds in Sierra Leone; although, their diamond mining activities in Sierra Leone had been going on since 1920.

The year 1803 right through to 1895 were years characterised by wanton violence. Those were the Treaty years when chiefs were deposed and coerced to sign entire land mass over to the British. It took over seventy years for the British to commandeer the hinterland. In about 1882, the British encountered the French in the northeast and the demarcating border drawn between the French territory of Guinea and the conquered territory of Sierra Leone. By the time the British onslaught was halted by the French, countless chiefs had been humiliated and kings who were spared death, were strictly warned against referring themselves as such. Their kin were also told to refrain from regarding their ousted kings as such because there was only one king and he is in Britain. Needless to state that those who dared to defy their new masters were swiftly dealt with, in many instances costing their lives. The savagery of the British pursuit for the colonial domination of Sierra Leone was incredible and beyond belief. The strategy to subjugate Africans within their continent to exploit them and the available resources was unravelling. Shipping valuable agricultural produce, a variety of minerals and other raw materials were to replace captured Africans in the holds of merchant ships for centuries.

Chapter 10
Taxation

In 1896 Britain declared the entire hinterland in Sierra Leone a Protectorate and placed it under the control of the colonial administration in Freetown.

During the struggle to take control of the entire hinterland, which lasted nearly a century, the Creoles and Mendes made considerable strides in educating themselves, albeit by studying British history, culture and religion. The ideals and ideologies of the occupying colonialists as a *superior race* were thoroughly inculcated into the psyche of Sierra Leoneans, leaving them emasculated and totally dependent on the colonialists as masters of their fate. The education curriculum was especially designed by the colonialists to completely re-programme the thinking of their subjects, re-orientate and influence or completely change the local culture. The people had to discard some of their traditions, which the British regarded as primitive and incompatible with Christianity, the more educated they became in the ways of their colonial masters.

By the time the Protectorate was conquered and a proclamation made, education had developed considerably through to the tertiary level of University studies in the Colony of Freetown. Fourah Bay College was established in 1827 by colonial missionaries as the first University in the west coast which attracted students from outside Sierra Leone, with aspirations to acquire further knowledge and understanding of European values. The Creoles played active roles in developing and promoting Fourah Bay College as an institution of further and higher learning.

The effect of British education had diverse impact on both the Creoles and subsequently the Mendes. The Mendes took keen interest in learning primarily from self-motivation with aspirations to emulate the Creoles. Through their affinity for the religion of the colonialists, they were able to gain scholarships to pursue higher learning after their elementary studies within the Protectorate.

Creoles had already been holding administrative posts as assistant commissioners in the Protectorate which became attractive to the Mendes. With time, Mendes who were educated and capable of taking employment within the administration of the Protectorate grew exponentially and posed a direct threat and competition to the Creoles.

The Creoles, on the other hand, viewed education from the dominant perspective of their British colonialists. They considered education as a right for all and a natural progression to personal development and equality with their British colonialists. Equality with their *colonial masters* was to put them in a precarious position with the colonialists and jeopardise the development they aspired to. Since they had historically been the subject of the Colony, the Creoles had been able to develop keen interest and skills that enabled them to assist their masters develop and proffer colonial policies. Over time, they became strident with their criticisms and expressed their opinions profoundly, when colonial policies both within the Freetown Colony and the Protectorate were deemed to be anti-African. The Creoles, however, never saw the Mendes as potential threats, from both the standpoint of their position and actions within the colony and their dominance of local trade in the Protectorate. Besides, they had always got on relatively well considering their obvious common genetic heritage through slavery.

One of the several issues that the Creoles had against the colonial administration was the arbitrary diversion of labour from agriculture to logging, road and rail construction and maintenance work. This policy was affecting local trade and had severe economic consequences for the Creoles. The colonialists were completely oblivious to the fact that even the people within the Protectorate were suffering too as food production was declining. Several petitions were made to the colonial administration to allow land to the people for farming and also for better working conditions in other commercial activities conducted by the colonialists. The colonialists increasingly became suspicious and irritable with the Creoles. They started to deny them access to information and controlled privileges. Some of the Creoles were sacked from their jobs for their stridency against colonial policies and behaviour of the colonial administration towards the people in general.

Creole traders who were resident within the Protectorate continued to pass on information to the local chiefdoms about pending developments from the colonial administration and made it their prerogative to explain the adverse effects of the actions of the colonialists. The colonialists maintained their suspicion regarding the actions of the Creoles and regarded them as a nefarious group of malcontents.

Nonetheless, following the elation from the success of bringing the entire hinterland under the administration of the colonial office and the declaration of Protectorate status, in accordance with the Berlin Conference, the administration thought it expedient for the people within the Protectorate to start paying taxes to the colonial office. The main purpose of this demand was symbolic and to emphasise colonial authority over the people more than to raise revenue. The amount of revenue that the British merchants and the government were making from exploiting the natural resources at meagre costs was enormous and adequate to finance the operations of the colonial administration. But as was usual, such decisions were made without compunction and consideration for the plight of people whose villages were destroyed and their families slaughtered during the quest for the control and establishment of the Protectorate.

On learning about the new proposal, the Creoles were quick to rouse the resentment of the people within the Protectorate against the colonialists. Chiefs and tribal heads were discreetly informed by the Creoles about the impending tax levy by the colonial administration and what they needed to do in terms of protesting their refusal to comply.

The district commissioners were instructed to inform the chiefdoms of the levy that was subsequently commonly known as the "*Hut Tax*" in 1898. The tax required the people to pay varying amounts to the administration depending on the size of the huts they occupied. The administration was obviously insensitive to the level of homelessness and poverty occasioned by their brutal actions within the Protectorate.

As soon as the chiefs and tribal leaders received the official instructions from the administration through the district commissioners, they launched collective and individual petitions for the administration to rescind the order. The first petitions came from the Temnes who historically were not on the most palatable terms with the colonialists. The governor was not going to back down as that would have been interpreted by the fledgling Protectorate as a weakness on his part. Instead of engaging in negotiations with the various chiefdoms, the governor immediately threatened punitive actions in the event of mass refusal to comply with his order. The Temnes in particular were incensed with the order as they had fought several battles with the colonialists previously to reclaim their land that was forcibly appropriated, in and around the Freetown Colony. During those violent encounters, the colonialists had subsequently re-entered their territories for the third time, deposing chiefs, burning down villages, killing people and confiscating more of their land. Those events had left a pretty poor taste for the Or Portos by the Temnes.

Some of the Creoles within the administration in the Colony, continued to urge the governor to exercise restraint and to engage with the people. These appeals were seen by the despotic colonialists as a ploy by the Creoles to get the administration to reverse the proposed tax and use it as a precedent to refuse to pay taxes levied on themselves. Since their first incursions into Sierra Leone during the slave raids, the British had maintained their only sure method of conducting business and that is the willingness to use force. With the effluxion of time, violence was dispensed with gratuitous, brutality and with increasing ferocity.

After warnings from the governor to the chiefs were not heeded, the administration strategically ordered initial military actions against the Temnes. Being situated closer to the coast it was much easier for British troops to launch attacks from their gunboats and most importantly, to use them as an example for the other districts.

The administration in their simplicity thought that they could apply the same model used previously to secure the Protectorate, in order to send stern warnings to others in the hinterland.

The initial use of force by the administration to intimidate and coerce the Temne chiefs into getting their people to pay the levy on dwellings was seen by the chiefs as an unnecessary and unfair aggression against them. They were ready and prepared to fight yet again to their death if necessary against the imposition of the tax. Word got to the colonial administration that a militant Tenme chief Bai Bureh, who had previously had violent encounters with the British, was planning an armed rebellion against the payment of the cruel and unreasonable tax. Irritated by the news, the governor launched a full-scale assault on the Temnes and ordered the capture of chief Bureh and his henchmen.

The Temne warriors organised a robust resistance to the attack on them by British troops and widespread violence ensued which lasted for more than a year. Although the British troops had superior firepower, the warriors managed to inflict serious loses on the British troops through stealthy guerrilla fighting tactics. After several bruising Battles with British troops, the Temnes became hardy and proficient in fighting. In the rampant violence that ensued, a few of the Creole traders who got caught in the fighting were brutally killed by the warriors. Some of the warriors saw the Creoles and other British traders within their communities as collaborators and as such saw no reason why they should not suffer a fate similar to that of the colonialists. Unfortunately, not all of the warriors were privy to the actions and the tacit support the Creoles provided their chiefdom leadership.

Observing that the British troops were not going to be able to defeat the Temne warriors as easily as was anticipated, the governor ordered that the assault on the Temnes be intensified and that all other necessary measures be employed to annihilate the warriors.

Meanwhile, across the Protectorate, the Mendes had themselves decided to react but not surprising, in a rather different manner to that of the Temnes and the other northern tribes.

Similar to the northern regions, Creole traders who lived and traded within the south and eastern regions took the opportunity to continue to sensitise the Mendes against the payment of the proposed tax which was based on occupied houses. A property tax. Although the Mendes were not overtly concerned about the tax per se, they were extremely displeased with the way the authority of their chiefdoms was eroded and usurped by the colonialists in the past years. Deposing some of their chiefs and replacing them with pro colonialist's puppets was particularly hurtful and insulting to the people. Unlike the Temnes, the Mendes by their nature were not impulsive and their reactions not always overtly spontaneous and incendiary. Some of the distinct characteristics of the Mendes were their elastic patience and their capacity to incubate pungent issues for prolonged periods before exerting vengeance. Therefore, the chicanery of the British colonialists to use some of the Creoles strategically within their ranks during the pursuit of the total domination of the Protectorate happened to be one such situation that left an indelibly bad impression in the minds of the Mendes. That the Creoles were double dealing, not to be trusted and would one day face their comeuppance.

Since the capture of their ancestors by British slavers into slavery, with the apparent collaboration of the Temnes, the Mendes had also been carrying hate and bitterness against them for the hurt and indignity they suffered during those dark days. But whilst waiting for the day of reckoning, they kept passing down a legacy tainted by pugnacity from one generation to another that required vengeance. The wave of violence that characterised the treaty years that the Mendes tactfully avoided in order to avert the extent of carnage inflicted on the northerners by the colonialist was purely strategic. The opportunity to vent out some of the rage that had been simmering for years had presented itself.

On learning that hostilities had started in the north to resist the payment of the proposed tax, the Mende chiefs called their warriors to arms and sounded the battle cry. But what resulted stunned the Creoles and left them practically numb with disbelief. Without any warning, the Mendes went on the rampage and attacked all non-Mendes living amongst them. British traders, colonial workers and countless Creole traders were targeted and slain mercilessly. Thousands of Creoles were brutally slaughtered by the Mendes. Unlike the Temne resistance which had a clear and direct purpose, the motivation for the ferocity of the rampage of the Mendes, especially against the Creoles, remained an enigma.

Forces of the British Royal navy were despatched to the east and south by the enraged administration to pacify the Mendes. The effort took at least two months to bring the desperate Mendes under control.

British forces however continued to battle the Temne warriors in the north, who were taking heavy losses within their ranks from intense bombardments. Villages on which the tax was to be levied were ironically torched and razed, and as usual, many innocent lives were destroyed. The governor was determined to see the battle through to the bitter end, lest he lost his authority. Chief Bai Bureh received an overwhelming support from other reputable chiefs in the northern region, and his warriors continued to inflict losses on the royal troops in retaliation to their aggression.

As the fighting continued, Chief Bai Bureh noticed that the colonialists had changed their tactics and were deliberately destroying not only their dwellings but their farms and crops upon which the Temnes and their fighters depended for sustenance and their survival. This reckless savagery caused unbearable hardship, malnutrition and deaths amongst the people. The strategy of the colonialists was to cause mass starvation that would induce the people to turn against the warriors. This approach was one of the models of domination in the chink of the British armoury. Used in varying ways and intensity, this scotched earth policy resulted in hardship that set people against each other, created hate and enmity towards their kind and finally, caused implosion and upheavals within communities. On realising the implications of this strategy and the severe impact on his people, Chief Bia Bureh consulted with

131

his warriors on the prospect of continued fighting of a war of attrition and the long term consequences. Towards the end of the year 1898, Chief Bai Bureh ordered his men to lay down their weapons, and he proceeded to surrender to the British troops who had been desperate to capture him. His move was to engage in dialogue with the pugnacious British colonialists, in order to spare his people from the unrelenting violence and cynical ploy to cause rampant starvation and suffering.

The colonial administration was in no mood to negotiate with him on any issue, and he was swiftly arrested, humiliated and detained as a sign of his defeat. Chief Bai Bureh and two of his senior accomplices were subsequently sent into exile to the Gold Coast (Ghana) where he remained for seven years under the protection of Royal West African forces.

Other followers were not as lucky as the chief. The colonial administration arrested hundreds of the battle-hardened warriors and executed them summarily without mercy.

British forces in operation in Africa

After the eventful years of fighting the resistance to the "Hut Tax", the British colonial administration turned their attention to the Creoles who they blamed for inciting the people of the Protectorate to resist the imposition of the tax. The Creoles were severely victimised, harassed and discriminated against by the colonialists. Though race discrimination was the hallmark of colonisation, the attitude and actions towards the Creoles were abject. In retaliation, the Creoles became extremely vocal and critical of the administration. Newspapers were set up by the Creoles writing and exposing the machinations and exploitation of the country by the colonialists. This made the governor irascible and his administration uncomfortable. Increased measures were put in place and action taken to frustrate the efforts of the Creoles to expose the shenanigans of the colonial administration.

The suffering of the Creoles during the hut tax resistance was immense, especially from the hands of the Mendes. They, however, continued trading within the south and eastern regions, nonetheless, but the actions of the Mendes created significant distrust between the two peoples.

Knowing that the Creoles were not particularly pleased with the savagery against them by the Mendes, the colonialists continued the cynical exploitation of their already febrile relationship, hoping to cause more problems and promoting hate amongst the Mendes for the Creoles.

Creoles who held clerical and administrative positions within district colonial offices were summarily dismissed and replaced mostly by educated Mendes. Because of their domination in education, the Creoles were proficient in carrying out the administrative duties delegated to them by their colonial masters. Many of the enlightened Creoles had travelled to Britain where they had received further advanced training in diverse skills and professions. The Creoles on many occasions, considered themselves better educated and far more intelligent than the colonial staff, most of whom were active or retired servicemen who had spent several years in one of the royal forces. Another reason for what could easily be characterised as hubris amongst the Creoles was the exaggeration of their resilience and seeming ability to overcome the perils of bigotry. Creoles who gained scholarships to travel to Britain to pursue further studies during those days of widespread ignorance and little exposure, suffered unimaginable discrimination and violence from British bigots, who prided themselves as masters and owners of Africans as slaves. Creoles were progressively subjected to the most horrendous and degrading treatment that would shock any human being out of shackles and chains. To have experienced the depravity, hostility and small-mindedness of the society from which the colonialists emanated and to successfully edify themselves within those adverse conditions, made the Creoles intolerant of the crude simplicity that characterised the colonial administration. Therefore, to replace a well-educated Creole with a Mende, who the Creoles thought were fledgling, was hurtful and degrading.

One of the governors during those earlier struggles, Edward Merewether, detested the Creoles to an extent that he felt that educating them to the level they were was a folly on the part of his predecessors and the British government. He applauded and avidly supported the policy to deprive Africans of books and literary materials, other than the Bible. Merewether, who most likely was a semi-educated man himself, saw not only education as a threat but an educated African as an error that should have been avoided. He proceeded to launch a personal crusade against the Creoles and instructed his administration to reject all Creoles from taking officer-ranked jobs in the police and defence forces. In pursuing this policy, Creoles were totally deprived of promotions, advancements and excluded from all potential recruitments into any of the forces on the basis that they were unreliable and untrustworthy. Creoles were summarily dismissed or suspended from work if they dared to complain or challenge the decisions of the administration.

The more the colonial administration victimised the Creoles, the more vibrant their news reporting and critique of the administration became. Cases of blatant racism and prejudice were openly reported in newspapers and challenged in the colonial courts in Freetown. Newspapers run by the Creoles were extremely powerful and gave them the platform to air their grievances against a system that was exploitative and against their interest. Corruption and excesses by the British colonial officers were exposed publicly to the continued annoyance of the governor.

In order to contain the increasing Creole antagonism, the governor instructed that tax records of Creoles to be thoroughly scrutinised and to proffer charges against anyone who failed to meet their obligations. Resulting from this order, false charges were raised against Creoles and many arrested, detained and imprisoned unfairly. The persecution of the Creoles was so intense, local suppliers were prevented from conducting business with them in the Protectorate by district commissioners. The administration embarked on recruitment and advertising for vacancies for colonial office jobs in England and encouraged mostly retired service men to fill posts that Creoles would otherwise have been appointed to locally.

Despite the undisguised hostility against the Creoles by the colonialists, they continued their evangelism and teaching in the south and east of the country with unrelenting verve. There was no animosity against the Mendes by the Creoles. What frustrated them mainly was the failure and inability of the Mendes to understand that they had far more in common with them than would ever be between them and their colonial manipulators. The apparent dominance and control of economic activity by the colonialists and the lack of recognition and appreciation of their altruism battered the already waning confidence of the Creoles. The Mendes were naturally seduced by the trickery and machinations of the colonialists and as such, gravitated towards them for security and job prospects. The seeds of distrust sowed between the Creoles and Mendes were germinating in the favour of the oppressor.

There was also frustration building between liberal Creoles and those who were advocating disengagement from the east and south. Creoles who thought that the Mendes were opportunistic and myopic with regards to the chicanery of the colonialists, advocated withdrawing evangelical services including education and training from the Mendes. Moderate Creoles disagreed with this hard-line stance on the principle of mutual benefits for all in the long term. They encouraged their compatriots to understand that unlike the colonialists whose motives were solely to exploit the entire country for the benefit of Britain, the Creoles had to collaborate and co-exist with not only the Mendes but with all the other tribal groups in order to guarantee their mutual survival and economic prospects.

Whilst the colonialists and the Creoles were fighting a psychological battle in the east and south for the hearts and mind of the Mendes, the Temnes were recovering from the brutality and hostilities of the hut tax war. Business relations between the Creoles and the Temnes continued as usual and the losses of the Creoles, which were far fewer compared to the numbers slain by the Mendes, were put behind them. The relationship between the two groups was made easier as Creoles who were Muslims found a common ground with their Temne brethren.

The Creole Muslims were very passive and led a different lifestyle to that of their Christian and secular compatriots. The Muslim Creoles were mainly re-captives from Nigeria, who settled on the fringes of the Freetown Colony. Re-captives who were Muslims were not motivated to travel to the mountain villages around Freetown as those villages were overwhelmingly Christian. The Muslim Creoles were avid traders and seafarers, and they managed to maintain a cordial relationship with all parties as was possible.

The increasing friction between the Creole press and the colonial administration created enormous political awareness within local communities. Workers were made aware of their rights and the vast differences in working conditions between them and the colonialists. The discriminatory social rules and conditions imposed by the administration were continuously challenged, exposed and written about. The number of unfair dismissals or beatings and killings of African workers were reported dispassionately by the Creoles. Workers were encouraged to report the goings on in their places of work and in particular, the abusive way their racist supervisors were behaving towards them. The press advocated for the reduction of working hours by exposing the ungodly hours Africans were made to work by their employers without commensurate compensation.

Artisanal workers formed alliances which became worker's unions to provide collective support for their members and to challenge the unfair practices of the colonialists. These alliances were disapproved of by the colonial administration and membership was prohibited. Workers who were found meeting with instigators were threatened with dismissal. The colonialists approach to the alliances was not surprising. Like all the challenges they faced, the only remedy they knew was force and the use of force was what they resorted to. Newspaper workers were targeted and beaten up, some were arbitrarily arrested and incarcerated. Leaders of the alliances suffered brutality and denied privileges. Public meetings were deemed illegal, and anyone who contravened such orders was severely dealt with.

The uncompromising approach of the administration only served to increase the tension between them and the workers. By 1919, at least three major industrial actions had been called by the generally oppressed workers. The collective actions of workers usually and invariably ended in mass riots and violence as a result of the sustained police brutality against them.

The administration in their exasperation with the Creoles unleashed a perfidious plan to wreck their trading activities and reduce them to indigence. British traders in collaboration with the administration embarked on a systematic campaign to influence the Mendes and, to some extent, the Temnes to refrain from dealing with Creole traders. British traders were supported and encouraged to undertake activities other than timber and mining operations for which they were given relative advantage and exclusivity over the Creoles. British traders with all the support systems opened to them failed to make significant impact on the Creoles local trading affairs in the short term. The reason for their abject failure was that logging and mining were done on larger scales at lower costs with poorly-paid oppressed African labour. They did not require the local network and personal interaction the Creoles had established in order to carry out their trade. However, their failure was ephemeral as an alternative strategy was quickly formulated by the colonialists to avoid conceding defeat to the dexterity of the Creoles.

During the protracted rancour between the Creoles and the colonialists, Lebanese Maronite Christians in the Middle East were being persecuted by the Muslim Ottoman Turks who ruled Lebanon as part of the Ottoman Empire, from Syria. Britain was aware of the plight of the Lebanese Christians who were fleeing persecution to seek refuge wherever they could. It was suggested that, through consultations with the British government, that many of the Maronite Christians were to be transported to Sierra Leone in pursuit of the plan to neutralise the gusto of the enlightened Creoles. The aim was to exploit the vulnerability of the Lebanese Christians and motivate them to infiltrate the Creole trading network as proxies of the colonialists. The hope and expectations of the colonialists were that the Mendes would extend the trust they had for the British to the Lebanese Maronite Christians. If that was achieved, then the Lebanese were to be given all the support they required to launch an unfair completion against the Creole trading methods.

The move by the British colonialists to encourage non-Africans to migrate to the Freetown Colony was an attempt to create confusion and instability amongst the predominantly Creole communities. There was an emerging threat from the edified Creoles and an overwhelming fear within the colonial ranks that control was slowly eluding their grasp. Collective bargaining and riots were replacing wild unstructured attacks, unproductive and unreasonable violence. The Creoles were metamorphosing into an intellectual force that the colonialists were incapable of combating. An intellectualism with the propensity to develop and promote strong ideologies. Ideologies that would have opened the eyes of Sierra Leoneans to the fact that they were one people who shared a common heritage. A union that gunpowder and bullet could not defeat. Creole enlightenment and economic power were clearly unsettling the colonial administration in Freetown.

There was urgent need for action from the colonial administration to either reduce or eliminate the educational structures and deprive the Creoles further access to learning or to make them indigent and unable to afford the expense of educating themselves and their offspring. The former was impractical as the structures of education had been permeating the Protectorate through religious evangelism with remarkable achievements amongst the Mendes especially. The alternative was much more plausible and would complement the unsuccessful efforts of the British merchants to outsmart the Creoles. The objective of the approach was to establish a choice between education and starvation amongst the Creoles. The Lebanese Christians, like the colonialists, were only interested in exploiting the resources of the country and would easily subscribe to the colonial patronage.

The British model of introducing foreign elements to the continent, in order to neutralise local resistance to their oppressive regimes, was widely replicated in East Africa and other parts of the continent. The introduction of indentured Asian workers within East Africa was a classic ploy to neutralise and marginalise the vibrancy of African development and resistance to colonial oppression and exploitation.

By mid-1890s, the first set of Lebanese Christians arrived in Freetown as refugees. They were extremely frail, emaciated and vulnerable. The Creoles unwittingly showed sympathy towards them and allowed them to settle around the fringes of the colony. Most of the Lebanese Christians slept rough in the streets of Freetown in front of shops and the porches of Creole residences. The population of the Lebanese kept growing, and the unsuspecting Creoles failed to recognise the potential threat to their economy and social stability. Rather, they were fascinated by the simplistic attempt of the Lebanese to eke out a living by selling ornamental beads made from glass, called *coral beads*. The sympathy and interest the Creole showed to this hapless people was mainly due to the ridiculous idea that the Lebanese could sell the colourful beads for a living, compared to the hard back breaking work that they had to undertake. They not only had to work extremely hard but were also fighting to stave off the persistent threats from the colonialists who were on a constant quest to oppress and subjugate them.

Coral beads, however, became popular amongst the residents of Freetown and were commonly used by women as fashion accessories. The poor Lebanese were ridiculed by the Creoles who called them "*Corals*" after the beads they hawked along the streets of Freetown. Coral eventually became the generic name of all Lebanese seeking refuge in Freetown. The naming convention was similar to the Temnes who generally called all Caucasians they encountered "Or Portos" derived from Portuguese slavers who kidnapped and shipped them into slavery. The Corals subsequently became helpers and workers to Creole traders and merchants in turn for generous handouts.

The Creoles widely believed at the time that the Lebanese Maronite Christians were Syrians because the Ottoman Turks who were based in Syria administered Lebanon as part of the Ottoman Empire.

The colonial administration was watching and observing the developing cordial relationship between the Creoles and the Lebanese to ensure that there was mutual trust between them. There was no point in pursuing the plans of the administration if there was suspicion amongst the Creoles regarding the intentions of the new Lebanese settlers. Africans are generally trusting and that has been the bane on their existence. One would expect that following the historical events of kidnappings and capture and the shenanigans of the British colonialists within the Colony and Protectorate they would be wary of such infiltrations. The Lebanese continued to live within the communities of the Creoles and began to understand the way they conducted their trading businesses with farmers and suppliers from the Protectorate. Lebanese were recruited by Creoles and were trusted with trade secrets and finances.

When the administration was satisfied with the knowledge acquired by the Lebanese, on the customs, culture and trading methods of Sierra Leoneans, they activated their plan. The administration commenced financing of the Lebanese through covert loans and logistical support to enable them compete directly with the Creoles. An alternative network between large British merchants operating within the Protectorate and the Lebanese was stealthily organised. District commissioners threatened local farmers and suppliers with arrest and prison detention in Freetown if they refused to deal with the Lebanese traders.

Unlike the perfidious methods used in Sierra Leone by the British to undermine the intellectualism and economic strength of the Creoles, in other African regions, gullible proxies in the form of indentured workers of the British were used effectively. They were misinformed that Africans were lazy, lackadaisical, and incapable of carrying out the simplest of tasks and could not be relied upon. Similarly, in the pursuit of their usual cynical plans to neutralise the native African resistance against oppression, their proxies were allowed access to resources and support systems that were denied the Africans. British proxies foreign to Africa were naïve but opportunistic. They failed to realise that they too were being exploited by the British like the Africans. However, because they were manipulated and made to feel privileged over the indigenous Africans by their benefactors, they were pleased with the delights they were accorded. They, like the British, were overwhelmed by their unnatural elevation and embarked on a sub tier of discrimination towards Africans who were generally denied any form of opportunity to continue to fulfil their natural ambitions on their own soil. The Proxies of the British, be they Asians or Arabs, never understood what it felt like to be asphyxiated and psychologically handicapped in your homeland. They never understood how painful and depressing it was to be unable to develop and practice their own culture. Instead, an alien culture was forced upon them. They were not expected to understand as they were seemingly under the protection and support of the colonial system and its well-oiled military machinery.

Africans were not allowed to dream, pursue and make their dreams become a reality. Their voices were muffled by oppression and subjected to multiple tiers of discrimination, exploitation and perpetual violence. Slavery was brought to the continent, kept alive and mutated into the most horrendous and vicious system of strangulation and deprivation that characterised the insidious colonisation of Africa.

Chapter 11
Colonial Surrogates

Living under the yoke of subjugation and the hostility of colonialism is by no stretch of the imagination normal. There is nothing normal about the regime as the existence of the people is fundamentally an economic factor of production. Life is a perennial battle for survival and to maintain mental stability. One wherein rights for the people are determined by masters who have little regard for their subjects as human beings. A life in which to appeal against social injustice is pointless and considered a crime. The psychological struggle was twice as hard for the Creoles as it was for the Mendes, Temnes and other minor tribes in Sierra Leone.

The impact of capture, the horrors of the slave holding centres like the *factory,* the perils of the merchant ships, the indignities of the slave markets, the brutal whippings and abuses on the plantations over centuries have all influenced and shaped the way Africans perceive themselves and importantly by others. For the Creoles to be tricked again into perpetual servitude on their own soil by the very people who brutalised them during those dark days was extremely hard to bear. What added to their pain was the counter narrative and misinformation received by the Temnes and Mendes from the colonialists about the Creoles, setting them up against each other and putting the lives of the Creoles in extreme danger. This was evident during the hut tax war when the Creoles were massacred by the Mendes. For moderate Creoles, it was increasingly difficult to get the other tribes to understand that they were all the same people. It was excruciating to observe the chasm growing wider between them and the other tribes due to the malevolence and perfidy of the colonialists in the pursuit of economic gains. Amongst the Creoles were hardliners who had lost confidence and trust in the tribes of the Protectorate. For them, the wholesale slaughter of their compatriots was not to be forgiven. The unprovoked mass killings of their kin by the Mendes in particular was particularly difficult to comprehend, not when they were supposed to be on the same side against the oppressive regime of colonialism.

Moderate Creoles were torn between the chicanery of the colonialists and the growing militancy amongst their own ranks. Creoles who were advocating strategic peaceful organised protests and the continued use of the print media as a weapon of attrition against the illegal and unjust system of colonialism, were losing to those who wished to pursue direct action. The spread of strikes and riots into the Protectorate gave credence to their approach, but however quick the results were, the effects were ephemeral and often cost many innocent lives.

Colonialism is borne out of extreme prejudice, an ideology that will never be defeated through the use of force. However, force, when used effectively, could prevent cohesion and logical thinking amongst the oppressed. This strategy is evident in the historical belligerence of colonialists in Africa. Violence begot violence which provided reason and the basis for the promotion of extreme ideologically motivated oppression through the use of force.

As time went by, the Creoles observed that their Lebanese workers were refusing to work for them and were conducting business of their own using the same channels as them. Because the infiltration of the Creole businesses by the Lebanese was surreptitiously done, the Creoles were unable to detect their creeping takeover. Ambitious Lebanese traders were provided with finance by the colonial administration whilst logistical support and assistance were received by them from British merchants operating in the Protectorate.

The rise of the Lebanese from being sellers of beads and workers and underlings to the Creoles to entrepreneurs was meteoric. The Creoles were unable to comprehend how the Lebanese were able to come by the ability to conduct business the way they did and the rapidity of their improvement. What added to their confusion was the fact that the Lebanese were able to take over their suppliers and customers without any resistance. Suppliers in the protectorate of the staple foods, rice and cassava were motivated to deal with foreign Lebanese traders who they scarcely knew. Competition for commercial exports like kola nut, piassava and palm kernels became serious, intense and rapidly became one-sided. The move of the colonialists to undermine the Creoles was becoming complete.

The dramatic rise of the "Corals", as the Lebanese were popularly known, was not without its setbacks. Stocks purchased from the Protectorate had to be transferred to the Freetown Colony and stored for retail or processing for export. The Corals had no storage facilities. Most of the Corals living in the Colony were homeless and those who were under the shelter of the Creoles were kicked out as a result of their suspected deceptions. Tension between the Lebanese and the Creoles became palpable. Creoles were unable to sustain the competition against the heavily-sponsored Lebanese, and sooner than they realised, their businesses were no longer viable or profitable. They started closing down rapidly giving way to full scale Lebanese takeovers and representation across the country.

The colonialists were pleased that their plans were finally working and that the Creoles would eventually be brought to their knees. The loss of economic power also had a corollary impact on the ability of the Creoles to continue to educate their children. In the long run, the threat that the Creoles posed would dissipate and the colonial administration should be able to operate with less scrutiny from the upstarts.

Another source of tension between the Lebanese and the Creoles was accommodation and business space. The growth of the Lebanese and the economic and financial decline of the Creoles put the two groups in a collision course. The Lebanese wanted to take over the shops of the Creoles to which the Creoles considered almost sacrilegious. They would rather die than rent their shops to the Corals. This apparent dispute between the Creoles and the emerging Corals was causing enormous problems for the flow of produce and the availability of staple food in Freetown. Creole merchants within the Protectorate also conspired to deny access to their stores and processing facilities.

The colonial administration sensing that things were coming to a head moved in to resolve the impasse between their protégés, the Corals and their arch enemies. Inadvertently, the colonialists blew the cover of their clandestine operations with the Corals. The Creole press went into overdrive, sensitising the Creole community about the apparent collusion between the Corals and the colonialists. Lebanese who had managed to secure accommodation from the Creoles were ejected from those properties. The press advocated that the Corals be removed from Freetown completely. But that was not going to happen. Not if the colonial administration had anything to do with what was going on.

To the utter dismay of the Creoles, the colonial administration issued an ultimatum to the Creoles to let out properties to the

Lebanese. Creoles who refused to comply with the order were to be arrested, detained and severely punished. The order naturally infuriated the Creoles and their resistance against the authoritarian colonial administration became resolute.

The colonial administration was not going to allow the Creoles to succeed in their defiance, neither in driving the Corals away from the colony, nor were they going to allow the Corals to become homeless again. The police were authorised to accompany Lebanese who wanted to rent shops from the Creoles. On refusal, the Creoles were summarily arrested and the shops forcibly opened and made available to the Lebanese. This apparent display of force in favour of the Lebanese sparked violence between the administration and the Creole community. After several months of violent resistance and protests, scores of Creoles were shot and killed. The ring leaders and several more arrested and jailed by the colonialists. The Creoles were defeated yet again, and their shops were to be taken over by the hated Corals en masse.

The farmers and suppliers in the Protectorate did not put up much resistance to the approaches of the Lebanese as they could hardly tell the difference between them and the colonialists anyway, at the time. They accepted the orders to trade with them without reservation. Their ever-growing doubts and suspicions about the potential Creole domination in the Protectorate, sown by the colonialists, made their decision to co-operate with the Lebanese even easier. However, what they were unaware of was that the Lebanese like the colonialists were not operating within their enclave to improve their lot.

Trade between Lebanese businesses in Freetown and the Protectorate faltered with severe effects, especially on food production. What the Lebanese and the colonialists were unaware of was the ancillary relationships that had existed between the Creole traders and the business communities within the Protectorate. Some of the Creoles had raised families with their fellow Africans, mostly Mendes. There were unofficial credit and pre-financing schemes established between them that facilitated the cycle of trade. The system was largely built on trust between the trading parties. The Lebanese traders who were fundamentally reliant on the support of the district administration were not allowed such latitude by their benefactors. Stifling the operations of the Creoles who in turn withheld pre-financing to the farmers had a significant but latent impact on production for the local economy in general. The effect was quickly felt when the availability of the staple food rice dramatically reduced in the market. It was not long before the blame was directed towards the Corals by the Creoles who felt vindicated by the looming food scarcity. They attributed the shortages to the inability of their rivals to conduct honest business. Neither the colonialists nor the Lebanese traders were prepared for what was to follow.

The desperation of the colonialists to reduce the influence of the Creoles by introducing the Lebanese into the production cycle, an operation they did not fully understand, was myopic and a terrible miscalculation on their part. This error manifested the intolerance of the administration and the despotism of a regime that functioned through brutality, oppression and exploitation.

Understanding the complexities of the food crisis eluded the capabilities of the colonialists who were preoccupied with emasculating the Creoles and eliminating their intense scrutiny and criticisms of their administration. The Creoles were far smarter than their colonial overseers and were quick to work out what the real issues were and were determined to make full capital out of the incompetence of the administration. They were also determined to take on and expose the hostility towards them by Governor Edward Merewether whose loathing of the Creoles had become a fixation.

Years of structured labour-intensified economic policies by the administration forced Sierra Leoneans to work on road and rail construction projects that lasted decades. This aggressive policy removed most of the effective labour away from the subsistence farming of the staple rice and other cash crops. British merchant companies like the United African Company, engaged in the commercial export of palm kernel, kola nut, ivory and piassava, drew significant numbers of labour from the same pool for their trading activities.

The increase in prospecting and mining for gold by British speculators required more and more people working in their labour-intensive operations. Sierra Leone was transformed into a labour camp with widespread malnutrition and death. The people were the equivalent of modern tractors and bulldozers working in despicable and appalling conditions that the administration prevented the Creole news agencies from exposing. The irritation of the administration was borne out of the need to reduce political and social awareness amongst the people. Also, there was an urgency to eliminate the increasing violent resistance to colonial authority amongst the Freetown population.

Another factor that the colonialists did not take cognisance of was the drop in life expectancy resulting from illnesses brought into the continent by British and other European merchants, to which Africans had no immunity or resistance. The summary killings of mostly men during prolonged periods of violent resistance against the autocracy of colonialism also contributed to significant demographic changes. Women, children and older men who could not work in arduous rail and road constructions were allowed to work in the rice fields in the south-eastern regions, whilst their compatriots in the north were predominantly growing tobacco in plantations for export by British merchants.

The introduction of education and religious evangelism, with all its merit, had long-term effects on the availability of agricultural labour in order to guarantee food security. The aspirations of those in the Protectorate influenced by whatever form of education was on offer gravitated towards religious evangelism, teaching or clerical work within the colonial administration. Another complexity that went unnoticed by colonialists was the structure and growth in the economy. The Sierra Leone economy by default had a net positive balance of Trade and Payment but did not reflect growth and wealth locally, neither was the surplus generated from export translated into reserves. Sierra Leone was a mere investment to the colonialists and therefore, sustainable economy and human development were not prominent features in their repertoire. The ethos was to produce extremely cheap raw materials through forced and relatively-unpaid labour for the British economy. The value of the enormous exports from the country, like many other African countries, was never credited to Sierra Leone in order to facilitate investments in health care, schools and infrastructure development. Instead, large bonuses were paid to colonialists in Britain for their achievements in the country. The strain on the people struggling to maintain some semblance of a local economy which was haemorrhaging enormous capital to the British economy was inconceivable. To exacerbate their woes, the colonial administration continued to demand taxes from the people who were being severely oppressed and exploited with little or no recompense.

As a result of the senseless and irrational way the country was run, staple food production was perennially carried out at below subsistence level with enough to keep the local communities barely alive. Colonialism is not a charitable venture.

The main incentive to the farmers who maintained the precarious balance between supply and consumption was the pre-financing scheme introduced by the Creole traders. This scheme operated with the collaboration of the chiefs ensured that seed rice was not sold or consumed and that farmers felt obliged to produce in order to meet their commitments and obligations. The encouragement of the Lebanese to take over the trading businesses of the Creoles meant a drastic reduction in pre-financing. Farm workers resorted to consuming and exchanging rice seeds for essential consumables. The Lebanese traders, even if they had the wherewithal, did not trust the farmers enough to facilitate advance payments as incentives for future production. Even if they had trust in the farmers, that was not part of the script, as their role was to promote the programme of their colonial sponsors. A programme that would keep the various ethnic groups apart, suspicious of each other and promote loathing and distrust amongst them. The Maronite Christian Lebanese were mere surrogates of the British.

By 1922, the scarcity of the staple food rice resulted in steep rises in price amidst increasing demand. The people were not impressed with the trajectory of the escalation and word quickly went around that the Lebanese (Corals) were hoarding rice in the hope of making super profits. This was a concept the people were unaccustomed to and especially not with their staple food. The Creoles in their revenge peddled misinformation that rice was being hoarded by the Corals, using both print medium and hearsay to spread mass hysteria successfully. Riots broke out. The Corals were physically attacked, their stores targeted by the marauding crowds and general unrest ensued. The colonialists, who were always suspicious of the Creoles, ordered the police to arrest and detain the miscreants. Oblivious to the reality, the administration embarked on the containment of what had quickly turned into full-blown mayhem. The administration was taken aback when news came through that similar riots had started in the Protectorate and Lebanese stores had been breached. Widespread looting, reprisals and deaths were reported.

The colonial administration went into a tailspin and started making proclamations and fixing prices. A committee was urgently appointed in order to monitor the food crisis. Eventually, a decision had to be made to import rice to make for the shortfall in the market. It had to take the mass loss of lives for the administration to realise the folly of their strategy.

The riot was popular across the entire country not particularly because of the insinuations and conspiracies of the Creoles but as a result of the culmination of several socio-economic and political factors that eluded the capabilities of the colonial administration. Although the riots were finally contained, some sectors of the Freetown colony were surprised and rather disappointed that the Lebanese traders got off lightly. Only one reported death amongst the Lebanese traders was recorded. The Freetown community was rather bemused because the Lebanese traders did not suffer a great deal as anticipated. This immediately brought back into focus the mass slaughter of the Creoles in earlier years by the Mendes for no apparent reason, other than them being manipulated by the colonialists.

Stores looted during the riots were quickly restocked by British merchants. Lebanese traders were compensated and continued to receive protection from the colonial administration. They generally lived a life of privilege throughout the colonial era. That preference accorded to the Lebanese traders which was sustained mainly by British finance institutions, continues to modern times.

Although the Creoles were not seeking a bloody revenge against the Lebanese per se, they were, however, seen as proxies of the colonialists and were a legitimate target in the fight against their continued oppression and exploitation. The post-riot events, in fact, increased the anger and rage of the Creoles who were extremely unhappy with the speed with which the stores of the Lebanese were replenished, whilst they were being hounded to pay taxes by the colonial regime. Another reason for their disappointment and exasperation was the leniency demonstrated towards the Lebanese traders by the Mendes during the riots. The psychology of the people had changed. The colonialists had succeeded. The distrust and hate between Sierra Leoneans as individuals and tribal groups had taken hold. Even the ruthlessness of the Temnes against the Or Portos had dissipated. The divisions between Sierra Leoneans was clear, and each group was foolish enough to think that they could survive independently of each other amidst the growing might and escalating chicanery of the colonialists and their surrogates.

With the passage of time, the people of Sierra Leone like others in the rest of Africa complied passively with the diktats of colonialism, albeit within an increasingly segregated and divided social environment. Attitudes towards each other as Africans were characterised by distrust, hate and suspicion. Curiously, the loathing usually manifested against the Or Portos slowly disappeared. Some sections within the communities opted for self-preservation instead of perpetual militancy. The increase in education and the perception of special privileges offered by the colonialists created expectations and rivalry especially between the Mendes and Creoles. People within the east and south of the country gradually switched their allegiances to the Lebanese whom they eventually came to accept and acknowledged that they had the irrefutable backing and support of the colonialists. This change was disastrous for all communities, especially the Creoles who withered away. Most of them became insolvent and subsequently went broke. Unemployment amongst them increased, and they became increasingly dependent on clerical jobs made available to them sparingly by the colonialists.

The policy of separation and divisions surreptitiously promoted by the colonialists was a major success for the administration and a respite from the increasing confrontation and perennial violence.

The privileges given to the Lebanese allowed them to replace the Creoles rapidly, improving themselves from selling glass beads and being homeless to major players in the economy whilst Sierra Leoneans were being gradually relegated to subservience and dependency. During the development and growth of the economy, colonial commercial banks like the Bank of West Africa cum, Standard Bank of West Africa (SBWA) offered generous facilities to Lebanese traders. The Lebanese like the colonialists were not committed to Africa and with the incredible change in their fortunes and collaboration with the colonialists, exploitation of the country continued unabated.

The Creoles were divided just like the rest of the country between those who were fatigued with fighting colonial domination and the educated elites whose determination for resistance was unrelenting. News reporting and criticism of the colonial administration continued undeterred. The activities of artisanal unions continued with riots and resistance to the increasing use of force by the colonial administration.

The introduction and support given to the Lebanese by the colonial administration finally saw the Creoles losing their control over the local economy. The colonialists had avenged for the Creole instigation of the war against their policy of taxing dwellings. The Hut Tax war. Although the plan took a long time to realise, the administration was pleased to see lots of Creoles trying to find jobs in construction sites, harbour side and the police they never used to countenance. However, they continued to be the preferred choice of workers for the Civil Service due to their mental agility and adaptability.

The Creoles struggled to send their children to school whilst those in the Protectorate were offered scholarships and bursary by

British Christian missions. Most of the Creoles fell back to the skills their forbearers brought with them from slavery; tailoring, carpentry, masonry and metal works. Nonetheless, it was an ideal to be educated, and they continued to purse education as best as they could.

Another event that affected the dynamics in the Freetown colony and the Protectorate during that time was the First World War. Although Sierra Leone was not directly affected, its location was ideal for bunkering war and other merchant vessels. There were increased activities at the docks as vessels seized by British navy forces were decommissioned in Freetown. War defence structures were built all over the country including civil works like the Freetown Water Works (FWW) in 1914 by the British colonial administration.

However, by late 1914, troops comprising, mainly Mendes, Korankos and Limbas were drafted to fight in Cameroon, which was then a German colony against the wishes of the governor, Edward Merewether. He made an official protest to the British government against using troops from the colony on the grounds that the administration would be vulnerable to and unable to combat local disturbances. His protest was dismissed by the British government on the basis of his extreme obsession and paranoia with Creole antagonism. Although to a large extent Merewether was right but, one might say, he was mainly responsible for the continued unrests due to his detestation of the Creoles and the shenanigans of his administration. He was subsequently replaced by the British government two years later in 1916, by Richard James Wilkinson as governor of Sierra Leone.

Large numbers of Sierra Leoneans were conscripted to work as labourers for the Inland Water Service to support operations in Mesopotamia, where they laboured for three gruelling years. These forced removal of labour from the Protectorate contributed also to the reduction in production of the staple food, rice and other essential produce.

The operations by Britain in Mesopotamia and the transportation of the Lebanese Maronite Christians to Freetown under the governorship of Edward Merewether caused some concern and unsettled the Muslim community in Freetown, who were usually passive and disinterested in the militancy of their Christian Creole counterparts. The Muslims had been keeping abreast with what was going on in the Middle East. The arrival of the Maronite Christians was interpreted as an emerging policy by the colonialists against them, bearing in mind the incendiary relationship that already existed between the administration and the Muslim Temnes. Their fears were based on the knowledge that Britain was on the side of the Lebanese *Druze* and their decision to let in the Maronite Christians might create religious tensions with the Muslims in Sierra Leone. In their panic and what was later regarded by the Temnes as cowardice, the secretary for the Committee of *Muhamadans*, in August 1914, wrote a letter to Governor Edward Merewether, sycophantically pledging the support of the Muslim community to Britain in the war against the Germans. They even went on to denounce the actions of their "Commander of the Faith" the Sultan of Turkey" and prayed for the victory of the British. The letter which was suspiciously patronising and redolent of Governor Merewether's antiques was countersigned by fourteen members drawn from across the Muslim community in Freetown. Not surprising, considering the nature and content of the letter of allegiance, only one Temne signature appeared on the letter. The Temnes represented the largest Muslim group in the country and were not in the mood to join in the hypocrisy of the Muslim Creoles.

Military service by the Sierra Leone proletariats during the First World War was through coercion by the colonial administration. The conditions in which they served were appalling and dangerous. The conscripts were severely discriminated against and were called "*darkies*" by their British trench mates. They were given laborious work: digging trenches, cooking and carrying heavy loads. When the going got tough, Africans were given rifles to face enemy fire and were killed in large numbers. Despite the inhumane treatment they received from the British, Sierra Leoneans were, nonetheless, magnanimous in adversity. A young Mende soldier amongst many other Africans, was given a British accolade for distinguished conduct in saving a British officer from certain death during the campaign.

One would think that in a war environment where the destiny and fate of combatants are identical and intertwined, common sense and rational thinking would prevail. That the ideology of supremacy based on the colour of one's skin would be overcome by the fear of the enemy and death which is common to all. Also, one might expect that Africans would be recognised not only for their bravery but as humans. Relations between British servicemen and African conscripts during the next World War were practically the same by all intent and purposes. Only that by the start of the Second World War, there were only a few educated and passive Sierra Leoneans who were regarded as sycophants, for volunteering to fight alongside the British following their experience from the previous war. Creoles who participated in the war were mostly volunteers, and although they faced appalling segregation and discrimination similar to the first war when serving alongside the British, they, nevertheless, gave their best. Despite the despicable plight they found themselves in, a few of the Creoles and Mendes were ironically elevated within the ranks of the British forces.

Volunteers during the Second World War were jeered at by their compatriots who managed to elude conscription. Their action was because of the blatant system of apartheid that was practiced in the Freetown colony. It appeared ludicrous and inconceivable for an oppressed indigent local person who was not allowed to sleep or eat in the same environment as his oppressor to want to sacrifice his life to fight for his course. A similar view was held by the then editor of the *African Standard*, one of the vocal print medium at the time. He was livid and irate and severely criticised the colonial administration and the objectives of the war. In his opinion, the war was as a result the excesses of capitalism and the furtherance of colonialism. I. T. A. Wallace-Johnson was swiftly arrested under an Emergency Act in force during the war for his radical thoughts. He was tried and incarcerated for twelve months on Sherbro Island.

Towards the end of the Second World War, the political landscape was changing in Sierra Leone. The platform no longer belonged to the vibrancy and lucidity of the Creoles. The Mendes and a few Northerners were also equipped with formal British educational values and ironically became confident to take on the Creoles advocating political change between the Protectorate and the Freetown Colony. Political debates between the two sides intensified in due course.

More worker's unions were formed and with these came more strikes and riots against exploitation by the colonial administration. Workers were increasingly becoming politically aware and interested in local and national administrative affairs.

The colonial administration was finding it increasingly difficult to exert the usual excessive, draconian and brutal punishments on recalcitrant subjects amidst such widespread awareness. After centuries of uninterrupted despotic authoritarianism, the need for British colonial oppressive rule to morph into a new form of governance and control beckoned. A new system that was going to hand over the whips, truncheons and prison keys over to local proxies was incubating.

Chapter 12
The Emergence of Multi-Party Politics

Colonisation is a modified form of slavery which involves the use of force, torture and fear to subjugate and control others. It is a concept borne of the ideology of supremacy of one race over the other. Colonialism extols the virtues of exploitation and repression, mainly for economic and material gains. It is a system that offers relative advantage to the coloniser, through illicit and improper access to a wide variety of resources for which they are not obliged to recompense those exploited. Controversial as it might sound, colonisation in all its forms should be classified as a crime against humanity. In particular, the widespread brutality and unrepentant abuse against Africans. The duration and magnitude of the despicable atrocities perpetrated against Africans during the dark days of oppression is the worst case of barbarism that humans have exerted on humans in living history. The spurious assumption of superiority by the coloniser and the assertion of divine authority to influence and change the cultures and way of life of others with force and impunity are the basic tenets that underpin the concept of *"White Supremacy"*. Colonisation simply replaces chains and shackles with prisons, labour camps and killing fields.

Racial segregation, oppression, hardship, deprivation and mass killings characterised colonialism in Africa. The reference to *"Colonial Masters"* in modern day parlance, when referring to certain European countries in relation to Africa, smacks of hubris and a total disdain for the integrity of Africans. Astonishingly, the status of colonial master still affords preferences and privileges in relation to economic and current geo-political activities within the continent. These were countries whose legacy in Africa could at best be characterised as genocidal. Africans are practically forced to continue to accept the master and servant, superior and inferior connotation in relation to Europeans. An instance of this vile concept is the contemporary engagement of Namibia and Germany. During the colonisation of Namibia which was then German South West Africa, an *Extermination Order* was issued in October 1904 that resulted in genocide against the indigenous Nama and Herero people. Scores of the victims murdered were decapitated and their heads shipped to Germany to support racial anthropological studies. This study was to justify the spurious belief of *white supremacy*, a practice that was common amongst European colonisers of Africa. Incredibly, Namibia has been demanding the return of the desecrated remains of their ancestors from Germany who, after several years of resistance, reluctantly handed over a handful of skulls to Namibia in 2018. No apology was given to Namibians for over a hundred thousand people slaughtered following the issuance of that single order in 1904. This exemplifies the "*Black and White*" ideologically unequal rankings in status that defines the co-existence of Africans with other races on planet Earth.

During the 1950s, there was an unexpected increase in the flurry of trade union activities across Sierra Leone. The colonial administration was not prepared for the riots that were associated with the various strike actions. Policing was overstretched, and there was a sense that the colonialists were losing control. The colonialists were torn between the emerging opinionated political elites from the Protectorate and the intransigent Creole political veterans in the Freetown colony. Not wanting to lose face, the colonialists decided to devolve some administrative authority back to the chiefs from whom they were usurped. The move signalled a significant change to colonial domination in Sierra Leone.

Chiefs were mandated to collect taxes which the colonialists were struggling with. They were also authorised to police their chiefdoms and most importantly, to continue providing forced labour for British merchants and speculators as and when required. In turn, the colonial administration created a false situation of privilege and power for the chiefs. Some of the chiefs did not fall for the ruse and saw through the colonialists no sooner they were approached. The colonialists did not waste any time with such intransigence. Chiefs who did not buy-in to the policy change were immediately deposed and replaced by more conciliatory ones. The chiefs found themselves in an extremely difficult position as they were perceived as the new faces of the colonialists. Most of their subjects became uncooperative and made life excruciatingly difficult on the one hand, with the colonialists exerting unrelenting pressure on them to do exactly what they expected of them, without exception on the other.

The dissent within the chiefdoms after the seeming delegation of power by the colonialists became increasingly uncontrollable, and the chiefs were failing in their duties. The colonial administration often had to step in and took charge of putting down the ubiquitous riots within the Protectorate. Violence that characterised colonial governance was frequently visited upon the people with familiar ferocity.

The budding politicians in the Protectorate took a rather dim view of the continued violence exerted on their people. The Creoles in particular were, as ever, vociferous about the behaviour of the colonialists towards their compatriots. In public, the administration showed no sign of weakness and remained unperturbed by the assault on their authority and credibility. In private, they were quietly concerned about the developing trend. British merchants operating across the country had recovered from the Second World War, and the economy was seemingly flourishing. Whilst the administration was contemplating how to adjust to the changing attitudes of the enlightened Sierra Leoneans, towards their autocratic rule, the British merchants were expanding their operations into mining and exporting diamonds, iron ore and gold. The economy was firmly in their grasp, and there was very little Sierra Leoneans could do about it. However, in order to ensure their protection and security, the British merchants needed the colonial administration to remain firmly in control of the political environment. Whatever it was going to take for this to happen, the administration and the British government had to guarantee this for their operations to continue unchallenged by the indigenes.

It was not long before the colonial administration realised the developing political and ideological rift between the Protectorate and the Freetown colony. The Creoles in the Freetown colony had been critical of the colonial administration for quite a considerable period of time. They had long since disapproved of the colonial intrigues following the return of their ancestors to Freetown and had realised that the British had never relinquished control and domination over them, neither did they wish to. Hence the brutality associated with their administration in order to get returned slaves to understand that freedom was not the underlying motives for the Freetown experiment in the first place. The prolonged attacks on their settlements by the Temnes, killing their ancestors as a result of the illicit acquisition of the land which they occupied; the carnage of converting the hinterland to Protectorate and manipulating each of the ethnic groups against each other; established the suspicion and deep seated distrust of the Creoles for the colonialists.

The more critical the Creoles became, the less inclined the British colonialists were to allow them closer to the inner workings of the operations of the colonial administration.

Conversely, the educated elites of the Protectorate had a different orientation to the Creoles. Whilst the Creoles disapproved of the colonialists, the elites of the Protectorates were not only distrusting of the colonialists, they despised the Creoles. Given the choice of being governed by the Colonialists or the Creoles, they no doubt preferred that of the colonialists. This strange phenomenon was displayed during the turmoil of the hut tax war, when scores of Creoles were slaughtered by the Mendes for no apparent reason other than believing the distorted representation of the Creoles by the British colonialists. Also, the ease with which the Protectorate capitulated during the introduction of the Maronite Christian Lebanese traders in order to undermine their trading capabilities left the Creoles profoundly frustrated and disenchanted with the British colonialists. Whilst these reactions by the Protectorate exasperated the Creoles, the British colonialists happily noted with satisfaction, the negative impact they had had on the psychology of the various ethnic groups across the country.

It was apparent to the colonialists that their subjects were not going to be easy to control anymore and the need for a change in their approach can no longer be procrastinated. The erstwhile governor, Edward Merewether had long since suspected that this situation would arise. Not that he possessed the ability and capacity to forecast such complexities but his disquiet arose mainly from the rapid intellectual development of the Creoles and his lagging competence to match them. Besides, he never envisaged a situation during his governance when mere slaves would pose any form of intellectual challenge to his cognitive capabilities and that of the administration he spearheaded. His violent and duplicitous behaviour and reaction to the increasing determination by the Creoles to edify themselves and, most of all, their unrelenting vocal opposition towards the mindless brutality of his administration, typified the inflexibility and inertia of bigotry. Nonetheless, his plan to emasculate the Creoles by encouraging and promoting the Lebanese traders was to him a master stroke. But whilst he succeeded on that score, he failed to suppress the desire and determination of the Creoles to pursue their own total emancipation.

The Creoles, like other Africans dreamt of the day when they would be the masters of their destiny in a life free of perpetual victimisation, oppression and violence against them. Their ambition never waned despite the financial constraints and hardship inflicted on them. The folly of their ambition was their desire to emulate the values of their oppressors. Those values were the only barometer they had in the pursuit of living life like ordinary humans. In truth, that was all they knew in centuries of dominance. They had inadvertently assimilated these vile alien values and cultures, whilst undergoing the process of formally educating themselves and working within the colonial administration. Innocuous though they might seem, elements of the British culture picked up during their pursuit of education conflicted with the morality, beliefs and way of life within African societies. One such issue was the emphasis on self and the tenets of capitalism which, in many ways, were at odds with the socialist-oriented governance driven by consensus that characterised African societies originally.

Although chieftaincies in Africa follow bloodline, the administration of the chiefdom itself is by consultation and consensus. Conflicts with other tribes or chiefdoms are often settled through effective diplomacy, negotiation and eventual agreement. The emphasis was on community building as opposed to corporate and individual aggrandisement that was manifested during the slave trading days and subsequently during the colonial era. The interests, immorality and unrestrained quest for profit by private merchants influenced decisions made by governments and impacted negatively on the lives of the ordinary people. The African model was obliterated by systematic manipulation, oppression and coercion. Africans still find themselves caught between the alluring advantages of individualism inculcated in them through western socio-economic and educational principles and the moral rectitude and selflessness of their traditional African societies.

The struggle for independent rule in Sierra Leone like many other African countries was characterised by the development of various hybrid ideologies and individual tribal idiosyncrasies. Conflicts between interested parties and ethnic groups ensued. Sierra Leoneans became engrossed with fighting each other for prospective political dominance and succession to colonial authority. They completely ignored the fact that their common enemy, the colonial administration that they were so desperate to get rid of, was still very much in control with no inclination to relinquish their stranglehold.

Since 1894, Sierra Leone had two systems of administration, the Freetown colony and the Protectorate. The Protectorate was administered by the Freetown colony which was in turn under direct British rule. Whilst the Creoles, essentially slaves who thought they were set free in Freetown, dominated the call for political change, the Mendes and Temnes were the main protagonists in the Protectorate. The Mendes, because of their relative enlightenment compared with the Temnes, championed the initiative within the Protectorate especially in the eastern and southern regions.

It was apparent that the quest for independent rule by both groups was beset by irreconcilable differences. The Creoles, who had vehemently and incessantly opposed their subjugation by the colonialists, sacrificing their lives, losing their properties and frequently being incarcerated for their troubles, were curiously myopic and narcissistic. They were diametrically opposed to the rational proposal for a single administration and political system adduced by the Mendes. This did not suggest authenticity of the proposals made by the Mendes as it was obvious to the Creoles that the colonialists were behind the proposed convergence of political opinion and governance.

The absurdity of the intentions of the Creoles to promote the idea of separate legislatures for both the Freetown colony and the Protectorate stemmed from historical events with the Mendes. The Creoles and the Mendes had mutual suspicions of each other following those historical encounters. Whilst the Temnes remained passive about the emerging transition, their position was always clear regarding land occupied by the Colony. The Creoles were reticent about their fear of being governed by the Mendes, hence their opposition to the proposal by the Mendes for a single national administration. The bickering between the two ethnic groups for political power prevented them from realising that the issues that confronted them were much larger than the duel for political superiority. The Creoles had been fighting against the composition and the undemocratic representation of the colonial administration for as long as they could remember but now faced with a new form of challenge. The coercion and use of forced labour and the inhumane conditions under which Africans worked were all sensitive issues to the course of the Creole political movement. Continuing with this worthy course required a united front irrespective of the prevailing disparate political opinions. The pursuit of these ideals was always threatened by the surreptitious meddling by the British colonialists.

The colonialists continued to ratchet the tension between their subjects and turned them against each other at every available opportunity. Although their covert support for the Mende proposal for a single legislature was correct, that was not the reason for their endorsement. The colonialists knew that the Creoles were very ambitious and were eager to send them packing from Sierra Leone. But packing was the last thing on the minds of the British colonialists. They knew that the Creoles were competent to take over the administration and would do better than the Mendes will ever be but that was not their preoccupation. In fact, for an administration that succeeded theirs to be characterised as effective, efficient or better than theirs was not a contemplation by the British incumbents. That was not going to happen pure and simple.

The colonialists' pursuit of a single constitutional governance dominated by representation from the Protectorate was a deliberate attempt to create chaos, confusion and rancour between the main opposing sides. An environment that colonial exploitation and dominance thrived on sustainably.

Another innovation by the British colonial empire was the creation of the "*Commonwealth of Nations*". This was another ploy to perpetrate the subjugation and control of mostly African countries amongst others. The organisation was formed on the basis of equality amongst the membership and freedom to govern themselves. However, within the Organisation was the *Commonwealth Realm* which constituted a collective sovereign rule with the British Monarch as head of state for the commonwealth membership. Sierra Leone was to be part of the Realm irrespective of whatever the political outcome of the proposed change was. The interests and security of British merchants and other British commercial institutions had to be guaranteed. Therefore, the radicalism of the Creoles which would lead to a total cessation of colonial control and domination was not to be tolerated. No matter how motivated they were for self-governance.

The sowing of hatred and distrust amongst the people, turning them against each other was the sterling approach to colonial domination. Individuals within the various ethnic groups demonstrated their own personal ambitions for political power without consideration for a holistic and common approach towards dismantling the intricate and vicious colonial system imposed upon them. What the Mendes were well briefed on by the nefarious colonialists was that they were in the majority and that they should by the principle of democracy, be the natural leaders of Sierra

Leone. Whilst that fact cannot be contested, the allure of political power clouded the judgement and reasoning of the Mendes.

Democracy, the new vocabulary was ironically not a feature in the colonial lexicon. Their administration of Sierra Leone, like others in the continent, was bereft of equality, fairness, morality, freedom and respect for African lives. However, the Mendes and other ethnic groups in a similar situation were being pressured to adopt and apply this nouveau political concept without exception. The introduction of democracy in such a hastily-cobbled manner was an indication of the desperation by the colonialists to remain as puppet masters. Ironically, the Mendes did not find it necessary to enquire from their mentors why they never thought of implementing the novel political principle of democracy they were espousing during centuries of bloody, tyrannical colonial despotism. It did not occur to them maybe for obvious reasons. The Mendes failed to ask the colonialists, why suddenly it became very important for the them to recognise their demographic advantage over other ethnic groups at a time when it was crucial for the country to unite in order to implement such a transformational change. A dramatic change that would have jeopardised their interests and continued exploitation of the country was not part of their agenda. Besides, unity is anathema to the ethos of colonialism. In any case, anything that resembled democratic egalitarianism would not have been tolerated by the British colonialists.

The introduction of general elections by the colonial autocrats was ludicrous and quite ironic. These were the very people who were deposing chiefs, dismantling kingdoms and appointing their replacements without any form of consultation or care for those the appointees were to preside over. Election was to be the weapon of choice by the colonialists to prevent a Creole hegemony. Universal suffrage was being drummed into the political discourse at every opportunity during the transformation. It was apparent why the Creoles were so exercised with what they considered the incessant meddling by the colonialists, even when they felt that the time had come for their departure. They knew that universal suffrage and a single political system would severely undermine their political influence and relegate them to the margins. The proposal for separate administrations by the Creoles, on the other hand, was neither a plausible alternative nor a progressive approach to an inclusive and effective governance. But should the autocrats in the colonial administration be the moderators in such a significant transformation or was it a change that will transform governance in any event.

It was clear why the colonialists were very keen on introducing a multi-party political system and universal suffrage. Divisive by nature, this was an invidious principle, conspicuously and deliberately calculated to replace muskets, gun powder, truncheons and prisons. These were the popular weapons of choice during one hundred and seventy-four years of colonial domination. The colonial administration was frantically trying to impose a system that appeared credible but fraught with controversy and problems in its implementation.

The scene was set for organised chaos and destructive tribal frictions and feuds. Sierra Leoneans were successfully pitched against each other and were on a collision course. This model was to be repeated throughout Africa with devastating effects. Africans were not allowed any thinking time by the British colonial empire to consider the implications of the dramatic changes that were being cynically thrust upon them.

The apparent irrational behaviour of Africans towards each other that emerged and followed the change to colonial domination was psychological and the roots run deep. African ancestors were captured and humiliated publicly, their chiefs and tribal leaders were deposed, whipped and dehumanised in the presence of their subjects. Hierarchy, order and status were obliterated from their culture. Loathing and disrespect for each other were grounded into their psyche through servitude and centuries of brutal oppression. The lack of individual self-esteem and mutual trust rendered the African race extremely vulnerable and perpetually susceptible to the scourge of bigotry, social engineering and exclusion.

The violence visited upon Africans in centuries past did not belong to Africa. It was the tool of the oppressor, gratuitously dispensed to disseminate hate and promote values characterised by prejudice. No amount of marching, sit-ins or violence will change the course of the destiny of Africans, where ever they find themselves in this planet but total unity and cultural transformation.

****

During nearly two centuries of colonialism, no less than ninety-five administrators, agents and governors ruled Sierra Leone in diverse ways but with identical job descriptions for dispensing authority and control over their subjects they believed to be lesser

161

humans. Many of them had the privilege to perform this duty multiple times but not a single one was chosen or elected by the people they governed. The legitimacy of colonial dominance, characterised by extreme abuse, exploitations, mass killings and other crimes committed against Africans, have never been challenged by Africans themselves. Most Africans have grown to believe that the suffering and extreme hardship they continue to experience in the hands of their erstwhile *colonial masters* is unavoidable. Africans, through centuries of oppression, abuse, domination and indoctrination, generally accept the postulations of their oppressors that their misfortunes and inabilities to achieve any form of potential as a race directly correlates to the colour of their skin. The mental and psychological fragility of Africans, they argue, predisposes them to failure and underachievement. Hence their justification to perpetuate the domination and paternalism of neo-colonialism.

The concept and perception of what political power was, by both the Creoles and the people of the Protectorate, in particular the Mendes, were mainly based on the colonial model of governance. Sierra Leoneans to a large extent, strangely appear to find the methods used by the colonialists to govern them, attractive and worth emulating in the absence of an organic alternative. A significant number of the Creoles in some peculiar ways also tended towards the British colonialist's approach to governance in Africa. Their motivations were the over-exaggeration of their educational achievements and their cosmetic presentation of themselves like their British oppressors. They presented themselves as superiors to the social underclass amongst them. Some of the Creoles did not disguise their refusal to accept their ancestral lineage to the Mendes and the Protectorate in general. Their asymmetrical thinking and behaviour to those of their less educated and well-off compatriots was uncannily similar to that of some of the liberated slaves in the Caribbean. This unusual behaviour and way of thinking resulted from centuries of forced culture change and subtle misinformation through servitude, colonialism and intense religious proselytising.

Liberated slaves in the Caribbean edified in British civilisation and culture were taught to believe that their ancestors were sold to British slavers by their kin in Africa. The manipulation and paucity of information made available to enslaved Africans by the British succeeded in infusing self-loathing, hate and division amongst them. African slaves held and subsequently liberated in the Caribbean were particularly vulnerable to such intense but subtle brainwashing in order to deflect the venom and dislike they harboured for the British and other European slavers to their own. Had such indoctrination not carefully choreographed and executed effectively, the Caribbean would have been ungovernable. Doubt was created in the minds of liberated African slaves by the British about how they and their forebears ended being enslaved and how better off they were in servitude compared to those left behind in Africa. The policy of the British was to keep them as ignorant as possible about the goings on in Africa. Those who chose to return to Africa never returned.

Conversely, the people of the Protectorate in Sierra Leone were surreptitiously led to believe through the mischief of British propaganda, that the Creoles in the Freetown colony were not Sierra Leoneans and bear no relationship to them and that they are not to be regarded as their kin. Hence the discriminative land laws that, to this day, preclude Creoles from owning freehold land within the hinterland. The contemporary perspective of such behaviour and beliefs of these groups of people would be nothing short of incredulity, considering the long-lasting effect such cheap colonial cultural manipulation and influences have had on Africans in general. The gullibility of Africans was a delight to the British.

The prospect of political independent rule of Sierra Leone from colonial domination preoccupied most of the people, but during the political discourse, not a scintilla of doubt was expressed by the Creoles nor the Mendes over the suitability of the concept of democracy that the British colonialists were prescribing to them. The fact that the colonialist themselves did not practice the espoused democratic principles, during nearly two centuries of domination, did not arouse the curiosity of the nouveau politicians. Their ambition and over exuberance did not allow them to scrutinise the proposed system and to spot the relative advantage and control that the colonialists were going to continue to exert on them. Their obsession was with who was going to be the new *Or Portos* with all the attendant trimmings of absolute power and control. The insistence by the colonialists that Sierra Leone should stay within the commonwealth realm of states mattered little to the aspirations for independent rule by the Protectorate. Their ambition was to displace the Creoles from the political arena and emulate the colonialists.

Multi-party political system was clearly unsuited to Sierra Leone and Africa in general. The fundamental weakness in the system is that it did not anticipate the diverse social and ideological

163

dichotomies between tribes. Or maybe the proponents did. Tribal allegiances do not always have democratic considerations within socio-political dynamics. Voting in democratic elections will mainly be based on tribal identity and association rather than practicality or feasibility of manifestos. Thus, the largest tribe will always win by simple majority votes. This was what the Creoles had envisaged during the build up to the transition from colonialism to independent political governance. They never articulated their concerns openly lest it be interpreted in the Protectorate as fear and weakness. They, therefore, chose to continue to harangue the colonialists, to desist from prescribing the way they are to govern themselves. Especially, when British colonial rule of the country for nearly two centuries was devoid of the political principles they were dictating.

Astonishingly, the Republic of South Africa is the most recent country to be ring-nosed down a similar path after two hundred years of brutal oppressive and discriminative rule by Britain, since 1795. The governance and exploitation of South Africa was so vile; the people could hardly cross the road without permission from their oppressors, let alone vote for political representation. No sooner modern civilisation rejected the repulsive draconian autocracy of *apartheid*, multi-party democracy was thrust on the people. The economy and control of their land remained firmly within the grip of their oppressors through cunning but intense pressure on the leadership of the African National Congress (ANC), the main political party that emerged post-apartheid. The hope for a socialist and egalitarian South Africa dissipated with the adoption of a modified apartheid socio-economic system. With time, tribal allegiances would define politics in South Africa. Chaos and violence would once again visit the poor people. The country would implode like the rest of Africa with destructive instability, undoubtedly sponsored by the hidden hands of their *colonial oppressors*. The reason for their failure would not necessarily be because Africans were incapable of governance, as popularly adduced by colonial interests but due to their inability to recognise the weaknesses and suitability of the political system they accepted.

When the Sierra Leone Peoples Party (SLPP) was formed in 1951, it was erroneously thought by the founders that the party would unite the people into a common course. The party was a tactical consolidation of the Peoples Party (PP), fundamentally a Creole movement, The Sierra Leone Organisation Society (SOS), significantly representing the Mendes and the Protectorate

Educational Progressive Union (PEPU), also dominated by the Mendes.

The configuration and composition of the Sierra Leone Peoples Party (SLPP) reflected the naivety and abject ignorance of the complexities of the political situation they faced. Although the SLPP brought a large group of people together under one umbrella, it mainly represented the ideology of the Mendes who predominated the party. The SLPP which in reality represented the Mendes who were the majority tribe in Sierra Leone went on to win subsequent general elections. Satisfied with the progress in the political transition which was overseen by them, the colonialists proceeded to appoint the leader of the SLPP party to the position of Chief Minister of the country as prescribed by the British sponsored constitution.

The apparent political latitude the constitution allowed the people quickly united the political foes to demand autonomy from the direct rule of the British colonial government. In April 1960, a high-powered delegation representing the spectrum of political opinions in the country was invited to meet with the Queen and representatives of her government in a conference to discuss the constitutional implications of a seemingly-independent Sierra Leone. After prolonged negotiations, Sierra Leone was eventually granted independence from British rule on the 27th April 1961 with a few dissensions from amongst the Sierra Leone delegates. The disagreement was regarding the issue of the continued military involvement of Britain in the purported defence of the country amongst other concerns.

This was a euphoric event for the people who were full of optimism and hope for the future. A future that British servicemen will no longer whip adults openly in public, one that is devoid of mass killings, race segregation, sexual and mental abuse and a future that will empower Sierra Leoneans to live like human beings. One might consider these to be reasonable expectations only that their political negotiators did not contemplate the enormity and complexity of the highly choreographed and carefully managed overtures by the British colonialists.

The notion that a set of people could be ambushed, kidnapped, captured and forcibly taken to market to be sold like animals for over three hundred years and subsequently colonised for another one hundred and seventy-four years is incredible. To ask the oppressed people to make the same journey of their ancestors to the slave markets, only this time around, they were to plead and negotiate the possibility of granting them some semblance of independent rule, challenges rational thinking. The process of requesting independent rule from the British colonial government was deliberately imposed to reinforce race and psychological superiority over the Africans. This was a process designed to humiliate Africans and impose further conditions on their conduct and behaviour within territories that were apparently owned by the colonialists. The expectation of total freedom and the relinquishing of colonial strangulation of the country was rather farfetched. This was a change that merely offered some semblance of political rule by Sierra Leoneans whilst total economic control was firmly retained by the British. The road ahead was going to be rugged.

Independent rule was entered into with high hopes and optimism, if only those were enough to guarantee a real change in their fortunes. Apart from the grandeur of self-governance, very little thought was given to the fact that it took the colonialists one hundred and seventy-four years to dismantle and replace the system of chiefdom administration and governance by consensus. African administrative systems largely constituted Socialism and humanism. These were completely and systematically uprooted and discarded by the colonialists. They obliterated most of the African cultures and stealthily replaced them by immorality, corruption and extreme violence. Through Christian evangelism, the people were pacified and led to believe in the unachievable and to sustain their unrealistic hopes in farfetched and unproven divine salvation.

One of the greatest mistakes Africans made was not to have created a religion themselves out of the savagery of slavery. A religion that would have cultivated new beliefs and values. One that would have galvanised the trust and hopes of the people to a common destiny. A religion that would have found meaning and restore dignity and humanity to Africans as a race.

In reality what was granted to Sierra Leone was restricted autonomy over certain aspects of their administration rather than what they perceived to be total independent governance. The country was to remain a part of the Commonwealth Realm with the British monarch as head of state.

Similar to other African countries, Sierra Leone inadvertently adopted most of tenets of colonial rule instead of challenging their legitimacy. The need for innovation and creativity, invoking the sterling principles on which administration in Africa was founded, long before the arrival of slavery and colonisation, were completely ignored.

The country continued to be operated as a trading outpost by Britain, perpetually recording negative balance of trade and payments. Tons of gold, palm kernels, piassava, kola nuts, bauxite, rutile, graphite, timber, spices, diamonds and artefacts were shipped out of the country without any form of accountability. In return, no proper infrastructure was built and the system of governance was deliberately convoluted and opaque. The country as it was meant to be, was totally dependent on the meagre imports by British merchants. Apart from a few missionary schools, a college and prisons, which ironically were well constructed, there was nothing to show for the enormous outflow of wealth from the country in almost two centuries of uncontested dominance.

A culture that was founded on consensus, trust and humanity was reduced to suspicion, hate, self-loathing, chaos, coups and counter coups. Guns and ammunitions became significant import items by the independent government of Sierra Leone. The brutality meted out to the people by colonialists was transferred to and placed firmly under the control of those to whom political power now belonged. The vessel of colonialism was sailing full steam ahead but with a new crew at the helm.

The quest for real independent rule in Africa did not always go without dramatic incidences. It all depended on from whom and how colonial power was to be wrenched. In the Congo, independent rule from Belgium was pursued avidly, and in 1960, this was seemingly obtained. Following elections held, Patrice Lumumba, a young intelligent firebrand was made the first Prime Minister. Independence Day was marked and celebrated on the 30th June 1960. During the independence ceremony, the king of Belgium spoke eloquently of the achievements of his country in Congo and in particular of his avuncular King Leopold II, who regarded Congo and the people therein as his property. His pomposity was evident and unrestrained. He proceeded to glamorise the innumerable and despicable atrocities committed against the Congolese by Belgians and King Leopold II whom he subsequently referred to as genius. He went on to admonish his Congolese audience and instructed them and made amongst other ridiculous utterances, *"Do not compromise the future with hasty reforms, and do not replace the structures that Belgium hands over to you until you are sure you can do better. Do not be afraid to come to us. We will remain by your side, give you advice when required"*. The speech was redolent of colonial hubris, bigotry and paternalism. The elected president and head of state proceeded to give his vote of thanks to the king in typical supine subservience.

Patrice Lumumba, full of enthusiasm and verve, was irate and in no mood to fit the stereotypical expectations of the colonialists. He rose and took to the podium to make an unscheduled and impromptu speech to his people stating: "*This independence of the Congo, even as it is celebrated today with Belgium, a friendly country with whom we deal as equal to equal, no Congolese worthy of the name will ever be able to forget that it was by fighting that it has been won, a day-to-day fight, an ardent and idealistic fight, a fight in which we were spared neither privation nor suffering, and for which we gave our strength and our blood. We are proud of this struggle, of tears, of fire, and of blood, to the depths of our being, for it was a noble and just struggle, and indispensable to put an end to the humiliating slavery which was imposed upon us by force*". He reiterated unequivocally the sufferings of the Congolese under the brutal colonial rule of Belgium. He highlighted the oppression, exploitation and injustices that characterised colonialism which Congo was all too familiar with and that independence was not achieved through Belgian altruism.

The speech infuriated the colonialists and was severely criticised by Britain, Belgium and other European governments. His fate was sealed. His words went through all the colonialists like hot spear for which he was not to be forgiven.

Although the speech was spontaneous and took the colonialists unawares, Patrice Lumumba's outburst was a culmination of years of pent-up anger and frustration. The Congo was run by Belgium like an animal farm. Despite the avaricious and unrestrained exploitation of the mineral resources of the Congo, the people were treated like lower animals. The declaration of the Congo as the personal property of King Leopold II in the first instance was a lunacy that should have been extinguished immediately. Instead, Europeans legitimised this illegal violation of a people by ratifying the resolutions of the Berlin conference in 1886. This conference not only legitimised this megalomania but the barbarism that it entailed.

Soon after Prime Minister Lumumba took office, unrest broke out within days following internal discord, which involved Belgian officers who incited the Congolese army to revolt against his new government. Events moved quickly and Belgium swiftly instigated an entire region to secede from the new independent government. Division on tribal grounds that multi-party political system cannot cope with was evident and capitalised on by colonial Belgium to overthrow the short-lived independent government. Prime Minister Lumumba was beleaguered and faced severe intimidation and threats from the Belgians. In a move to recover from the colonial-sponsored anarchy and having being disappointed by the United Nations to intervene, Prime Minister Patrice Lumumba turned to the then Soviet Union for military assistance. Britain and the United States wasted no time to swoop in to finance and complete the overthrow of the anti-colonialist Prime Minister.

Patrice Lumumba's decision to seek help from the Soviet Union was a mistake, either through naivety or ignorance of the fact that the Congo was still under the intense spotlight of the British MI5 and CIA of the United States. The Congo possess the largest deposit of the highest quality grade of *uranium* in the world. The Chinkolobwe mine in the Congo supplied this rare potent material for the making of the bomb that was dropped on the Japanese city of Hiroshima on the 6th August 1945. British and American secret services besieged the Congo, preventing the ore falling into the hands of the Germans, Japanese and the Soviet Union. To seek the military intervention of the Soviet Union was political suicide by Prime Minister Patrice Lumumba.

Prime Minister Patrice Lumumba was subsequently arrested by the United States and British sponsored-coup leader, detained and nefariously handed him over to a regional administration in the Congo that was heavily partial towards Belgium. The price that Patrice Lumumba paid fighting against slavery, oppression and colonialism was the ultimate. He was summarily tried, found guilty of some trumped up charges. The sentence was the ultimate price he had to pay for freedom. Patrice Lumumba was shot dead by Belgian officers who were under instruction to dispose his body immediately afterwards by the Belgian authorities. What the Belgians did subsequently was beyond reasonable human comprehension. The body of Patrice Lumumba which was interred at a local cemetery, was later exhumed because Belgium was not satisfied with him being buried, to prevent a shrine being made out of his grave by his people. Belgian officers under further desperate instructions later proceeded to dissect his body and dissolve it in concentrated *sulphuric acid*. His teeth, fragments of Patrice Lumumba's shattered skull and the bullets that killed him, which were not completely dissolved by the acid, were morbidly taken and unbelievably kept as souvenirs by two of the Belgium officers who carried out this despicable, horrendous and heinous crime.

The Congo example is one that clearly showed that slavery and colonialism were not going to be a thing of the past. Those who had grand optimism about independent self-rule, free from colonial interferences, had some serious thinking to do, and the Congo experience was a severe warning and indication of future developments in Africa.

Needless to mention that the sponsored leader of the coup against Patrice Lumumba, Mobutu Sese Seko, with the collaboration of Belgium and other colonialists, went on to exploit Congo of an estimated $9 billion. A significant amount that could have made a difference to the life of the people. Mobutu's exploit was an indication of the magnitude and immeasurable amount of wealth that slavery and colonialism had extracted from Africa without any form of accountability. This was also a crystal clear case and warning to the rest of Africa that it was going to take a lot more lives and intelligence to eliminate the threat that colonialism poses to the prosperity of Africa.

The struggle for independent rule in Sierra Leone was less dramatic. Preoccupation was more with individual attainment and who would best emulate the British colonialists through materialism and abuse of power. Unlike many other African countries, colonial indoctrination and systematic cultural change achieved the desired psychological effect on the people. Subservience, docility and inferior politeness towards colonialists or Europeans in general were distinguishing features of Sierra Leoneans.

Post-independent Sierra Leone was fraught with political intrigues. This was, no doubt, the expectation of the British colonialists during the granting of independent rule. The first Prime Minister Sir Milton Margai was a frail old, placid gentleman who would easily be placed on the extreme end of the spectrum of independent activists like Patrice Lumumba and others like him. Milton Margai posed no threat to the interests of the British and was the perfect candidate for the job. One of his achievements was the founding of a University in Njala in the southern province in 1964 in order to improve the quality of life of his people. Following his death, three years after independence, his younger brother was appointed leader of the ruling SLPP party.

On his accession to office as Prime Minister, Sir Albert Margai, did not disguise his feelings and views of the other ethnic groups in the country. The Creoles in particular, who were the adversaries to the colonial regime, did not escape his ruthlessness. He proceeded to dismiss and removed a lot of them from central government administrative jobs that they had dominated. There was a resurgence of tension between the Mendes and the Creoles. The Temnes were passive observers in the political maelstrom. Tribal politics became fashionable, and the Protectorate and Colony dichotomy became apparent once again.

Although his political manoeuvrings did make him unpopular not least amongst the Creoles, Sir Albert Margai unwittingly discovered the weakness in the multi-party democratic political system. He may have realised that numbers mattered significantly to sustain that system and that advantage was what he had. The SLPP would always dominate politics if he did things that would keep the Mendes and some of the others in the Protectorate happy. In hind sight he failed to do just that. Impatience, intolerance and hubris characterised his fledgling career, and whether it was due to his admiration for colonial autocracy or the near-certainty of perpetuity through the numbers game, he ventured a change in the rules of politics.

Sir Albert swiftly proposed a single party political system and laws to alienate the main opposing party the All Peoples Congress (APC). That was an error which at the time bore the hallmark of a despot. His proposal met with ferocious opposition culminating into widespread riots and vandalism that popularised the erstwhile British colonial administration. The Creoles who were at the twilight of their political influence and vibrancy, left an indelible legacy on his fleeting political ambition. Sir Albert, in a dramatic climb-down, conceded to, in his own words, the "*significant minority*" the Creoles, who championed his political debacle. In his confusion and his quest to repair his severely-damaged reputation, he resorted to the colonial antique of universal suffrage and called for early general elections. This was a strategy to quiet his critics and assailants once and for all with an anticipated majority vote from his kinfolks.

The request for general elections by Sir Albert brought tribal politics sharply into focus. However, to the dismay of Sir Albert, the outcome of the elections was not to his expectations. The numbers game had been played against him by his wily opposite, Siaka Stevens the leader of the opposition APC party.

The alienation and victimisation of the Creoles was not such a smart idea by Sir Albert Margai. The political interest of the Temnes and other northern tribes which had remained passive for a long while, were aroused by the nepotism and tribalism that characterised the brief rule of the SLPP. The master stroke of Siaka Stevens was to garner the support of the aggrieved Creoles who were once aligned with the Mendes. That move and his gerrymandering marginally tipped the balance in his favour. Coups and counter coups were what followed the elections in 1967. The military that had a significant Mende officer corps executed the first coup d'état and detained the Governor General who represented the British Crown in Sierra Leone together with the leader of the APC, Siaka Stevens. A couple of days later, the junta was itself overthrown. The charade continued and after another coup, Siaka Stevens was installed as Prime Minister a year later.

To state that the British colonialists did not anticipate and influence this turmoil was to underestimate their sophism. The people had been thoroughly indoctrinated by the colonial administration to be suspicious and hateful of each other in order to create confusion and discord amongst them. The colonial strategy to set up the military and equip it with enough weapons to destroy the entire population had succeeded and played well to perpetrate their planned indirect control.

Sierra Leoneans were killing each other senselessly to emulate the colonialist regime. To a large extent, the colonial regime was the only benchmark of governance they had and were familiar with in a hundred and seventy-four years. The politicians, their stalwarts and the country as a whole failed to grasp the dire state they were in. The statistics were grim for a country that had contributed significantly to the development of the British economy. A people whose blood had been spilled from slavery, colonisation and fighting wars they had nothing to do with, were now poised and set up to fight and destroy each other. The economy was febrile. Britain continued to use the country as a trading outpost with transfer pricing of exports and overpricing of imports. Life expectancy was very low resulting from infections and deceases, some brought over by the colonialists, and with poor healthcare facilities the country was always on the margins. Illiteracy was thriving at an alarming rate, and poverty, well, almost everyone was poor in relative terms. This was the legacy of colonialism.

These statistics are all too common everywhere Africans could be found on Earth. In the United States and other western societies, poverty, illiteracy and life expectancy amongst Africans are not dissimilar to those in Africa. Unlike Africa, social engineering, relaxed ownership and use of firearms, highly-curtailed resource allocation, poor education and exploitation, relaxation of drug use, disproportionately-high levels of incarceration, physical and psychological abuse pervade African communities within western countries. Bigotry and race discrimination against Africans do not usually help their cause. Africans in their desperation over the years have chosen to fight the adverse conditions against them by attempting to influence a change in the culture and ideology of Caucasians through affirmative actions and the use of low-level violence when required. Although it took Caucasians centuries of brutality and slavery to influence the culture and traditional practices of Africans, this method might not necessarily work on the reverse. Africans must concentrate and endeavour to reverse years of oppression and the negative impact on their psyche through intensive re-education and a Cultural Revolution. Race equality will never be achieved through the attempt to change the ideologies of Caucasian. Marches and sit-ins will only create and maintain awareness and focus on issues relating to race inequality and bigotry. Actual change will happen when Africans develop their own ideologies through effective social and cultural transformation and cohesion through effective and generally sound education.

The principles that underline colonialism in Africa are identical to those that support race discrimination around the globe. Africans within Africa need to abandon the strenuous and unproductive effort to try to emulate the methods of colonialism and expend more energies on developing their own distinct cultures, ideologies and socio-political systems through unity and collaboration.

Chapter 13
A New Republic

Like many countries that have been subjected to prolong subjugation and oppression, the first ten years of apparent independent governance was turbulent and traumatic for Sierra Leone. The brutality and violence against the people during colonialism was difficult enough to take, but when killings of Sierra Leoneans by their peers continued in a fashion ever so familiar to them during colonisation, it all became hard to bear. During the chaos, the people tended to forget that Sierra Leone was still under the leadership of the British monarchy and a member of the commonwealth realm. The influence of the British government was significant, more so as the country was also considered as a strategic military outpost for Britain. Arms and ammunition were supplied by the British in significant quantities to the military, which was largely run by Sierra Leoneans but trained and cultured by Britain.

During those earlier post-independence years, governments struggled to understand and apply multi-party democratic principles against the complexity and backdrop of tribal allegiances. On his assumption of office, Siaka Stevens who knew exactly what his predecessor Sir Albert contemplated, pursed the same single party political system but for different reasons. The motivation for pursuing a single party political party system was in a way to mirror the colonial administration which never had democracy in their repertoire. Also, it was an attempt to unify the Protectorate which admittedly had noticeably dominated the political discourse for independent rule. Siaka Stevens genuinely believed that a single party would bring all the tribes together politically, which was rather simplistic. Maybe like his predecessor, he was naïve and oblivious to the fact that it took the ruthlessness of colonial Britain seventy years to dismantle the political and cultural systems in the protectorate. He initially thought himself capable of uniting the people through his association with the northerners, his maternal connection with the southerners and his union activism with the Creoles. The divisions between the people were cultivated by colonialism and thoroughly managed through coercion and trickery for nearly two centuries. The chasms created were not going to disappear by a mere constitutional change or political gerrymandering.

During the late fifties and sixties, African politicians who were trying very hard to extricate themselves for the shackles of colonialism started courting with the political ideology of communism. The Soviet Union was very attractive and offered a less burdensome alternative to the convoluted and oppressive colonial style of governance which was dominated by major western governments, most of whom participated intensely in the trading of Africans as slaves. The pursuit of communism was not going to be free of perils. The dichotomies in Africa would have to be addressed, and time was not going to be on the side of those advocating a long drawn out cultural change. Importantly, the world geo-political landscape changed significantly after the Second World War.

Changing the orientation of governance to suit a single party political system was a reasonable prospect to Siaka Stevens by his standards. He was the only member of the party of politicians who left Freetown marshalled by the British to discuss colonial cessation and independent rule but refused to sign the accord for very good reasons. His aspirations were quickly smothered by colonial Britain and the covert machinations of the United States of America. Not wanting to be seen as a puppet of colonialism, Siaka Stevens pioneered a constitutional change removing the British royalty as head of state. That brave move made him the first President of the Republic of Sierra Leone in April 1971, exactly ten years after independent rule was proclaimed.

If only it was that easy to shake off over three hundred years of slavery, one hundred and seventy-four years of colonialism and ten years of indirect rule. Siaka Stevens thought that the introduction of republicanism would irradiate the political meddling by Britain and the United States of America who had emerged as the new world power after the conclusion of the Second World War. His deft move to introduce a republican constitution triggered yet another mutation of colonialism. This time the objective was to asphyxiate the aspirations of Siaka Stevens to adopt socialism as the official political ideological system of Sierra Leone.

Having succeeded with the introduction of republicanism, Siaka Stevens was confident that his ambition was going to be realised and more importantly, he felt satisfied that he had taken the idea of his predecessor a significant stage further. The path towards achieving his goal was set, but his intolerance of divergent views quickly became apparent. After four years of political instability and a few sombre incidences, Siaka Stevens was able to pass through a bill in the APC-dominated parliament to introduce a single party system of governance. The party of the Mendes, the SLPP, was immediately relegated to obscurity and was to remain in that torpid state for twenty-five years. In spite of the familiar colonial style violence that dogged his single party system, Siaka Stevens still believed that he could unify all the tribes by presenting an inclusive government, but little was achieved on that score. The Mendes had him in their sights.

No sooner republicanism was introduced, the pressure from Britain and the United States of America, escalated on Siaka Stevens who was determined to pursue an alternative to the unfamiliar political system that was thrust upon the people during the declaration of independent rule. He was very lucky to have survived the political roulette he played with the changing faces of colonialism on the one hand and courting communism on the other. The interests in the wealth of the country, which in turn stimulated their colonial paternalistic behaviour of control and monopoly, was an obsession and a weakness of the *colonial masters,* Britain. Siaka Stevens thoroughly capitalised on the avarice of the neo-colonialists for his own political survival. The British did not want to jeopardise their economic interests by overtly precipitating political instability, and according to their subsequent assessment, Siaka Stevens was a viable partner they could work with in order to perpetrate the exploitation of the resources of the country. So whilst Stevens looked towards the East in his pursuit of an alternative political system, subtle pressure mounted on him through various international organisations orchestrated mainly by colonial Britain. The United States intelligence agencies were the hidden force behind most of the new colonial initiatives. Meanwhile, exploitation of the country continued unabated, impoverishing the people as best as is possible.

Other weaponry within their armoury used to continue to subjugate Africa were a raft of economic regulations ranging from transfer pricing for exported resources, sanctions and conditions from economic bodies dominated by the very colonialists. The ease with which these sanctions and conditions took effect in Africa was astounding. Numerous independent states within the continent found themselves struggling to adopt the prescribed democratic principles which the colonialists were aware was incompatible with the oppressive regimes they bequeathed to them. As if integrating democracy and autocracy was not enough to keep the politicians in complete disarray, African states were tactfully encouraged into the membership of various international organisations they had little or no influence within. Some of these innovations are now dispensing political justice to Africans who had suffered the worse forms of atrocities in the hands of colonialists. Others ensure that economic progress is stifled by the imposition of perilous conditions incredibly on the pretext of poor governance and human right abuses. Ironically, poor governance in Africa is always cited by neo-colonialists as a pretext for their continued involvement in various aspects of political, economic and social life.

The absurdity that a country in Africa can be producing billions of dollars of resources and still running extremely high percentages of illiteracy, poverty, infant and adult mortality is mind boggling. The socio-economic statistics for most African countries have hardly changed since the days of colonialism. The absence of proper industrial and socio-economic infrastructure during the seeming transition to independent rule made it extremely precarious for start-ups in African countries and created an environment of total dependence on their *colonial masters*. The new democratic independent governments in Africa were constructively undermined by their erstwhile colonial benefactors and made to feel inadequate and incompetent to govern themselves.

Zimbabwe, as a modern example, has been struggling to extricate itself from such a dependency. A country where eighty percent of the arable land was owned by non-Africans who constituted less than five percent of the population. Zimbabwe was considered the food basket of Africa through colonialist propaganda, when tobacco, cotton and precious minerals dominated production for British markets. The people of Zimbabwe endured nearly eighty years of untold brutality from colonialism. The country's resources were plundered like many other African countries, but rather strangely, the perpetrators somehow escaped justice. Ironically, the brave Africans who had fought against colonialism in all its guises are those who are charged with human rights abuses. Sanctions of varied characteristics have been imposed on the country, stifling economic growth and sometimes causing internal strife and instability, all aimed at forcing the people to rebel against their gallant African leadership. Their motivation is also to surreptitiously apply pressure on the poor people to relinquish control of more of their land to their oppressors.

During the 1800s, Zimbabwe was conducting its affairs peacefully, until the arrival of the British who purported to have obtained a signed concession for mining from King Lobengula of Ndebele. If this concession was obtained as easily as proclaimed, one wonders why it was necessary for the British government to despatch armed forces to the country to brutally depose the King and massacre his people. The British took over the control of the country and relegated the people to obscurity and indigence. The country was renamed Rhodesia after Cecil Rhodes, the accomplished racist and self-acclaimed businessman, who purported to have obtained a dubious written concession from native Zimbabweans to support its violent occupation. That resulted in his appropriation and confiscation of extensive land belonging to the natives. Zimbabweans eventually lost eighty percent of the arable land to Rhodes and his British comrades through extreme violence and oppression. The actions of Cecil Rhodes and compatriots were nothing less than criminal. The land confiscated from the people was dedicated to the production of tobacco and cotton for the British market. For centuries, Zimbabweans were relegated to the margins through a system of unimaginable oppression, segregation and apartheid. The legacy of Cecil Rhodes in Southern Africa is characterised by extreme racial discrimination, segregation and subjugation. Ironically, the British public still benefit from his ill-gotten wealth obtained on the blood and countless number of Zimbabweans and other Southern Africans lives.

In the late 1990s, British colonial resurgence in Zimbabwe, purposefully to remove the leadership of the country, intensified. This was motivated by their resolute opposition to the leadership's determination to reclaim and retain land originally confiscated from Zimbabweans by British farmers. The leadership doggedly resisted advances from the British government for the return of some of the land that were already reclaimed from British farmers. The erstwhile British colonialists had employed all available measures to influence the position of the Zimbabwean government leadership regarding the exploitation of their ancestral land. Meanwhile, the then Prime Minister of Britain Tony Blair who reneged on an agreement between the British Government and that of Zimbabwe, to pay compensation to dispossessed land owners, was furtively planning the overthrow of Robert Mugabe the president of Zimbabwe. Blair, a typical neo-imperialist, was impatient with Robert Mugabe for his refusal to accede to the overtures of colonial Britain. It subsequently became public that Britain had even identified people in the Zimbabwean military who they were going sponsor to overthrow and succeed Robert Mugabe.

Astonishingly, during the protracted and consolidated colonial effort to replace the leadership of Zimbabwe because of his refusal to conform with British demands, the archbishop of the English Diocese of York, an African himself, stunned the modern world by an unusually-strange behaviour. In his commitment to Britain, the archbishop removed his collar, an official symbol of his status in the Christian faith, and cut it to shreds on a live *British Broadcasting Corporation (BBC)* television programme. The pretext of his unusual behaviour was due to his devout opposition to the leader of Zimbabwe, Robert Mugabe, for his determined refusal to allow the re-colonisation of his country. Rather curiously, the archbishop strangely pronounced that he would never wear the symbol of his religious apparel until Mugabe was gone. Meaning, his ouster or maybe death. This extreme display of surrogate colonial hubris by an African occupying such a high religious office left a lot of Pan-Africanists and anti-colonialists seething.

Bigotry and Colonialism are cancers to Africa, the cure for which might be known to but a few.

Although colonial Britain was relatively at ease with the introduction of republican constitutional rule and single party political systems, there was a marked reduction of colonial personnel in Sierra Leone. This was either due to concerns for their general security or the anticipated changes to the laws and the potential implications for them, in what was evidently becoming a hostile environment. However, changes in the management structure of most of the colonialist-owned organisations were accompanied by huge capital flights to Britain from Sierra Leone. A business practice that disrupted economic activities in the country. This was similarly experienced by South Africa when the African National Congress (ANC) took control of governing the country. Such dramatic fiscal changes could bring a country to the brink of economic collapse with disastrous social and political consequences. Also, actions of such nature demonstrates the lack of commitment that colonialists had in the country other than for the sole purpose of exploitation.

In Sierra Leone, the dramatic changes in the economic structure resulted in widespread corrupt practices, which to a large extent were encouraged by the erstwhile colonialists. During the colonial administration of Sierra Leone, merchant companies were only accountable to the British government. Profits and excess funds were not reinvested in the country or within Africa but were syphoned away to Britain. The enormous difference in remuneration between colonial staff and locals stimulated the first wave of corruption when management structures changed, replacing colonialists with indigenous personnel. Local Africans who elevated to positions previously occupied by colonial personnel quickly found out the dubious ways funds were squirrelled out without any form of transparency. Commercial banks, which were colonialist owned, were in cahoots with merchant companies to syphon funds away from the country. The Lebanese colonial surrogates were encouraged to fill in the void where practicable. They continued to perpetrate the despicable practices of colonialism, with the collaboration of local sycophants, to the detriment of the country.

As far as the shipment of valuable minerals was concerned, Sierra Leone was noted for its value and quality of alluvial diamonds. Diamonds were exploited for centuries by the British, and there was no intention on their part to stop doing so. All sorts of measures were taken to ensure diamonds left the country with little or no accountability. Commercial quantities of gold were extracted and shipped out as by-products to diamond mining. These malpractices deprived the country for centuries and made it impossible to build a decent and viable society.

During the republican single party system of governance, President Siaka Stevens was determined to seek a change to the political ideology of the country before his retirement in 1985. He was seen by the erstwhile colonialists as a threat to their sphere of influence by avidly pursuing communism and Maoism like some other African states. He was quite clear in his mind that the colonial oppressive regime had done no good to Sierra Leone in nearly one hundred and eighty years but the pressure on him by them was all too much.

Unlike Sierra Leone, the leadership of Ghana, Kwame Nkruma was able to concentrate on building industrial and social infrastructures to make up for the reckless exploitation of his country by colonialism. Siaka Stevens and his political predecessors in Sierra Leone spent their time wrestling with the ideological differences between their tribes, which was entrenched during colonialism. They failed to recognise the decay left behind and to halt the phlebotomy of the country by colonialists. There was an all-round socio-economic malaise in the country. There was no foundation on which a sustainable economy was to be built. The preoccupation with the destructive distrust and suspicion that pervaded the country by the new politicians did not help in any way.

The attributes of single party politics espoused by Siaka Stevens did not resonate with the Mendes who felt isolated and perceived to have been denied the right to govern Sierra Leone. The clamp down by Siaka Stevens on dissent and opposition to achieve his goals to some extent alienated the Mendes. Several of them fled the country to live in neighbouring Liberia. There they found refuge with distant relatives and their compatriots who were displaced during the irrational demarcation of Africa by European colonialists.

Although a few prominent liberal Mendes were offered positions in the single party government, the resentment against northerners was palpable. This mind set was due to the belief that the membership of Siaka Stevens' political party was northern biased. Despite several failed attempts to overthrow Stevens, the Mendes remained petrified of the ruthlessness of the Temnes, who were seen to exert influence in the single party government of President Siaka Stevens.

During the period of the first republic, Siaka Stevens, like many African leaders fighting for the freedom of their countries, contended with the ugliness of their divided and fragmented societies and the search for a suitable alternative to colonial repression. Whilst most of the leaders gravitated naturally towards communism with the prospect of returning their countries back to politics by consensus, prior to slavery and colonial oppression, Siaka Stevens took a swipe at the British and American intelligence services by supporting the Palestine Peoples Liberation Organisation (PLO). This was at a time when Israel's popularity could do with some propping. Pressure mounted on Siaka Stevens to relinquish his radical behaviour, but to make things worse, he went further to establish diplomatic ties with the Democratic People's Republic of Korea (DPRK). By then, the Israelis had closed their embassy in Sierra Leone and left town. The unseen hands of what was generally referred to as Neo-colonialism was turning nasty. With the Soviet Union, DPRK and PLO prancing around the country, the colonial intelligence and secret services were all over Siaka Stevens like bees.

Attempts were made to assassinate and overthrow Siaka Stevens, allegedly instigated by foreign agencies. Military officers still loyal to the Sierra Leone Peoples Party and other parties sympathetic to the course of the opposition were covertly influenced to rid of Siaka Stevens. International media reports became negative and his human rights record was ironically put under the spotlight by the erstwhile colonialists. The economy was repeatedly sabotaged through various international organisations controlled by Caucasians. The sole purpose was to cause instability and insurrection that might lead to his overthrow. Siaka Stevens was caught between the intrigues of the cold war, the kaleidoscope of colonialism on the one hand and the inherited conflicting internal ideologies of his own people on the other. Also, the values and principles of the emerging Pan-African movement were compelling, and Siaka Stevens, like other radical African leaders, was keen to promote the integration and unity of Africa.

Colonialism in its modern form is ever so complex that the less organised and fragmented the African continent is, the harder it will be to contest the aggression of imperialism and neo-colonialism. An array of tools is at the disposal of colonial interests that are utilised effectively to perpetrate the exploitation and subjugation of the people of Africa. The broadcasting media had been a preferred tool of choice for mass propaganda by colonialism. The *British Broadcasting Corporation (BBC),* known as the colonial radio in Africa, is a strategic tool used effectively by the British to maintain and continue to influence the cultures and attitude of Africans. The majority of Africans still regard information disseminated by the *BBC* as gospel. The *BBC* broadcasts directly to various tribes and ethnic groups within African countries. They promote individualism, separatism in some cases and entrench the ideologies impressed on the people during the dark days of repression.

Zimbabwe was particularly targeted by the colonial broadcasting corporation during the active British sponsorship of political opposition to Robert Mugabe, the President of that country. He was a sworn enemy of Britain for reclaiming land from British landowners, who once commandeered eighty percent of the arable land in Zimbabwe. He was persistently caricatured as a deranged despot who killed his own "starving" people. The Broadcasting Corporation did not disseminate information about the number of British-sponsored sanctions and restrictions in place causing untold suffering of the people. These sanctions and embargoes were to stimulate widespread rebellion and carnage, that would eventually lead to the overthrow of President Mugabe. This was all due to the politics of land. Land that actually belonged to the people of Zimbabwe that the British cynically commandeered from them. The control of the air waves in Africa by the British colonial empire had long-term negative cultural influences on Africans and increasingly promoting distrust amongst the people.

Modern times have seen the uncontrolled and effective use of social media to influence the culture of the continent, specifically targeting impatient young minds to adopt and practice values that invariable conflict with the ideals and aspirations of their leaders.

There is a plethora of international organisations that African countries have de facto membership to through their colonial associations. Some of these organisations have been wreaking havoc within the continent causing instability, carnage and untold hardship amongst the people. Colonial intelligence agencies often use these organisations to embed operatives within Africa to whip up anti-government sentiments and instability in order to facilitate regime change whenever they deemed it necessary.

Direct military interventions as "*colonial masters*" is another modern approach to effect regime change or to enforce policies or colonial diktats in Africa. In Cote D'Ivoire, the outcome of elections held in 2010 after a brutal civil war was marginal, leaving both presidential parties disputing the result. Instead of encouraging the forming of a coalition government by consensus, the French colonial "*Masters*" swooped in with overwhelming force, smashed their way into the presidential palace, humiliated the incumbent and took him away to face charges of human rights abuses at the International Criminal Court. The colonialist's-favoured candidate, who was himself tainted by war crimes, was installed and propped in government by the French colonialists. A country that was virtually divided equally through tribal affiliation and had suffered from intense violence could have benefited from a coalition through consensus which was an African ideal. The usual demonstration of colonial force in deciding who governs was only temporarily suppressing the other side and deferring inevitable conflict. That is how a master behaves to his servants. Straight forward *Colonial Mastership*.

In Sierra Leone, Siaka Stevens had brushes with the subterfuge of some of these colonial apparatuses. During his long term in office, one of such encounters was the arrest and incarceration of a former rebel leader and president of Liberia. Charles Taylor was intercepted in Sierra Leone on a secret mission to overthrow the incumbent president of Liberia. Siaka Steven, whose action was in accordance with a sub-regional arrangement, the Mano River Union (MRU), was ordered by the CIA to release Taylor as quickly as he had arrested him. It subsequently became public that Charles Taylor was an operative of the United States intelligence agency, the Central Intelligence Agency. This is what colonialism had morphed into. Ironically, African lives are still lost through sponsored wanton violence. Such actions by colonial interests are usually described as necessary for the protection of Africans.

****

The encounter with Charles Taylor by Siaka Stevens was not going to be the end of that episode. Charles Taylor was to progress with his ambition to take over political rule in neighbouring Liberia, an American colonial outpost. A feat that Sierra Leone was to be inextricably entangled.

The partitioning of the continent by colonial zealots, who had no consideration for the suffering caused to families separated by the forcible imposition of borders within the continent, was one of the significant and irrational actions that upset the dynamics of African societies. The Mendes, unfortunately, were directly affected by this arbitrary action, with a large section of their community partitioned into Liberia. The Vai is one of the tribal group and dialect of the Mendes found in both sides of the south-eastern border between Sierra Leone and Liberia.

During the initial period of the first republic, the declaration of single party governance and the alienation of parties in the opposition including the Sierra Leone Peoples Party (SLPP), which was dominated by the Mendes, led a few key SLPP members to seek refuge in Liberia from the Stevens government, which lasted eighteen years. Communication contact with their compatriots left behind in Sierra Leone was well maintained. The general unease of the Mendes who took political positions within the government of the ruling All People's Congress (APC) party, was known on both sides of the border.

After eighteen years, Siaka Stevens retired and in a neatly choreographed political process, handed power over to the head of the military who became president for another seven years. Siaka Steven's departure aroused the interest of the Mendes, more so that of the exiles in Liberia who had already established a symbiotic relationship with Charles Taylor. Charles Taylor by then had launched an incursion into Liberia, and fighting was raging between various tribal factions within that country. The successor to Siaka Stevens was not going to enjoy the fear and respect that characterised the regime of his predecessor. No sooner he assumed the office of president, he came under pressure from the Mendes and the British to revert to multi-party democracy.

In Liberia, the United States of America was very concerned with the threat posed to their interests by the guerrilla activities of Charles Taylor. The incumbent who himself took over power by force of arms was heavily sponsored by the United States. The primary interest of the US was for Liberia to relinquish ties with the Soviet Union, a connection that was established during the cold war years. President William Tolbert like President Siaka Stevens in Sierra Leone was not convinced about the viability of the colonial imposed multi-party democracy and capitalism in Africa. His preference for socialism, like many of his peers, was to put him at loggerhead with the United States of America. It was widely believed that President William Tolbert was killed by American agents during the United States of America sponsored coup that toppled his government.

Colonial Britain was also keen to re-engage and continue their influence in Sierra Leone after President Siaka Steven's apparent geo-political shift to the eastern bloc. Pressure mounted for political reforms by Britain who sponsored economic and other subtle sanctions on the government in order to precipitate political change. These measures where ratcheted especially after a series of executions of very senior members of the government and the military, by President Siaka Stevens.

During the seventies and eighties, there were increased political and social interactions with the Soviet Union, China and North Korea. Although the Soviet Union was keen to promote communism in Africa, it was not in the position to do so by brute force as was the case during the partitioning and colonisation of the continent by western European countries. Their approach was to extend cultural exchange programmes and set up pedagogical centres. China, on the other hand, undertook extensive economic activities in order to gain influence and exploitation of resources. That approach was not going to last as it took colonial Britain nearly two centuries to change cultures, in Sierra Leone as an example. Another major impediment was the rivalry that resulted after the Second World War between the Soviet Union and the United States. Wherever possible, lethal force was used to maintain their sphere of colonial influence in order to prevent the overtures of the Soviet Union taking hold anywhere in the African continent.

British and American secret service operatives were imbedded in most African countries, and Sierra Leone was no exception. During the height of apartheid rule in South Africa, sixty-nine people were shot and killed in cold blood for protesting against the apartheid regime in 1960; the infamous Sharpeville massacre. The African National Congress (ANC), perceived to be a communist organisation, was forced to change its strategy in combating the barbaric regime, opting for guerrilla warfare and widespread sabotage. Nelson Mandela who was the head of the military wing of the ANC became the world's most wanted *terrorist.* A terrorist for fighting extreme oppression of his people by Caucasian occupiers. Several attempts were made to capture Nelson Mandala who was known as the "*black pimpernel*" amongst his Caucasian adversaries. It was the American CIA that eventually tracked down Nelson Mandela and betrayed him to the ruthless South African police force. That malicious betrayal resulted in the illegal and unfair incarceration of Nelson Mandela and his compatriots for 26 years. Centuries of collaboration and coordination amongst Caucasians made the oppression of Africans sustainable.

Siaka Stevens and other African leaders were certain that the political system forced upon them was incompatible with African traditions, particularly when the colonialists themselves never attempted to practice any aspect of the democratic principles they extolled. Siaka Stevens was not keen on communism per se but was unable to craft a novel political system amidst the insurmountable colonial pressures he faced. He was quite aware of the African traditional systems of governance by consensus, which was fiercely obliterated through sheer brute force by Britain. These systems perfidiously replaced by authoritarianism and separatism resulted in social tensions, distrust, hate and anger between various tribal groups.

The establishment of a single-party political system under a republican constitution by Siaka Stevens was an attempt to galvanise the political interests of the various tribal groups within the country towards a common goal. Straight forward as it may have appeared, the move unsettled colonial interests with drastic consequences for him and the country. In the absence of a blueprint of what he was aspiring to, one could easily surmise that his ambition perhaps was to achieve a hybrid political system between communism and western democracy. A transformation of that significance could only happen in an environment of unity and total commitment by the people of the country.

The SLPP exiles in Liberia, keen to re-establish their political influence in Sierra Leone, had recruited the services of an ex-military mutinous corporal, once jailed by Siaka Stevens, as the commander of the military wing of their revolutionary front. Charles Taylor was already fixated with avenging his detention in Sierra Leone and the country being used as a military staging post for a United Nations sponsored military intervention force into Liberia. He saw the United Nations intervention force as an American ploy to stall his military advance on Monrovia, the capital of Liberia. Charles Taylor made available sufficient logistical and military support for the incursion of the SLPP exiles into Sierra Leone. The sole purpose of the incursion was fundamentally to prise power from the northerners back to the eastern and southerners. The divisions between the major tribes were clear and long-lasting. There had never been any attempt to reconcile the two major tribes in Sierra Leone. The Mendes had always been bitter against the Temnes for their treachery in collaborating with European slavers to capture, abuse and inflict untold suffering on their people, historically. The Temnes, on the other hand, believed they had to do what they did as a strategy for their survival. Needless to state that the motivation for the ensuing violence was quite evident.

Colonial influence and meddling were evident in both Liberia and Sierra Leone during the years of violent upheavals. There is hardly any country in Africa that had not experienced instability and violent conflicts post colonialism. Such situations will persist as colonial structures remain in place and represent symbols of exploitation and divisions.

It did not take much for the insurgency to gain momentum and take hold within the east and south of Sierra Leone. Amidst the chaos and confusion, mercenaries hired by unknown interests began operating freely in Sierra Leone. Diamonds and gold became a lucrative pastime for colonial surrogates. Unidentified European flights often landed with tons of lethal weapons delivered directly to the revolutionaries. The country quickly became awash with guns and bombs and the all too familiar violence experienced during colonialism resurfaced. Sierra Leoneans had hardly recovered from centuries of brutality and oppression and the resulting fractured and dysfunctional social structure that had no facility for dialogue and consensus.

The escalating violence precipitated a military coup d'état that took over power from President Joseph Momoh, the protégé of Siaka Stevens. President Joseph Momoh subsequently fled into exile in neighbouring Guinea, amidst the looming aggression from the east and south of the country. A series of coups and counter coups resulted. This aroused the concern of the *colonial master*, Britain, whose strategies within the country became ineffectual during the Siaka Stevens hiatus. Conflicting orders and threats were made by the erstwhile colonialists in desperation. The country's military was merely playing out the discord and disharmony that characterised tribal relations in the country. On the assumption of office by the military coup leader in the first instance, who by some rare chance happened to be a Creole, Britain was quick to move in urging the re-introduction of *democratic* rule and to conduct general elections as quickly as was possible.

Two tired and uninspiring Sierra Leoneans who were former United Nations bureaucrats were sponsored by Britain to facilitate and expedite political change that would conform to their paternalistic interests. The primary duty of the duo was to influence the junta to hand over power back to civilian rule who were usually easier to corrupt and manipulate with less security issues. The two underlings immediately set to work in Freetown reviewing and making changes to the country's constitution, whilst fighting was still raging in the provinces. By the time the beleaguered junta leader realised what was brewing, it was curtains for his regime. The two United Nations retirees had pencilled him out of fulfilling his ambitions to become a civilian president, by manipulating the constitution to preclude the gun-toting Creole army captain from running for elections.

A palace coup was swiftly activated by a member of the junta, a captain himself, to remove the aggrieved leader for attempting to revisit the amended constitution that had been manipulated to eliminate him from running for presidential elections. The junta leader's successor was from the Mende tribe that predominated the revolutionary fighting force. The takeover of the new junta leader, unsurprisingly immediately influenced and reduced the momentum of the revolutionary activities in the east and south of Sierra Leone. A ceasefire was easily negotiated by the new leader with the revolutionary fighting front. He wasted no time to accept and carry out the instructions of Britain to hold general elections. The elections were presided over by one of the two former functionaries of the United Nations, who subsequently went on to become the finance minister in the government that emerged from the elections he directed. Interestingly, the other retired UN functionary with whom he spearheaded the change to the constitution of the country emerged as the *democratically* elected President of the country. Needless to state that the results of the elections, however skewed, satisfied the demands of the *colonial master*. The intrigues of colonial legacy in Africa is quite baffling.

The long wait by the Sierra Leone Peoples Party (SLPP) appeared to have come to an end after twenty-five years in the doldrums. The main protagonists of the revolutionary movement, who had been in exile in Liberia, dramatically and opportunistically abandoned the revolution to take up positions within the new government that emerged from the hastily conducted elections. The military commander of the revolutionary front, who for obvious reasons happened to be a Temne, was left to manage the remnants of the movement which was in disarray but still seriously armed.

The elected president received the undisguised and enthusiastic support of Britain, the "*colonial masters*", who were quite pleased with their influence on the affairs of the country once again. However, their elation was to be short lived as the division and segregation that they established and promoted during centuries of colonialism was to militate against their interest. Although the SLPP was the colonial preference, President Tejan Kabbah, the new civilian leader, turned out not to be from the predominant Mende tribe. Though he was born in the south, the president was from a smaller tribal Mandingo group. This did not actually resonate well with all the Mendes, and a significant section of the fighting force became rather remote and indifferent to his political overtures.

Britain, the "*colonial masters*", cynically continued to support the fragile government of President Tejan Kabbah for obvious reasons. The tenuousness of the government did not require much expertise to figure out, but the opportunity to take control of the country once again was irresistible to Britain. The British government gave their support irrespective of whether the system they were promoting suited the prevailing conditions or might end up widening the chasm they created between the tribes. The level of hate and discord for each other were infused in the minds of the people and had far-reaching consequences.

High unemployment characterised the colonial era, but because of the trickle down economic approach by the administration, the people felt their lot was endurable. A few Sierra Leoneans were exposed to British cultural education but were never exposed to

189

environments that inspired strategic and innovative thinking. Planning had always been done by the colonialists, albeit against the interests of the people. This classic trait was displayed by their sponsorship of the inept, ill-timed and badly-organised elections, during which a few of the opportunistic revolutionaries defected to what they felt was mainstream politics after over two decades in the political wilderness.

The British "*colonial masters*" failed to recognise that the bitterness that had created the upheaval was ideological, which to a large extent was cultivated by them. Their interest in the country after the shambolic elections was greatly publicised as humanitarian even with mercenaries and arms popping up everywhere in the country. Stocks of diamonds left the country with reciprocal increase in aid and mercy missions, channelled through various makeshift organisations, creating the illusion of stability and prospect.

Colonial dependence was not hard to see or experience in Sierra Leone during the upheaval. At specific times during the day, almost the entire country came to a virtual standstill to listen to updates from the British colonial broadcasting corporation, the *BBC*. These were regular reports on the resurgence in fighting in the southern and eastern regions in their country. The hopelessness and the puppetry of the government tested the patience of the people. The government was overly dependent on briefings from Britain. The president practically approached the conflict from a United Nations bureaucratic standpoint, making speeches over the *BBC* and regularly consulting with the British government instead of engaging with the people who were fast running out of patience with his inertia. The country depended on handouts and other subventions from its "*colonial masters*", whilst commercial quantities of diamonds, gold and timber were being shipped out of the country by unscrupulous agencies of the very "*colonial maters*". Such was the culture that the people were accustomed to in centuries, to sit idly by whilst the colonialists and their Lebanese proxies exploited their wealth in return for donations and patronage.

It was not long before the British sponsored Tejan Kabbah government was overthrown and replaced by another military officer. This change surprised not only their protégé but also the British government that thought they were back in control. Their distorted perspective of what was going on in the country was severely exposed yet again. Their persistent meddling resulted in the impotence of the government which was totally dependent on them for direction. This was the democracy that was proffered and avidly propped by them. Those who for a brief while thought that colonisation and its oppressive methods had faded away could not be ever so wrong. The malignancy of colonialism could not be merely wished away, although there were periods when it appeared that it was all over. This perception created a false sense of security, disguised by spots of seeming altruism through strategic aid packages that achieved hardly anything. The objective of such handouts was to distort fiscal activities and deflect attention from the vigorous exploitation of resources of the country by Europeans and other foreign interests.

Chapter 14
Merchants of War

The complexity of the civil strife in Sierra Leone typified most social instabilities in and around Africa. The separation of tribes and pitching them against each other during hundreds of years of slavery and colonisation created a culture of distrust and hate that could only be addressed by a collective and unified nonviolent, systematic and organised Cultural Revolution. These divisions had been used repeatedly to perpetrate the exploitation of the continent and its people.

When the Tejan Kabbah government in Sierra Leone was overthrown, he and all his hangers-on sort refuge in neighbouring Guinea where they continued to receive hand-outs from the British government. The reaction to the overthrow by the British government was one of indignation and fury.

Although the upheaval was characterised by extreme violence, the solution was not necessarily military and whatever was going to be achieved through military force would only suppress the deep ideological differences between the factions.

After the sponsored elections in 1996, when opportunistic members of the military revolutionary front surfaced in the capital and participated in the Tejan Kabbah government, those moves created a false sense of security and eventually conceit. It was generally thought that the long awaited accession to political power by the proscribed SLPP party during the single party system, had been achieved but the story was not going to be that straightforward. The defection of the few who joined the government was not viewed particularly favourably by many of the other militants who decided to continue the fight. The membership and fighting force of the Revolutionary United Front (RUF) comprised of nearly hundred percent Mendes. The military wing of the Front was, however, led by an ex-military corporal who was from the Temne tribe. This was a situation that those who defected to the Tejan Kabbah government subsequently became too embarrassed to associate with. He was recruited by the SLPP exiles in Liberia for his credentials and the common destiny they shared at the time. Corporal Foday Sankoh's appointment as the head of the military wing of the Revolutionary Front was time bound. He was to be disposed of immediately after the SLPP got back in power. However, the mass defection to the hastily formed SLPP Kabbah government, without considering the opinion and consideration of the rest of the membership, further complicated the dynamics of the Revolutionary Front as a movement and a fighting force.

The younger officers of the Front who were not politicians per se were fighting not only for the SLPP to achieve power but for better employment, economic prospects and fulfilling their individual aspirations. They were unimpressed with the swift capitulation of their predominantly older comrades to the Tejan Kabbah government. Their political philosophy appeared to be at variance with the rest of the younger fighting force. The younger squad proceeded to make their position quite clearly. That they were not prepared to be political bed fellows with Tejan Kabbah who they scarcely knew and had not proffered any cogent plans for economic reforms and most of all addressing the political rift and social discord within the country. The government issued instructions for all armed personnel to surrender and hand over their weapons to the United Nations monitoring group stationed in Freetown. The fighters had little or no confidence in the United Nations peace keeping and monitoring group because of their perceived impartiality. The defectors who had joined the Tejan Kabbah government promised to order a complete cessation of hostilities as a condition for their participation in government. They were however left seriously embarrassed when the military wing under the command of their uncompromising northern leadership rejected their orders and resumed hostilities.

It was the resumption of fighting and the cavalier attitude of the British sponsored Tejan Kabbah government that precipitated yet another coup, staged by some elements of the country's national armed forces. The coup leader immediately offered an olive branch to the remnants of the Revolutionary Front and invited them to participate in the formation of an all-inclusive government which appeared reasonable and attractive at the time. This move added a further complication to an already political quagmire. The defectors who earlier joined the government which hand been overthrown took flight and sort refuge together with Tejan Kabbah in Guinea.

No sooner they settled down in Guinea, against the wishes of the president of that country, who by then was playing host to the third overthrown president, they went on a disinformation overdrive. With the tacit support of their British sponsors, they adopted a tactic similar to the colonial years. Through the *British Broadcasting Corporation* and allied neo-colonialists media, they attempted to rouse the Mendes to rise against the Temnes using the pretext that the corporal leader of the militant revolutionary front movement, a Tenme, was waging a war against them. This was a deliberate move to increase tribal tension between the majority Mendes and their Temne foes. The rhetoric designed to apportion blame for the upheaval to the northerners. The propaganda was very effective, aided by the British government who had set up a special broadcasting station with jamming devices to prevent divergent views from hitting the airwaves. The north and south-eastern divide was laid bare yet again. The cracks were visible even within the national armed forces whose senior officers, predominantly from the south and east, covertly and expertly manoeuvred troops to take hostilities into the northern regions. This move when juxtaposed with the propaganda appeared to be a calculated and an obvious act of revenge for historical events, using the involvement of a northerner in the revolution as a reason for all-out cross-regional war.

The British *colonial masters* who were only focused on increasing their participation and exploitation of the resources available in the country completely ignored and took little cognisance of the continued and serious divide in the country. Economic interests usually precede morality in geopolitics. Divisions and discord amongst the people created an environment that made for good feeding grounds. The prospects were alluring, and Britain asserted itself and adopted a strident approach towards the coup plotters who had collaborated with the Revolutionary Front. The British government continued to bankroll the Tejan Kabbah government in exile.

Meanwhile, Tejan Kabbah, the exiled president, in his well-founded enthusiasm for returning to power, somehow established contact with a notorious businessman and financier with a less than colourful reputation, who was held in detention in Canada for various alleged improprieties in Thailand. Rakesh Saxena promised to reinstate Tejan Kabbah as president of Sierra Leone in return for considerable diamond mining concessions in the country. Tejan Kabbah in his eagerness and desperation to return to power acceded

194

to the request and set out plotting away profitable mining fields and recklessly signing contracts with the miscreant.

Rakesh Saxena, whilst in detention, managed to recruit the services of a mercenary company called Sandline International registered in Britain. The appointment of the mercenary company was not in itself a coincidence. The company and its front man, Lt Col. Tim Spicer, an ex-British Army officer were well known to the British government. The proposed activities of the mercenary company in Sierra Leone was to create carnage and destruction that would facilitate the return of the puppet Tejan Kabbah government. The plan was redolent of colonial intrigues and reminiscent of the expeditionary forces that operated with unrestrained force under British Royal warrant, committing appalling crimes and abuses in the pursuit of total domination and subjugation of the people. Such was the reputation of this mercenary, that the once Senator, who became president of the United States, Barack Obama indicated in a letter to his constituents in 2005 that "The CEO of Aegis Defence Services Tim Spicer has been implicated in a variety of human rights abuses around the globe… given his history, I agree that the United States should consider rescinding its contract with his company". This was the man that Tejan Kabbah with the overt support of his colonial mentors were desperate to recruit to unleash terror on the unsuspecting people of Sierra Leone.

The exiled Tejan Kabbah government and the British government were engrossed with political power on the one hand and diamonds, timber, gold and colonial influence on the other. Their fixation, coupled with the proposed antiques of the maverick mercenary, obscured their moral judgement and were completely oblivious to the potential carnage they were about to cause in the country. The intervention of *colonial masters* in African conflicts is usually subtle. Their involvement in conflicts usually is to supply lethal weapons to both sides in conflicts, hedging their bets and wreak havoc and wanton slaughter of innocent people. On the pretext of humanitarian consideration, they always conjure compelling and altruistic reasons for their intervention. Their initiative usually receives overwhelming psychological and moral acclaim based on their seeming generosity and philanthropy. The additional purpose for this intricate scheme was to re-install a government that was apparently highly receptive of colonial paternal patronage.

The Revolutionary Front fragmented into two factions following the political debacle. One faction allied to the military junta led by the recalcitrant Temne corporal and the other led by one of the returned defectors to the exiled Tejan Kabbah government. The latter rebranded themselves and ironically called their break away movement the "Civil Defence Unit" or in local Mende parlance, "*Kamajors*". The kamajors were rapidly armed with lethal weaponry from their colonial sponsors and promptly went on the rampage, facing off with the military junta and their former Revolutionary Front compatriots. Total carnage ensued and thousands of innocent and poor people were slaughtered en masse. Colonialism is synonymous with violence and violence terrifies people into submission and unconditional acceptance of values and practices that are normally incompatible with their cultural ideals.

No genuine effort was made to reconcile the fighting factions and to bridge the tribal divide. Instead, the British continued to bombard the people through their broadcast medium with incendiary and threatening rhetoric. They used their leverage within the United Nations to support an increase in military activity through the enforcement of peace by the United Nations and the unconditional return of the exiled Tejan Kabbah government. The reason the exiled president was encouraged by the British to sign away land that did not belong to him was purely to support their continued exploitation of diamonds and gold for the exchange of lethal weapons and for the hire of mercenaries. Most of all, the urge to install a government that was easy and amenable to colonial overtures could hardly be resisted.

Sierra Leone is quite unique to be used as an experiment to implement the change in strategy from trading Africans in slave markets to enslaving them on their own soil by the British. This change in strategy motivated by the need to be unaccountable for their actions had caused nothing but perennial carnage, destruction, pain and hopelessness in that country. The introduction of guns and gunpowder during the slaving days and during the fight for control of the hinterland caused untold deaths of innocent children, women and men. Violence was widely used to suppress Africans and to promote the ideals of the infamous colonial administrations across the continent. This violent practice sadly and rather unfortunately become part of the culture of the people.

As with many conflicts in Africa, where ideological divisions between tribes are capitalised on by foreign interests, it is spectacularly amazing how conflicting sides easily and quickly have access to arms and ammunition. The fascinating aspect of all this is, quite often conflicts are instigated by colonial interests for reasons obvious to all, whilst their proxies and corporations tend to carry on with the plundering of resources or whatever attracts their interest. Amazingly, such proxies usually remain unscathed amidst the ravages of hostilities within the conflict zones. The model has hardly changed since the proliferation of British Slave Companies all over Africa. The Sierra Leone Company was one such creation that kept changing its form to suit prevailing environments and conditions.

Whilst the Tejan Kabbah government and hangers-on were receiving tokens and pocket money for their sustenance in exile, the British *colonial masters* were merrily rubbing their hands in glee at the ease and the prospect of taking control of Sierra Leone once again. Sandline International's Tim Spicer wasted no time to engage with the relevant bureaucrats in the British government. This was reminiscent of the colonial days when decisions were made by colonialists on behalf of Africa remotely. A flurry of meetings and palm squeezing ensued with functionaries within the Foreign and Commonwealth Office in London, where designated officers charged with responsibilities for affairs of the Gambia, Sierra Leone and Liberia formulate policies promoting British hegemony. Their charge obviously does not include building schools, hospitals, preventing rape and abuse of vulnerable people or pillaging the resources of these countries. Rather, their brief is to monitor the political situation, policy development and strategic direction of these countries and to destabilise them whenever necessary if their actions tend to contravene their interests. Although the situation in Sierra Leone was conducive to the nefarious operations and practices of the foreign office, the number of interested parties however become a concern and required some order and control. But that was not going to be done in the comfort of their Whitehall offices. Britain had to assert itself in the usual manner and that was through force. Thirty-five tons of assorted lethal weaponry, described as Bulgarian arms, to the cost of £6m were swiftly procured and shipped to the battle ground. Not surprising, the end user certificates were endorsed by the British Department of Trade for use by Tim Spicer in Sierra Leone. The modus operandi of Lt Col. Tim Spicer included training and arming thousands of unemployed youths as militias with the objective of overthrowing the military junta and its allies. No flexibility for dialogue between the factions and the people of the country was allowed. Ultimatums and sanctions were issued by the British government, some routed through the United Nations, as they quite often do. The rhetoric of distrust and hate was ratcheted by the colonial broadcasting corporation and many other neo-colonial media. The people were made to believe that there was no alternative to the ousted government of Tejan Kabbah. The backing of the ousted government by British military force seemed to offer false assurances to the ill-informed people. The presence of the British armada along the Freetown estuary, like it used to be in the slaving and colonial days, was amply publicised, instilling fear amongst the already bewildered and confused people.

Colonialism is a system borne out of an ideology that supports the notion of race superiority of the coloniser over those colonised. A claim that colonialists believe entitles them to unrestricted access into territories they deem to be theirs to exploit and abuse with impunity. The motivation for colonial Britain to intervene in Sierra Leone the way they did was evident. Whilst there might not be a clear winner in the conflagration, the losers were going to be the innocent the people.

The Revolutionary Front which had fragmented into a Civil Defence Unit (*Kamajors*) was fighting against the Armed Forces of Sierra Leone (Junta) and their erstwhile compatriots who are allied to the armed forces. However, loyalty within the Armed Forces (Junta) was surreptitiously split between the Civil Defence Unit (*Kamajors*) and the original Revolutionary Front. The remnants of the original Revolutionary Front were committed and open to a negotiated settlement of what had rapidly became an impasse. Their philosophy appealed to a large swathe within the military armed forces who were hoping for an inclusive government. On the other side were with those who believed that governance should be the preserve of the Mendes, hence their covert association with the *Kamajors*.

Another complication was the presence of a South African private mercenary company, Executive Outcomes, which had strong links to the former apartheid regime in Southern Africa. They were supposed to be fighting alongside the country's armed forces but rather curiously confined their operations mainly to the diamond rich areas. Included in the fray were the Economic Community of West African States Monitoring Group (ECOMG), a Nigerian led force mainly promoting the interest of their president Sani Abacha. The United Nations under the influence and guidance of the *colonial master, Britain*, also added their armed peace enforcement troops in the mix. Not forgetting the British Navy and Sandline International led by Lt. Col. Tim Spicer. All of these protagonists were armed with enough fire power to exterminate the entire population. A total quagmire that left the people totally vulnerable and confused amongst such potent fighting forces with conflicting interests and loyalties.

The pivotal role played and the involvement of colonial Britain in this debacle, though not surprising, typifies the chicanery and exploitation that went on during a hundred and eighty years of hubris, autocracy and repression in Sierra Leone. How this whole enterprise was put together, staged and managed, stunned not only Sierra Leoneans in particular but Africans in general who thought colonialism had long gone and a thing of the past.

After the British-sponsored deliberately ill-timed elections that brought in an ineffectual government to office in 1996, the services of the South African Private mercenaries, Executive Outcomes were recruited and were alleged to have the capability to keep Tejan Kabbah in power in exchange for diamonds. This was against the backdrop of a mainly disloyal armed forces who preferred the president of the country to be from the Mende tribe. The United States expressed their unease about the capability of Tejan Kabbah as an effective leader initially, but his mentors, the British, were comfortable with his simplicity and offered some reassurance to the United States of America. They continued to support Kabbah avidly on the pretext that he was the legitimately elected leader of the country.

Tejan Kabbah's desperation to return to power at any cost after he was ousted, even to the extent of sacrificing the lives of the people he intended to rule, did not sit well with the United States. However, his colonial mentors continued to prop him steadfastly.

The export of thirty-five tons of weaponry from Britain in 1998 was intended to be a covert operation, but the secret was blown into the open when the illicit transaction which violated the provisions of the very British Sponsored United Nation Resolution 1132 on Sierra Leone was found out by the Customs and Excise Department of the United Kingdom. The customs department was inadvertently left out of the plan by the Foreign Office. The cargo of weapons was transported by a British registered company, Sky Air Cargo Services with export licences and end user certificates from Britain.

The weapons were flown directly to Sierra Leone where they were promptly intercepted by the Nigerian dominated Economic Community of West African States Monitoring Group (ECOMOG). No one in Sierra Leone knew who the weapons were for, as Lt Col. Tim Spicer who was supposed to be the consignee, was unknown to the Nigerian troops who by then had occupied and had control of the international airport. Even if the Nigerian troops were aware of Tim Spicer's dealings, there was no guarantee that they would have wanted to participate in his adventure. His objectives were inconsistent with theirs and their leader Sani Abacha, the president of Nigeria.

The great British counter-coup or whatever was being planned, was over without a single bullet being fired from the confiscated arsenal. The confiscation of the illegally-imported weapons by the Nigerians resulted in a thoroughly embarrassing situation that caused a political storm of accusations and denials amongst British government officials. The British government and to a large extent, the United States, were not particularly supportive of the Nigerian operation but could have done very little to influence their military activities. The Nigerians who ironically were also operating on the pretext of restoring democracy had established themselves in Sierra Leone and were ahead of the other players. The issue was with the Nigerian president Sani Abacha, whose human rights credential was considered bad and his corrupt ways were under scrutiny by the United States especially. It was public knowledge that Sani Abacha was keen to have Tejan Kabbah back in power as he had personal designs in Sierra Leone for the purpose of concealing some of his questionable fortunes. The paradox was that the British government, Rakesh Saxena, Tim Spicer and the *Kamajors* were all on the same side in this high stakes game but with differing agendas. The imposition or restoration of *democracy* was what appeared to be the common objective they all espoused.

An inquiry was ordered by the Foreign Secretary of the British government to find out how such a botched illegal transaction could have received government approval in the first place. The Secretary of the Foreign and Commonwealth Office, who vigorously promoted an ethical foreign policy, was apoplectic when he found out his department was not only at the centre of the deal but had approved the botched transaction. It subsequently became public that some of his functionaries had orchestrated the transaction. The foreign secretary was a man of detail and shown a lot of interest in minutia within his department but, however, somehow missed the deal. He probably would not have missed a few documents pertaining to the arms deal that filtered through his dispatch box if indeed they did, as his functionaries alleged. The British High Commissioner to Sierra Leone, Peter Penfold, was described as an "*old Africa hand*", having served in and witnessed a couple of coups in Uganda, a revolution in Ethiopia and a war in Nigeria. It was he who instigated and masterminded the grand plan to supply the arsenal of lethal weapons, presumably to the faction that Britain perceived would serve their interest. The venture was consistent with his colonial credentials. To destabilise, control and exploit. His posting prior to Sierra Leone was Governor of the British Virgin Islands, an excellent résumé of a typical colonialist. The urge for Penfold to restore colonial order and control in Sierra Leone was instinctive. The days of obtaining treaties and deposing chiefs through deception and coercion must have appeared distant, maybe too distant for him and his associates. Therefore, Tejan Kabbah's unreasonable desperation to be restored to power at any conceivable cost complemented Penfold's primordial colonial ambitions.

Tim Spicer, mercenary merchant of trouble as was known in some circles, was, however, not unfamiliar with the goings on in Sierra Leone. He had a security contract with a company, Diamond Works, in the country which ran out just when the opportunity to restore the ousted government came knocking. He claimed he was contacted by Kabbah who introduced him to Rakesh Saxena, who already had business interests in the country. By some strange coincidence, his compatriot, Peter Penfold, the British High Commissioner with an impressive colonialist credential, also made contact with him on the same issue. The issue was to reinstate Tejan Kabbah to presidency of the country as Tejan Kabbah was the preferred choice of candidate of the British government. Peter Penfold further expressed the British government's apprehension about the Nigerian dominated Economic Community of West African States Monitoring Group (ECOMOG) troops and his government's plan to neutralise them as swiftly as possible. The use of the concept of democracy by neo-colonialists to promote their sphere of influence within Africa is always suspect. Colonialism has never been synonymous with democracy however which way the concept is interpreted. The purpose of propping weak governments in Africa under the guise of democracy is clearly to promote exploitation and nothing to do with the interest of the people.

In a rather bizarre turn of events, the then Prime Minister of Britain, Tony Blair amidst the consternation caused by the illicit weapons deal chose to extended an official invitation to the exiled president Tejan Kabbah to attend the meeting of Commonwealth heads of government in Edinburgh in 1997. Sierra Leone had been suspended from the commonwealth, and Tejan Kabbah was not representing the country for all intent and purposes. In his desperation to reassert his government's position and authority, following the botched arms deal, Tony Blair further proceeded to invite Tejan Kabbah to attend a conference at the *Royal Overseas Club*, giving him the opportunity to make a distress call to the international community at large for his reinstatement as president of Sierra Leone. The British Foreign and Commonwealth Office at the same time issued stringent undiplomatic warnings to the Junta to relinquish power and hand over back to their protégé Tejan Kabbah. The colonial machinery was put into full operation by the Prime Minister of Britain, Tony Blair, in order to overshadow the embarrassing illicit arms saga by his government and to regain lost credibility especially to their ally the United States of America.

Wary of his previously failed adventure in Papua New Guinea, Lt Col. Tim Spicer, when told that the arsenal of weapons and a helicopter were ready to be shipped to Sierra Leone, did not hesitate to consult the Foreign Office to obtain protection and clearance for the export. The mercenary merchant who prior to this gambit, managed to obtain a contract to crush a rebellion by separatists in Papua New Guinea. That enterprise ended in a fiasco, with him being rejected by the military of Papua New Guinea that hired him. He was dramatically asked to leave the country and was spared jail. He was not going to let this opportunity in Sierra Leone fall through due to lack of planning and co-ordination, hence his meticulous engagement with the functionaries at the British Foreign and Commonwealth Office. Several meetings were held with officials from the Foreign and Commonwealth Office, briefings with United States of America State Department officials and Peter Penfold, the fixer.

Whilst the British government continued to deny any involvement in and approval of the botched arms export to Sierra Leone, accusations were levelled against a British liberal government opposition member for sympathising with the military Junta in the country. The Liberal Lord of the House of the British parliament who did not attempt to conceal his interest in the people of Sierra Leone was contacted surreptitiously by one of the foreign office functionary about developments in Sierra Leone. Lord Ashdown, after researching into the proposed counter-coup plot to return the exile president to power, by the British government, found out about the mercenary plan of operation amongst other things. He immediately warned foreign office officials that their escapade would breach the United Nation's Resolution and "that would be wholly inconsistent with any believable concept of an ethical foreign policy". Lord Ashdown was ignored and communications with him ceased. Despite of his knowledge about the country, his position was not considered consistent with the colonial way of thinking within the Foreign and Commonwealth Office.

Tim Spicer eventually shipped the consignment of arms with the facilitation of the Foreign Office and the Department of Trade of Britain. When the arms transaction unexpectedly became public and that the United Nations' resolution prohibiting the export of arms to Sierra Leone had been breached, the Foreign and Commonwealth Office functionaries promptly denied knowledge and giving any approval of the deal. Tim Spicer was incensed. He was not going to allow himself to be scapegoated by the Foreign and Commonwealth Office. Tim Spicer had no reason to believe that he was acting without the approval of the British government.

Although the consignment of weapons was eventually confiscated by the Nigerians, Tim Spicer somehow managed to take delivery of the helicopter and operated it for a considerable period of time covertly within Sierra Leone. The helicopter was in fact serviced and maintained by the British Royal Navy from their war ship that was moored just outside Sierra Leone waters during the upheaval. This debacle thoroughly embarrassed Her Majesty's Government of Britain. The fury of the secretary of state who pleaded his innocence promptly ordered an inquiry which further complicated the affair. The worse was to come for the distressed Foreign Secretary who was renowned for promoting his ethical foreign policy.

The exiled president Tejan Kabbah was eventually returned to Sierra Leone in March 1998, mainly as a result of the operations of the Nigerian forces. The death toll amongst civilians was alarmingly high which also attracted the attention, concerns and criticisms of parliamentarians in Britain as well as international outrage. A further nightmare for the foreign secretary was when the information minister of the reconstituted Tejan Kabbah government was interviewed on *BBC Radio 4* in England about the illicit arms deal and the disproportionately high death toll of civilians in his country. The information minister when asked whether the carnage was all worth it and if they were aware of the embarrassing breach of the United Nations Resolution by Britain, he remarked rather unwittingly that "*if the British government officials assisted us, the British people should be proud of their government. Even if a British law was broken, people in Britain should be happy that it was for a good cause*". These ill-advised and irresponsible remarks by Tejan

Kabbah's naïve information minister left British Foreign and Commonwealth Office staff and the Secretary of state in particular incandescent with rage. A good cause that has cost the lives of thousands of people could hardly be consistent with an ethical foreign policy. A policy that was deemed to have returned an incompetent democratically-elected person to office after being ousted by his people. That was a severe blow the Foreign Secretary never recovered from. The thought of him ardently pursuing his ethical foreign policy he genuinely believed in, whilst his leader and head of government, the Prime Minister, showed no interest in such philosophy, left the credibility of the British establishment, much to be desired. The Prime Minister Tony Blair's unsurprising display of innate conservative hubris during the episode made the trappings of colonialism very attractive.

Tim Spicer was to be the loser and fall guy in a web of complexity and intrigue. He had received an initial $70,000 down payment from Rakesh Saxena to cover his planning and arranging expenses. How much he collected from the $10m contract he had with Tejan Kabbah remain unknown. What is however public is that the Nigerians who had the moral high ground, instructed Tejan Kabbah not to make any further payment to Tim Spicer and that the contact entered with him should be cancelled.

The reaction of the Tejan Kabbah government information minister was characterised as reckless and ill advised by the British government. But what Tejan Kabbah's minister displayed was his ignorance of the complexity of the geo-political environment within which he was operating. Contracts were entered into, monies changed hands, power achieved and abused by a few and several innocent people killed.

Although Sandline, the mercenary company attracted significant negative attention, other British companies were prepared to supply military hardware and weapons to Sierra Leone in anticipation of participating in the fortunes of war. One such company that was detected and prosecuted by the Revenue and Customs Prosecutors in Britain was a company called Milestone Trading Ltd that was to ship military vehicles to the country against United Nations' imposed embargo. In as much as the nature of these transactions violated United Nations Resolution 1306, the real concern was, for whom were all these military hardware and weaponry intended?

Those who thought that colonialism is a thing of the past are merely wishful and naïve. Colonialism mutates with time to suit the environment for which its doctrines are surreptitiously compatible. Aspect of colonialism that do not change are the principle of separatism and repression, division, exploitation and culture change.

The way democracy was introduced to Sierra Leone and most former African colonies was deliberately planned to cause maximum mischief and instability. Colonial administration was intolerant of diverse opinions. In fact, no other opinion mattered other than that of the colonial administration. Cultural, ideological engineering and religious proselytising during colonialism left some societies deeply divided and entrenched. Democracy had been a massive setback for most of these countries who believed that they were free to rule themselves with a political system that was forced on them. A system that was not only alien to colonial repressive administrations but could only be enforced by lethal force. A particular weakness in this political concept is the varying electoral processes depending on how democracy is interpreted and applied. Minorities do not stand a chance of active political representation or participation, especially in environments where tribal groups are defined by ideology and historical beliefs. Values that are fundamental and almost irreconcilable.

The peculiarities and perceptible differences amongst various tribes were capitalised on and thoroughly exploited by colonialism. This relative advantage of colonialism was what angered and equally motivated some of the immediate post independent African leaders and pioneers like Lumumba, Nkrumah and Stevens to avidly pursue an alternative political system that would unite instead of divide their people. An alternative system that would recognise and cater for the needs of their people and to serve them in an innovative and creative manner through consensus. It was, however, not hard to fathom why these pioneers failed to achieve their objectives. The colonialists cum *colonial masters* were not going to relinquish the political and economic stranglehold on African countries and never was it their intention to do so. West African leaders who ventured and failed to seek alternative political systems embarked on their quest at a time when western and central Africa were under intense surveillance by spies and secret agents. The mission of British and American secret agents was primarily to prevent the rich *uranium ore* produced within the region from being controlled by Germany, Japan or the Soviet Union. This uranium was used to build the infamous *Atom Bomb* that caused so much death and suffering in Hiroshima Japan by the United States of America. The untold suffering of Congolese who were forced to work the mines and the environmental pollution caused by Belgium, still remains a secret. The other mission of British and American secret agents was to ensure tons of industrial and diamond gems and gold were exploited and transported to Britain and the United States of America. Colonial economic structures like the banks, petroleum companies, colonial airways such as the British Overseas Airways Corporation and Pan American Airways were all instrumental in the operations of MI5 and CIA operatives.

These covert operations were so intense that there was no conceivable possibility for any of the budding African politicians to institute any transformational political change other than what was thrusted upon them. Their gravitation towards the Soviet Union tantamount to suicide. Patrice Lumumba, Kwame Nkruma and others dared and paid the ultimate price. Siaka Stevens, on the other hand, played the political roulette and managed to see out his retirement.

The number of personnel in modern western governments dedicated to watch and monitor activities in their former colonies is significant. Incredibly, they are empowered to influence and facilitate change through subterfuge in those countries when things are not tending the way they expect. Their duties are complemented with the services of secret agencies. The aim is always to destabilise and sabotage anything that might suggest a deviation from colonial norms. Hence the reason why most leaders are corrupted and are usually taken out, in some instances violently, when necessary. The functionaries that are paid to destabilise and engage with African countries often ironically operate under the cover of human rights. Interventions could range from negative influence on political electoral processes to full scale military bombardment.

In Libya in 2011, *colonial Masters*, Italy, Britain and France, under the guise of protecting the Libyan people from their leader, orchestrated a catastrophic invasion of the country with the primary aim to replace the regime. A country which once had the most impressive socio-economic indicators in Africa, if not the world. An upheaval was instigated by the colonialists, propagating misinformation that the leader was killing his own people. The colonialists harboured a historical grudge against the leadership of Libya, for which enormous financial compensations were extracted from the country by Britain and the United States. Using the pretext that the leadership was committing or intended to commit human rights abuses and capitalising on the ideological and tribal differences between the people, a coordinated military campaign was launched against the country under the aegis of a British Sponsored United Nations Resolution No.1973. The damage caused by the colonialists was near apocalypse. The leader was brutally slain, allegedly by colonial Special Forces. Opposing factions to the deposed Libyan government were aided and encouraged to complete the takeover by force of arms. The colonialists presided over the physical, social, economic and political ruin of a once prosperous country. Libya regressed into medieval carnage and instability in an instant. The fate of the country's enormous gold reserves and foreign investments after this brutal episode remained a mystery. Such is the ruthlessness of colonialism and the avarice of capitalism that perpetually pursue the subjugation and exploitation of the vulnerability of Africans.

Whilst slavery and colonialism were underpinned by the ideology of supremacy based on skin colour, capitalism thoroughly exploits the inequality and fear inculcated in Africans through the brutality and chicanery of colonisation. The outcomes of instability and marginalisation introduced through the majority versus minority concept of democracy, coupled with the diversity of tribes in Africa, created an environment for the immorality and avarice of profitability over humanity.

Africans are generally led to believe and are of the illusion that colonialism is a thing of the distant past. The preoccupation and aspirations of modern Africa to achieve the elusive perfection of political democracy in a bid to impress their *colonial masters* have always been a source of social tension within the continent. Colonial capitalism paradoxically allows significant minorities to control economic wealth and influence political trends in spite of the general belief of majority rule within the concept of democracy. Whilst the methods of capitalism are not democratic by nature, the principles of free market espoused by democracy, encourages and sustains acute economic and political imbalances within African countries. The use of force and intimidation to uphold and promote such inequality within a democratic environment is not unusual in Africa. When the majority of Zimbabweans sort to reclaim their ancestral land from the minority British and other European settlers, social and political anarchy ensued, accompanied by severe economic sanctions. Threats of indictment for human right abuses were made against intransigent Zimbabweans who were determined to pursue the recovery of land. A minority political party in Zimbabwe was ardently sponsored by the British in order to take over political power. The enterprise failed to overturn the democratic principle of the significant majority. The consequences for the majority of Zimbabweans who naturally expressed their wish to retain the leadership they chose was severe and dire.

Democracy is very fluid in its interpretation and implementation in Africa depending on the strategic view of the *colonial masters.*

In Congo where colonialism wreaked centuries of unprecedented social devastation, the immorality of capitalism through neo-colonial patronage is evident and very much alive. A British oil exploration and investment company, SOCO International, somehow surreptitiously secured exploration rights within the Virunga National Park that offers sanctuary to the nearly-extinct mountain gorillas of Africa. The nefarious activities of the company included inciting violence and promoting high levels of corruption within the country's administration. The company was found to be paying a senior Congolese military officer to ambush and summarily execute people who opposed their unethical practices within the Park. This is a typical colonial approach to exploitation and capitalism in Africa. The shareholders of this company are all British. They use their ostensible status as *colonial masters* to continue to create havoc within the country whilst the plunder of resources carries on.

The ease with which colonialists usually promote or instigate violence within the African continent is incredible. Their ability to use force at will within Africa with impunity, often inciting the minority against the majority when the democratic philosophy they espouse, fails to achieve results they expect is classic. Surprisingly, the financial performance of SOCO was hailed as exemplary within the British media and the Stock Exchange of London, despite the reported malpractices. Curiously, whilst all these unethical practices were going on in the Congo, British shareholders were meeting in London to discuss the profitability and potential returns from the operations of the company in the war-ravaged country. Congolese like many other Africans continue to suffer unbelievably despite the enormous economic wealth of their country. With the incessant peddling of wars, a strategy of the colonial masters, their suffering is unlikely to ever abate.

British newspaper cuttings pertaining to the illicit arms supplied to Sierra Leone:

all me a feminist, but I
do think it degrades
women to expect a
grown-up lady to dress as a
birthday cake to wish the
Prime Minister a happy birthday.

You knew as soon as you
saw Jean Corston's pink outfit
that this was going to be
somebody's big day. Hers.
The Labour backbencher flut-
tered into the chamber yesterday in extraordinarily shiny
pink silk, secured at the front
with a row of dozens of little
pink buttons. The effect was
spoilt only by the omission of

plumes and a drum. Her
question was second in the
list. One's heart sank.

But first came David
Crausby. Oddly, the Prime
Minister did not look surprised by his question. He
seemed to have guessed that
the Labour MP for Bolton NE
might ask how we could best
ensure that "all our children"
got a good education. Could
the answer be, one mused
that we should all vote Labour
in today's local government
elections so that Labour's very
excellent policies on education
could be applied by Labour's

very excellent local coun-
cillors?

Yes indeed?" The answer is
to vote Labour!" trilled Tony.
Oddly, Mr Crausby did not
look surprised.

There followed an interlude
in which William Hague, who
has been warned by pollsters
not to rain on Tony Blair's
Ulster Parade, chose to drizzle
on it instead.

In one of those "while I
would be the first to applaud
... " homilies — an ill-
intentioned shove masquerading as an arm on the
shoulder — we watched what

Tories presumably think demonstrates that no fuzzy-
brained dream-merchant can
pull wool over the eyes of this
tough-minded Tory anti-ter-
rorist. Hague wants to ride
two horses: public approval of
the agreement and the hostility of the Orange-tinged Tory
Right. We sigh and look
away.

Our eyes return to find the

Labour in hurry after SNP boost

By SHIRLEY ENGLISH

LABOUR attempted to re-
gain the political initiative
in Scotland yesterday by
announcing plans to bring
forward the opening date
for the Scottish parliament
by six months.

The move, on the day
that Scottish Nationalists
surged ahead of Labour in
the opinion polls for the
first time, was labelled a
"panic measure" by oppo-
sition parties but was
broadly welcomed.

The System Three sur-
vey on voting intentions,
published by The Herald,
revealed that the Scottish
National Party had opened
a five-point lead over Labour. Donald Dewar, the
Scottish Secretary, re-
sponded swiftly by an-
nouncing that he was
about to consult opposition
parties on proposals to
open the new parliament
in July 1999 instead of
early 2000. He said that,
after the elections on May
6 next year, he saw no
point in delaying the trans-
ference of powers from
Westminster to the new
parliament, provided that
the necessary structures
were in place.

In the poll, the SNP
moved up one point to 41
per cent. Labour slipped
by four points to 36 per
cent compared with last
month. The Conservatives
rose three to 11 per cent.

Cook announces Sierra Leone arms inquiry

By NICHOLAS WATT, POLITICAL CORRESPONDENT

ROBIN COOK announced an
independent investigation yesterday into allegations that
senior Foreign Office officials
approved the sale of arms in
Sierra Leone in breach of a
United Nations embargo.

In an unusual move, the
Foreign Secretary expressed
"deep concern" at the Foreign
Office's handling of the affair
and said that the inquiry
would examine allegations
that civil servants failed to
keep ministers properly
informed.

Mr Cook said that the
independent inquiry would be
carried out by an outsider
after a separate customs investigation had been concluded.
"I am determined to establish
the full facts," he said in an
emergency Commons state-
ment. His announcement
came after Tony Blair de-
clared that ministers and
officials would face discipl-
inary action if they were found
to have breached UN
resolutions.

The investigation will examine claims that civil servants secretly sanctioned the
supply of weapons and mercenaries to Sierra Leone by a
London company. Sandline
International. The company
claims that the Foreign Office
gave it approval to send arms
to forces who restored Presi-

dent Kabbah in March, a year
after he was deposed in a
military coup.

Mr Cook, who denied that
ministers approved the alleged activities of Sandline,
faced embarrassment yesterday when the Government of
Sierra Leone welcomed the
British involvement.

Confirming that weapons
were delivered, Julius Spencer, Sierra Leone's Information Minister, told The World
at One on Radio 4: "If British
Government officials assisted,
the British people should be
proud of their Government.
Even if a British law was
broken, people in Britain
should be happy that it was
broken for a good cause."

Foreign Office officials were
irritated by Dr Spencer's remarks because Mr Cook has
pledged to pursue an "ethical
foreign policy".

Mr Cook's difficulties over
Sandline deepened when he
was forced to disclose that his
officials referred the allegations to Customs and Excise
on March 10 without inform-
ing ministers. This meant that
Tony Lloyd, the minister with
responsibility for Africa, denied allegations of British
collusion in Sierra Leone in a
Commons debate on March 12
without mentioning the Customs investigation. Asked by

Michael Howard, the Shadow
Foreign Secretary, whether
officials were "wholly out of
control", Mr Cook said that
their conduct was a "matter of
deep concern to me".

He added: "I do believe that
it is unsatisfactory that [Mr
Lloyd] was put up to the
dispatch box in Parliament to
speak in the House without
being informed that a customs
investigation had been re-
quested. I think that is unfair
to the Minister of State and it
is unfair to Parliament. That
will almost certainly form part
of the independent inquiry I
have announced."

The confusion within the
Foreign Office meant that Mr
Cook had to clarify remarks
by Mr Lloyd, who told a
Commons committee on Tuesday that no minister knew of
the customs investigation until
Friday. The Foreign Secretary
said that Mr Lloyd was shown
papers about the customs
investigation in mid-April, but
was not fully informed about
the matter until last Friday.

Paddy Ashdown, the Lib-
eral Democrat leader, said
any breach of the UN
resolutions would be "wholly
inconsistent with any believable concept of an ethical
foreign policy".

Diary, page 22

TIM11

First proof of navy role in c[...]

Pictures refute ministers' denial of British aid to mercenaries

Nicholas Rufford
Defence Affairs Editor

PHOTOGRAPHIC evidence obtained by The Sunday Times that reveals for the first time proof of official British involvement in the coup that is shaking the Foreign Office.

The photographs show Royal Navy mechanics repairing a [...]-built military helicopter used by mercenaries.

They are the first evidence that servicemen played a direct role in restoring Sierra Leone's legitimate government. It is embarrassing because that Britain had no [...] in the Nigerian-led [...]

Sandline International, the firm responsible for military [...] cannot by supplying the [...] and aim, in under [...] investigation by Customs and Excise for breaking United Nations sanctions. The [...] helicopter was vital to [...] troops and equipment in [...] throne. It is shown being [...] in Freetown on [...]

1 to airlift food and [...] approved the action and [...] of the military's participation power last year.

Lloyd, the Foreign [...] MPs in March that the [...] played an "invaluable" [...] delivering food and medi- [...] supplies to the region. [...] He made no mention of [...] personnel had actively [...] the mercenaries.

Diamond dogs of war Focus special, pages 13-15

The pictures, supplied by [...] learn that Sandline gave a de- [...] those involved in the coup, will [...] tailed briefing on its operation [...] called briefing on its operation [...] to Whitehall's defence intelli- [...] allegations that the foreign Of- [...] gence staff, which advises the [...] fice the escalating row over [...] government on operations over- [...] sanctions-busting mission. [...] seas and reports to George [...]

The affair is already linked [...] Robertson, the defence sec- [...] to supply David, who [...] retary. A security team [...] ...over the affair. Last [...] gave an officer called Major [...] week's Sunday Times reveals [...] Sandline's executive director, [...] how Sandline's executive director, [...] German detailed tactical plan. [...]

Sandline is accused of [...] breach of UN resolution 1132, [...] which Britain helped draft. The [...] arms were flown to Lungi air- [...] port outside Freetown of Feb- [...]

Caught on camera: Royal Navy mechanics with Sandline's helicopter in Freetown in March and [...]

Cook snared in arms for coup inquiry

by Nicholas Rufford
Home Affairs Editor

CRIMINAL investigation has been launched into British-backed military moves to overthrow a foreign government.

Cook has exposed an unhappy foreign policy and support for the UN. The Labour party.

Investigators centre on Lieutenant-Colonel Tim Spicer...

A Department of Trade official said: "Either Cook gave his blessing for the operation or he did not know what his Af-rican desk was doing."

...companies in the foreign business.

... the board of trade, ... ministry is responsible ... was under pressure ... to make an immediate ... Lord Avebury, the ... Democrat vice-chairman, said: "an extremely serious breach of our obligations seemed to ... spokesman said officers...

Penfold: facing questions

At least 200 people, many of them civilians, were killed when local militia men and Ni-gerian military forces drove out a military leader who had seized power.

The inquiries centre on Lieutenant-Colonel Tim Spi-cer... a British company that helps to arrange the supply of military equipment and mercenaries, and Peter Penfold, the British high commissioner to Sierra Leone, who is accused of asking Spicer to help re-gain the country.

The events that followed resembled Frederick Forsyth's novel The Dogs of War. In a £10m operation in February, Sandline shipped Bulgarian guns and ammunition to forces opposed to the government, which seized power last year.

And train 40,000 militia fight-ers. In collaboration with the Nigerians, they helped to topple the government in March.

Ahmed Tejan Kabbah was restored as president and militia-ry by Paul Koroma, the military.

Ousted: Johnny Paul Koroma, the overthrown military leader, and Lieutenant-Colonel Tim Spicer, who is said to h

regime's leader, Jock Kabbah and Ministry of Defence... Sandline Silim by inter-... he interviewed by customs officers, is said to have paid diamond concessions.

Britain stands to regain the Force's resources... in Guinea, Si-erra Leone's neighbour.

The investigation began when it emerged that Sand-line's operation defied UN...

bosnia and Ministry of Defence... resolutions passed last October...

Security Council... Sandline Silim by... law Resolution 1132 explicitly prohibits the supply of arms to the war-torn country.

MPs came on tip-off from... search warrants at the London headquarters of Sandline and Spicer's home last month. The Cook, Beckett, and George...

His lawyers believe the company had Foreign Office per... mission to supply arms...

Civil war: more than 30,000 people have died in fighting since 1991

Revealed: Sandline's helicopter in Sierra Leone, far right, with British military personnel (dark clothing) lending assistance and, left, helping to service engine

counter-coup. He suggested it would contravene the UN resolution. He received in response copies of Sandline's strategic and tactical plan for Sierra Leone were taking on a momentum of their own.

SPICER'S plans were begin-

terms learnt, had not only been briefed by Spicer but had been made over to his colleague, David Mathison. "What do you make of this?" he asked. ... its "concept of operations". In the documents was was no need for discussion. Cook was in Brussels chairing a meeting of European foreign ministers, but when he

its covert operation, Hood made no mention of the customs inquiry and had consistently denounced a report about meetings between ... "An ill-informed and scurrilous article," he called it. "We reject the nonsense in that article." Now, under a

mid-April. "However, he was not fully informed of the allegations by Sandline of storing Sandline since 1997.

Foreign Office contacts until Friday May 1," said Cook. ...

they monitored everything they were up to," he told his did he need to be? How much did Lloyd already know about

found no evidence that Sandline's men ... Others find it incredible that a mission so openly canvassed by Sandline with friends in America and London, Britain and have been ... from colleagues in the army and intelligence world. Such suggestion prompted escape the attention

Chapter 15
Tricks of the Trade

Africans do have their differences, both physical and ideological. There have always been ways and means by which ideological, cultural differences and other issues are settled amongst them. The violence that was associated with kidnappings, abductions and colonialism induced a change in the political process, cultures and the way Africans regard each other.

In Sierra Leone, it took the British several decades of brutal killings, widespread pillaging and destruction of properties and societies to be able to instil the terror that led to the overrun and domination of the entire country. If Africans were killing each other so much as was alleged, it certainly would have been much easier to pick them up into slaves and to gain unfettered control during the colonial era. The change to their cultures could have been executed without the resistance encountered. There would not have been the need to mete out the level of wanton violence on the people with such ferocity. Colonialism introduced the use of lethal weapons to settle scores between tribes as opposed to dialogue and decision making by consensus. It is this system of administration that many post-independent African leaders attempted to reshape and reintroduce into the fledgling political system forced on them. The objective was to form a hybrid political system that would have deviated from the divisive democracy imposed on the people. Their intentions posed a clear threat to the sphere of colonial influence in Africa which in turn provoked a series of heinous crimes against Africans in order to maintain the status quo.

The failure to develop a new form of governance that will suit Africa, especially after centuries of repression, increased the vulnerability and instability within African countries post colonialism. African leaders found themselves inadvertently implementing draconian colonial practices in diverse ways with devastating effects on their own people. Leaders with strong Pan-

African ideologies who persisted in the pursuit of an alternative system to western democracy suffered the wrath of colonialists.

Resentment between tribes and social groups increased immensely since the seaming independence from colonial domination. This surge was primarily due to the availability of the same lethal weapons used on them by their former oppressors. Additionally, a widespread mental manipulation of the people was embarked upon distorting the facts and creating a culture of dependency. Weapons are supplied to various African governments at extortionate costs by the very *colonial masters* to be used on their own people and against opposing tribes. This cynical trade has severely inhibited the ability of African governments to govern effectively, impartially and to provide essentials that meet the needs of the people they govern. The indebtedness resulting from the astronomical costs of procuring non-essential and unnecessary arms and ammunition has left African governments incapable of developing policies and generally submissive towards their *colonial masters*. Ironically, the very *colonial masters* would turn around, capture and whisk the puppet and ineffectual African leaders to stand trial in international courts for their inept performances and purported human right abuses, when they are considered dispensable.

African leaders end up adopting the modus operandi of their erstwhile *colonial masters* characterised by violent behaviours and actions, which to a large extent mirror those meted out on Africans during slavery and colonialism. The political upheavals in Sierra Leone and Liberia during the 1980s and 90s were characterised by such unprecedented violence and mass slaughter of innocent people.

The return of the exiled president Tejan Kabbah by the military forces of Nigeria was hardly without cost to the people. Thousands of innocent people were killed through indiscriminate shelling and the inappropriate use of artillery within populated urban areas. Rampant pillaging, sexual and other human abuses were successfully passed off and attributed to "rebellious" activities. Who the rebels were amidst the conflagration of British mercenaries, Nigerian forces, British Royal Navy, Armed Forces of Sierra Leone, the Revolutionary Front and the Civil Defence Units (*Kamajors*) remains a mystery. Colonial conspiracies and counter plots, tribal ideological and political differences, high unemployment and geopolitical interests resulted in a quagmire with combustible consequences. These potent socio-political issues were completely ignored and the failure to address them by successive governments, renders the country vulnerable to exploitation and leaving most of the people disaffected.

The return of Tejan Kabbah as the democratically-elected leader on the blood of the people did not stop the carnage. His immediate priority was to use the backing of colonial Britain to wage his own personal war against those who he felt were against him or conspired to overthrow him from government. He swiftly rounded up, conducted a badly-choreographed trial and executed twenty-four predominantly senior ranking officers from the national armed forces by firing squad. This gruesome act pitifully included a female medical officer. Apart from the half-hearted condemnation from some quarters, no actual charge was made against him for the dastardly act.

The absurdity of the relationship between Africans and their *colonial masters* is one were the master remains superior and untouchable, irrespective of the depravity of their actions. Whilst the servants, on the other hand, must exhibit absolute subservience at all times and accept the exploitation and unbearable oppression of their people. They, unlike their *colonial masters*, are usually inevitably held accountable for their own actions. In that vein, the question is, how the illicit export of a military helicopter and thirty-five tons of lethal weapons to any country to support democracy and promote peace be ethical. No one was prosecuted or held accountable for this affront against the people of Africa.

The *British Broadcasting Corporation (BBC)*, one of the relics of colonial propaganda, led the survivors in Sierra Leone to believe that the carnage was caused mainly by the "Rebels" of the Revolutionary United Front. That British participation and contribution to the mayhem was altruistic and noble. But who were the rebels? These are the people who have been left disenfranchised by a system forced upon them that only recognises the opinion of and celebrate the successes of the minority who dispenses the requirements of their masters. A system that is a diametrical opposite of original African cultures. A system of deprivation, oppression and exploitation. Whilst colonial administration involved the minority imposing their values on the majority mainly through force, the democratic system cunningly introduced to their colonies like Sierra Leone was also surreptitiously sustained through coercion and manipulation.

The British, not wanting to be outflanked by the apparent success of Nigeria, launched a military operation code-named "*Palliser*" within the country. The primary aim of the mission was to take the moral high ground and seize the limelight from the Nigerians who were masquerading as the liberators of the once besieged capital, Freetown. Freetown, a British creation and colonial administrative outpost. The opportunity for the British arose when a group of United Nations Peace Enforcers were abducted by Revolutionary Front militants who were still active around the country. British troops wasted no time to engage with the United Nations forces to launch a rescue mission of the hostages. Operation "*Palliser*" was executed without any reported problems. However, the operational activities of the British forces in the country were not monitored neither were they accountable to anyone. Not even by the democratic leadership of Tejan Kabbah who by all accounts owed his political survival to the British government.

Hostilities by various forces continued within the country despite the installation of the Tejan Kabbah government from exile. A breakaway group of guerrilla fighters called the "*Westside Boys*", a splinter from the Revolutionary Front, had strategically held on to territories including an arterial motorway connecting the capital and the provinces. The British in their eagerness to dominate the political headlines and to vindicate the botched arms export that violated the United Nations Resolution which prohibited such transactions, approached the camp of the Westside Boys on the pretext of positive engagement. A group of British soldiers from the Irish Regiment who made contact managed to access the camp of the guerrilla fighters. The purpose for their actions remained unclear as they were not part of the United Nations peace enforcers. Whatever transpired between the British and the guerrilla fighters resulted in the British emissaries taken as hostages by the militant group. After intense negotiations, five of the British troops were released and the rest were retained by the group. What became clear was that the remaining soldiers, being special forces, were able to assess the capabilities of the guerrilla fighters and secretly transmitted the co-ordinates of their precise location. This information was vital for the neutralisation of the camp. The British *colonial master* had finally created a situation and the opportunity to make their presence felt and most of all, increase the publicity of their military engagement with the hope of consigning the Nigerians to history. There was also the desperate need by the British government to placate the vexed members of the British parliament, who were seething with rage and embarrassment over the illicit arms shipment to Sierra Leone.

Lame efforts were made to engage the guerrilla fighters in some form of negotiation to release the detained British troops. This was calculated to give the world the impression that the fighters were inconsiderate, untrustworthy and that the lives of the British hostages were in mortal danger. There was hardly a consultation with the government of Sierra Leone prior to the grand military operation that was planned. Supposedly, this was not necessary and would have been merely academic as the government of Sierra Leone and the country were almost back under their control.

A second operation, code-named "*Barras*", was swiftly put in motion, comprising the British Special Air Service (SAS). Operation "*Barras*" subsequently received approval from the British government and dawn on the 10th September 2000 was declared ShowTime. Initially, two nearby towns were savagely attacked by British paratroopers in order to diffuse any potential counter attack by the guerrilla fighters. The exact casualty of women, children and the infirm within those towns was undisclosed.

The main assault was reserved for the main camp that created the bottleneck of the highway, obstructing commercial activity within the capital. In colonial terminology, this amounted to a "*stockade*", an activity that Africans who were resisting colonial subjugation, usually staged but paid for heavily, ultimately with their lives. The violence of those dark days when British expeditionary forces were despatched to obtain signed treaties from chiefs was about to be visited upon the camp of the guerrilla fighters. Chiefs were coerced to sign treaties ceding powers to the colonial administration, but when they and their compatriots refused to comply with the conditions of the treaties, villages were often razed to the ground. Recalcitrant chiefdom subjects were summarily executed publicly to instil fear and to ensure unconditional compliance by the people.

In King Leopold's Congo, the brutality meted out to Africans was beyond human comprehension. Men, women and children who failed to tap enough rubber for the King's agents in the Congo had their right hands amputated instead of being shot. The stock of right hands was submitted to the local Belgian administration to prove that they had been frugal with the usage of expensive bullets used to enforce compliance by the reluctant people. The crimes that the Belgians committed were in many ways similar to the coercion and heinous atrocities committed during the signing and enforcement of treaties.

During the first hour of operation "*Barras*", the hostages were extracted from the camp with only one fatality. Although a few others suffered non-life threatening injuries, vengeance for the slain SAS officer by the remaining forces was to be swift with unprecedented brutality. The camp and the entire surrounding village were annihilated with all detectable living being ferociously slaughtered. Traumatised Sierra Leonean witnesses who were embedded in the British force as interpreters described a scene of indescribable wholesale murder. The stench of blood pervaded the tropical air like an abattoir. The corpses of women, children and men, some of them blasted beyond recognition, strewn deserted compounds. The evidence of extreme savagery was present everywhere. This was colonial supremacy and bigotry in action and at its primordial best. The British forces displayed their prowess and invincibility within an environment of vulnerability and hopelessness.

At the end of what seemed like eternity, the approximately five-hour operation "*Barras*" came to an abrupt end. The deafening silence devoid of rapid heavy arms fire and the apocalyptic death scene suddenly brought the rampaging British service men back to humanity. Realising the consequences of what they had done to scores of innocent and unsuspecting people, desperate effort was instinctively made to dispose of the incriminating evidence of the aftermath of a gruesome and mass slaughter of predominantly defenceless civilians.

British military helicopters were called in to remove and dispose of corpses, especially those of women and children whose execution could prove difficult to justify in the event of an investigation. Helicopters laden with corpses with blood trailing on take-off flew several sorties to the mouth of the Rokel River where the corpses were dumped. After several flights, it was then decided to bury as many of the corpses in mass graves. The operation was eventually called off after as many of the corpses as possible had been buried. The rest were left to decompose in the open. There were reports of bodies being washed back to land to the bemusement of people leaving along coastal villages.

Crass as it may sound, the Special Forces even found time to drag and arrange corpses of Sierra Leoneans they had executed in a despicable and appalling manner to form rows in order to take trophy photographs for their war diaries. The practice of taking home such trophy photographs and stolen artefacts as souvenirs is consistent with those of the colonial expeditionary forces. Such souvenirs not only adorn the mantelpieces of British homes, they instigate bigotry and race supremacy amongst successive generations. It was later disclosed that the appalling Operation *"Barras"* was incredibly used by the Special Forces as a training exercise for similar operations in the future as much as it was for geo-political gains. A training exercise conducted without any modicum of morality or legal propriety. The lives of Africans have historically been valued by slavers and colonialists on the basis of their potential to be productive in plantations. Beyond that, Africans are expendable without compunction or any form of accountability. These sort of operations were commonplace in African communities such as South Africa, Namibia and the Congo.

British Special Force sources revealed that they had to drop the bodies in the river, some dropped across the jungle, and as many as possible, buried in mass graves hurriedly to prevent detection. *"It was just not politically acceptable to have so many dead after a rescue operation"*. *"Such actions do not sit well with British New Labour's supposedly ethical foreign policy"*. An ethical foreign policy that allowed thirty-five tons of lethal weapons and a military helicopter to be exported in violation of United Nations Resolution to the country. An ethical foreign policy that strikes deals with mercenaries to carry out nefarious military activities in Africa.

The actions of the Special Forces during Operation *"Barras"* was completely unbridled. Even the members of the forces could not believe the latitude they were allowed. Operation *"Barras"* was a practical demonstration of the attitude, value and regard colonialism had for the lives of Africans. The carnage of operation *"Barras"* was kept very secret and nothing significant was said thereafter. The Special British Forces took and kept their war trophies just like the Belgian troops who kept undissolved body parts of Patrice Lumumba as souvenirs following his brutal execution in Congo.

Tony Blair, who was the prime minister of the British government at the time, was conspicuously reticent during the scandalous arms shipment. The intriguing aspect of his action though was to invite Tejan Kabbah to the Commonwealth heads of government meeting. This was particularly noted as Sierra Leone's membership to the colonial conclave was suspended at the time. The Prime Minister even organised a conference at the Royal Overseas Club giving Tejan Kabbah an official platform to solicit support for his ill-fated government in exile. These overtures bore the hallmark of a colonial empire. The Prime Minister, the grand puppet master and the President, the sycophant and stooge. After the elaborate cover-up of the mass slaughter of innocent women and children during the purported rescue of service personnel by the SAS, the Prime Minister made a contrite statement paying tribute to the British officer killed *in the line of duty* and commending the bravery, professionalism and courage of those who put their lives on the line to rescue their colleagues. He expounded on Britain's historical ties with the dysfunctional country of Sierra Leone and as *colonial masters*, would stand shoulder to shoulder with the puppet government to resist those who are fighting against the virtues of democracy. The unsuspecting people of the country, in their abject ignorance of the heinous crimes that British troops had committed, instantly held the Prime Minister as a hero for ending the upheaval in the country. In a bizarre turn of events, Peter Penfold, the erstwhile British High Commissioner, the principal facilitator and protagonist in the illicit arms deal and the inexplicable activities of mercenaries in Sierra Leone, was also adulated by the poor ignorant people. Tony Blair and Peter Penfold became a double act and were given high honours usually awarded to great chiefs and warriors, in appreciation of their perceived effort to end of the upheaval. The people were oblivious to the fact that both Prime Minister Blair and the duplicitous Penfold were very much aware of the despicable acts of the British troops but chose to conceal the gruesome details of the massacre at Gberi Bana for political expediency.

The atrocities committed were horrendous and with impunity. The perfidy of the British *colonial masters* was shocking considering the hypocrisy of promoting ethical behaviour and equality in race relations. The people did not have the opportunity to even challenge their actions. Those who witnessed the shocking series of deadly events were traumatised to their very core. They were petrified of the backlash if they dared to go public with what they saw and experienced during that violent episode. The entire country was pummelled by propaganda from the colonial broadcast machinery, extolling the bravery and courage of their military and mercenaries in liberating the people of Sierra Leone. The involvement of British forces in a combative role in Sierra Leone was not entirely surprising with the emerging geo-political shift towards China. Their rules of engagement and how their bloody massacre in Gberi Bana came to be regarded as practical training exercises for the Special Forces were duplicitous but effective. The actions of Colonialists in Africa remain unchallengeable.

Some of the abuses against the people by the guerrilla fighters included the mindless amputation of limbs of innocent people. These were mostly carried out in revenge for local disputes and disagreements. These despicable acts were alien to Sierra Leone and shockingly disturbing. Amputations of the nature perpetrated and inflicted on Sierra Leoneans were first introduced to the continent by the megalomaniac, King Leopold II of Belgium and his depraved urchins in the Congo. Rubber was greatly in demand, and Congo had the capacity to produce enormous quantities. The Belgian's unquenchable appetite, avarice and bigotry motivated them to initiate and implement the despicable act of amputation. In many cases, men were coerced to provide bondage labour to their oppressors for the tapping of rubber, which was one of the main economic activities in the Congo. Men who failed to turn in significant quantities of the sap, the raw natural material that rubber is made from, were brutally punished. One such punishment was to cut off their right hands or even castrated. Families of men who refuse to cooperate were made to witness the hands of their wives, mother and children being cut off. The severed hands were handed to them to keep as an inducement for them to increase their production in the future. The following is a photo of a Congolese child who suffered this barbarism by the Belgians because her father failed to produce enough rubber sap for Belgian King Leopold II:

Child victim of Colonial Brutality – Congo

In the Congo, just like in Sierra Leone, where diamonds were a motivator for the untold savagery meted on the people, the company responsible for these mindless barbarism in the Congo was the Anglo-Belgian India Rubber Company (ABIR). This company was owned by British and Belgian shareholders, registered in Belgium and was awarded concessions to tax Congolese. A euphemism for free slave labour and the setting up of labour camps. The following photo depicts British "missionaries" posing with timid Congolese men who had the hands of their peers or loved ones cut off for failing to meet the daily rubber sap delivery quota:

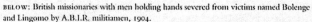

BELOW: British missionaries with men holding hands severed from victims named Bolenge and Lingomo by A.B.I.R. militiamen, 1904.

Congolese men with the severed hands of those who failed to make the daily rubber sap quota (www.worldpress.com)

What happened in Gberi Bana in Sierra Leone was a mere re-enactment of unaccountable and uncontrolled exuberance of ideological supremacy. The rampant amputations carried out by militants equally replicated the barbarism of the British and Belgians in the Congo.

The statement by the British Prime Minister eulogising the virtues of democracy amidst the unethical practices of the Foreign and Commonwealth Office and Special Forces was hollow and opaque. His repertoire was reminiscent of colonial nihilism and the clarion messages of altruism, success and grand achievements of the *colonial master*. Suppressing information regarding the carnage occasioned by British troops on the people of Sierra Leone could hardly be characterised as virtuous.

The defeat of the Westside Boys and the annihilation of the town of Gberi Bana created a feeling of completion and satisfaction amongst a cross section of the country. The intense positive spin by the *BBC* on the achievements of British Special Forces rapidly asphyxiated any rational or objective assessment of the situation by right thinking individuals. Sierra Leoneans were made to believe yet again by colonial propaganda that the mass slaughter of their compatriots was a price worth paying for what was regarded as their freedom. The *British Broadcasting Corporation* in the same breath reported to their domestic audiences that Britain had carried an exemplary job to restore democracy to the former colony ravaged by a senseless civil war. The Broadcasting Corporation further reported that British Special Forces were involved in one of the fiercest battle ever in Sierra Leone to liberate the country from the rebellion. Although some British service personnel were killed or injured, scores of the savage rebels were killed in return, the Corporation reported. A colonial speak, for Africans who dared to take the life of a British would pay dearly for such a brazen act. Whilst the people of Sierra Leone were made to feel grateful for the illegalities of British Forces, the British public was manipulated into feeling a sense of superiority and accomplishment. The reasoning of the Prime Minister and his government was that the illicit shipment of arms in contravention of United Nations Resolutions was acceptable if the situation was so barbaric that the invincibility of the British was tested to the point of losing one of their own. In all of this, the *British Broadcasting Corporation* remained a very potent instrument used effectively to promote imperialism, culture and social change in many former colonial outposts. Things have hardly changed from the days when Africans within their colonies would tune in to listen to "London calling" a colonial broadcast by the BBC to the British Empire.

The Prime Minister of Britain, Tony Blair's paradoxical move to invite the exiled president Tejan Kabbah to a Commonwealth Heads of Government meeting, when technically he was not a head of state and that the country was suspended from the organisation, was not serendipitous. The exposure he gave Tejan Kabbah to make an appeal to the rest of the world, bizarre though it may have appeared at a time when his government was at war and with the arms scandal, exemplifies his paternalistic colonial instinct. He not only placated his critics with the bloody achievement of the Special

Forces in Sierra Leone but tactfully used the carnage to launch his post ministerial interest in Sierra Leone.

No sooner things appeared to have quieten down in Sierra Leone, the first move by the British *colonial masters* was to initiate the review of Sierra Leone's diamond exports system by incorporating the country into the Kimberley Process for a Fully Integrated Certification System (FICS). Whilst the new Certification System did not eliminate conflict diamonds, it assured Britain's increased participation as *colonial masters* once again in the monitor and control of diamonds from Sierra Leone.

The upheaval in Sierra Leone was also associated with diamonds which was commonly known as "blood diamonds". Diamonds have always been associated with blood in Sierra Leone since the early days when missionaries first found out that the valuable crystalline carbon could be picked up from the ground with no effort. Colonialist interests promptly shifted and widespread seizures of the precious stones were ordered by the colonial administration.

After years of free pickings, the colonial administration decided to go into proper commercial mining. The Sierra Leone Selection Trust (SLST) was set up by the Consolidated African Selection Trust Ltd. The company quickly obtained a monopoly guaranteeing exclusive mining and marketing rights for ninety-nine years.

Since diamonds became a feature in the colonial administration's economic activities, Sierra Leoneans started paying for this valuable stones with their blood ever since. The colonialists raided houses, burnt down villages and killed anyone who was found hiding diamonds or refusing to surrender their stock to them. When the Sierra Leone Selection Trust was formed, things deteriorated as they officially owned every square inch of land that diamonds could be found on. Agriculture became extremely problematic as anyone found digging was liable to severe corporal punishment. Food production became a perennial problem with an increased dependency on foreign imports, by the Maronite Christian Lebanese, the colonial protégés. The people could not believe what was happening to them. To build a house to live in suddenly became a nightmare. No one was allowed to dig foundations without permission and adequate supervision. The quality of life of the people deteriorated immensely.

Unemployment became the norm, and children grew generally malnourished with diminishing life expectancy.

Sierra Leone Selection Trust enjoyed years of uninterrupted and uncontrolled exploitation of Sierra Leone diamonds. As time went on, the Lebanese traders too became interested in diamonds. Some of the people who still had access to and possessed diamonds were willing to exchange their possessions in payment for farm implements, food and anything to ensure their general upkeep. This batter system incentivised the people to take risks to go out finding diamonds to exchange for foodstuff and other bare essentials.

The company subsequently found out that the people were increasingly violating the orders of the administration. The Company became increasingly ruthless with the enforcement of orders forbidding Sierra Leoneans from participating in the exploration of diamonds. Security patrols by British ex-servicemen accompanied by vicious attack dogs became ubiquitous, and several people were mauled and killed in their daring adventures, hoping to provide for and to keep themselves and their families alive. As the operations of the company grew bigger, and with the improvement of technology, helicopters were introduced into the armoury of the security service. Untold number of people were shot and killed as low flying helicopters were used to impede their ability of escape the pursuit by security operatives. The security personnel would shoot at anyone who breaches the colonial order. They would land their helicopters and search corpses of people gunned down for diamonds. Corpses were even eviscerated in cases were suspects had swallowed the diamonds in trying to make their escape. They would confiscate the implements used by the ill-fated local explorers, whose corpses were left where they fell in order to deter others from making the same mistake. The brutality of the company against the people could hardly be expressed in words. The fear of death and the suffering that was associated with diamonds scared Sierra Leones who shied away from anything diamond. The company showed no iota of social responsibility. Villages were destroyed, farm lands were commandeered and mined beyond any prospect of future agricultural activity. No compensation was paid to the displaced people, and no form of infrastructural development, reparation or rehabilitation of the environment was done. Up till the present day, the main diamond areas in Sierra Leone are left looking like craters on the moon surface.

Diamonds destroyed the lives of many and continues to do so. Agriculture which was the speciality and mainstay of the people was almost erased from their psyche and culture. Large swathes of land were made barren and uncultivable. The colonial administration was not accountable to anyone for proceeds generated from this or any other economic activity. The country has nothing to show for the suffering inflicted on it through bigotry and avarice. Unemployment became the norm, hence the ease with which the upheaval during the nineties took hold.

During the upheaval in Sierra Leone, an opportunity was inadvertently presented to Britain and the Prime Minister to revive British military presence in the country just like it used to be under direct colonial rule. The pretext this time around was that there was a need for the *colonial master* to provide the country's armed forces with training and support. A few British business interests quickly materialised after the supposed liberation of the country. Another intriguing result after all the destruction and carnage was the regularity and almost permanence of the presence of Tony Blair in Sierra Leone after he left the office of prime minister of Britain.

Tony Blair ceased to be prime minister of the British government in June 2007 blighted by his decision to invade Iraq in 2003 and his involvement in Sierra Leone that was less spoken about or referred to, following an elaborate cover-up and information management. Incredibly, he proceeded to engage with successive governments in the country and conducted private businesses and exploited the resources of the country as a true *colonial master*. His private dealings within Sierra Leone reaffirmed the duplicity of the British government, to hire mercenaries and the illicit arms export, which cost the lives of over fifty thousand innocent Sierra Leoneans, including the massacre at Gberi Bana. In true colonial fashion, Tony Blair established himself firmly in Sierra Leone masquerading as a messiah to the unsuspecting people of the country. In gratitude for his purported heroics, he was honoured and made a Paramount Chief of "Kaffu Bullom" chiefdom.

Paramount Chief Tony Blair of Kaffu Bulom Chiefdom

Whilst the people and the puppet government were besotted by his intrigues, his sights were set on the wealth and business potential there were to be exploited in the country.

Ironically, Tony Blair was made a chief in one of the Chiefdoms were incumbent chiefs were brutally deposed by British expeditionary forces. This was one of the chiefdoms where brave Temnes fought selflessly to defend their ancestral land and chieftaincy. Thousands of men, women and children were slain with towns and villages razed to the ground in the quest for land and domination of the country by the British. The installation of Tony Blair as a ceremonial paramount chief of a chiefdom steeped in the history of British barbarism, atrocities and abuses, defies rational thinking. This is a manifestation of the severe mental and psychological damage to Africans resulting from centuries of oppression, information management and colonial patronage. Heroes like Bia Bureh confronted British aggression stoutly in defence of their right to self-determination and paid the ultimate price with their lives. The strategic capitulation of Bia Bureh and his men in order to spare the lives of his people was as a result of the scotched earth policy of the British calculated to cause prolonged starvation and mass death of his Temne people. The British administration, in celebrating their victory over Chief Bai Bureh within their Freetown enclave, deliberately misinformed and taught children and adults alike, a song that extolled British invincibility and superiority to Sierra Leoneans:

"Bia Bureh was a warrior
He fought against the British
The British made him surrender
He hollers kortor maimu
Ah kortor maimu,
He hollers kortor gbeketor"

This song was taught to children in Freetown by British missionaries as part of the culture change and fundamentally to emphasise the superiority of colonial Britain. Cannily, this was not taught anywhere else in the Protectorate.

Colonial administration and governance in Sierra Leone was anything but democratic. Creole newsagents and journalists were severely brutalised and exploited workers were gunned down if they dared to protest against their working conditions. Creole bourgeois were emasculated and replaced by Maronite Christian Lebanese and their properties expropriated. Land was commandeered without recompense; taxes were imposed arbitrarily that proved burdensome on the people. Resources were exploited with no accountability. Sexual and other abuses against Sierra Leoneans by colonialists went on unabated and with impunity. Apartheid was introduced and tribes kept apart and were instigated to turn against each other in order to facilitate easy management of them by the colonialists. The values, beliefs and traditions of the people were suppressed and almost obliterated and replaced by alien practices. A thorough mental reprogramming of the people was achieved within centuries of brutal oppression. Such were the characteristics and legacies of colonialism that lasted for a hundred and seventy-four years in Sierra Leone. Within a few years of the quest for independent rule, when the colonialists realised that an irreversible change was looming, they surreptitiously introduced the concept of democracy within an oppressive and extremely traumatised environment.

The conduct of Prime Minister Blair and his regime amounted to a Déjà vu to some Africans. A recurring nightmare that Africans can do without and Sierra Leoneans will never forget. On the seeming departure of colonialism from Africa, copious quantities of arms and ammunition were left behind and supplies continued in order to prop various chaotic political systems across the continent.

In most so-called democratic African countries, the voices of the people are hardly listened to neither do their hopes and aspirations considered. Capitalism and its vices pervade the very nature of governance in Africa. Corporate interests now precede that of the people. In the United States where Africans and mixed-race Africans constitute a significant proportion of the population, no one could honestly articulate that the government is really and truly of the people and for the people, espoused by democracy.

In the United States of America and Europe, poverty and illiteracy within African communities, on whose blood, sweat and tears, the foundations of some of these modern societies were built, remain astonishingly high. Capitalism has created dynasties and oligarchies from which only those who can afford the price of leadership emerge. A leadership like that of King Leopold II of Belgium that will conspire to deprive the very people on whose blood their destiny was charted.

Most of the African leaders who emerged during and after the quest for independence from colonial rule were quite aware of some of these frailties and were suspicious of the type of political system that was forced upon them. The fact that the principles of democracy were inconsistent with the colonial administration they were familiar with, made it increasingly untenable. However, because of the precipitousness of the transition and the imperious characteristics of colonial administrations, the African leaders were constrained to adopt the political system thrust upon them, mainly as stop-gap measure until suitable alternative forms of governance were envisaged. That was not going to happen as the intentions of the colonialists were to create as much chaos and confusion within territories so they would still consider theirs, in order to maintain control and perpetuate the exploitation of the continent.

Prior to the scramble for and colonisation of Africa, there were socio-political systems in place that ensured tribes engaged with each other even in times of conflict. Africans respected their Chiefs and Kings. Order and fairness prevailed throughout chiefdoms. Inter-chiefdom disputes were settled through the exchange of designated emissaries who conveyed the details of issues to be addressed. Aggrieved chiefdoms despatched whole entourages on the invitation of other chiefdoms where conferences were to be held. Proper rites and rituals were followed and fair exchanges and hearings were given to all sides. Decisions were arrived at through consensus and were respected and carried out without contest. These were traditional values and beliefs that held African societies together. Those were the values, order and respect for humanity that British and other Europeans took away from Africans and deprived future generations. They usurped the powers of the Chiefs and Kings and perpetrated untold criminality and abuses within the continent. The apparent success of colonisation, subjugation and abuse of Africans is what gave rise to and resulted in bigotry and the ideology of colour supremacy which continue to bedevil Africans.

This ideology results in an overconfidence that quite often leads to the reckless, unreasonable and generally unnatural behaviours towards Africans by Europeans. Such was the attitude of the son of a former British Prime Minister. In 2004, Mark Thatcher, very well edified in colonial exploitation and prejudices, masterminded and attempted to overthrow the government of the African state of Equatorial Guinea with the collective sponsorship of likeminded bigots in Britain. As if inspired by the actions of British Special Forces in Sierra Leone four years earlier, another ex-British SAS Officer Simon Mann was hired by Thatcher to execute a coup d'état in Equatorial Guinea. The country is rich in oil and natural gas but has a relatively small and uneconomic population. A legacy of the arbitrary demarcation of the continent following the Berlin Conference in 1886. Simon Mann proceeded to recruit his South African accomplices who were erstwhile operatives of the 32 Buffalo Battalion and the reminiscent Sandline and Executive Outcomes mercenaries. These were operatives who had perpetrated unimaginable atrocities against Africans, south of the continent. They underpinned the elaborate oppressive structure of apartheid. The objective of the heist was to overthrow the incumbent president of the African country and to replace him with a rogue African politician who was in exile in Europe. A typical British colonial hubris displayed by Tony Blair towards Zimbabweans in his attempt to depose their president Robert Mugabe, who resisted British attempts to commandeer their land.

The audacity of Mark Thatcher and his British associates who financed the escapade was astonishing. Similar to Sierra Leone, not a scintilla of regard was demonstrated for the opinion and lives of the poor people of the African country, who by all account were considered expendable by them. The outcome of a successful coup was to subject the people who might survive the carnage yet again to conditions akin to colonial repression. But this time, colonial repression would be exerted by their own kin, the feckless African who they would install as leader.

After what he thought was a dexterous and meticulous plan, all worked out in South Africa, Mann decided to put his daring adventure in motion. Unwittingly, his plan was to acquire his arsenal of lethal weapons from Zimbabwe where Simon Mann was to board a chartered flight and collect his dangerous cargo bound for Equatorial Guinea. To his shock and amazement, Simon Mann was intercepted and detained no sooner he arrived in Zimbabwe. The others who were already in situ within the Equatorial Guinea were also arrested and detained following a credible tip-off. Mark Thatcher, the architect of the grand plan, was subsequently arrested in August of 2004 in South Africa. After his elaborate prevarications and denials, the preponderance of indisputable evidence relating to his dealings with several others precipitated his acceptance of guilty in January 2005. Interestingly, following his guilty plea, he was only sentenced to four years in jail but suspended. Incredibly, he was only fined about half a million United States dollars by a South African court and set free. Simon Mann who was extradited to Equatorial Guinea by Zimbabwe to face charges of treason was tried and sentenced to thirty-four years and four months in prison in 2008. After serving just over a year of the prison term, he was released in November 2009 incredibly on humanitarian grounds. Enormous pressure was exerted on the government of Equatorial Guinea by colonial Britain for the release of the miscreants. Threats were made by Britain to freeze assets worth millions of British pounds held in Britain and France by the president of the country who they intended to overthrow. The behaviour of colonialists in Africa through centuries of dehumanising slavery and brutal colonisation up to modern times is a clear indication that the apparent freedom that Africans envisaged during their struggle for independence is far from reality.

Bigotry creates an unnatural and unrealistic confidence within those who claim to be superior but when confronted by the unexpected, invokes a sudden paroxysm of fear and insecurity which unleashes racism, sometimes in its crudest form, as a defence mechanism.

Today, Africans are berated and harassed everywhere they find themselves in the world because of the scourge and legacy of slavery. In modern democratic Britain, children grow up in environments where Africans are shoved out of trains, told to "*go work on the buses*", "*go clean toilets*" and shouted at in the street, "*Why don't you fuckin coons go back to Africa*"? It is not unusual for Africans to be confronted in public spaces and asked when they are going back home. This is often met with incredulity and utter bemusement. Africans hear songs espousing racism, with lyrics such as, "*we are racists and that is the way we like it*". Often, civilisation is cited as a justification for colonising Africa but the political and social experiences of Africans from their *colonial masters* both within and away from Africa do not appear to support that postulation.

In the United States of America, Africans are shot and killed like hunted animals in modern civilisation. Africans are used by the justice system to populate correction centres and penitentiaries to generate profits for their Caucasian capitalist compatriots.

Members of the police and armed forces are themselves products of the bigoted and racist systems they grew in. They are very accustomed to and familiar with ideologies that promote separatism and the hubris of supremacy. Therefore, when *colonial masters* intervene in African affairs often through military force, motivated by economic interests, they take with them these weird values and beliefs that characterise their appalling behaviour towards Africans. The actions of the Special Forces in Sierra Leone and the conduct of the British Prime Minister who concealed details of the atrocities and massacre of the people were all driven by the ideology of supremacy and colonial paternalism. The danger of such pernicious ideologies to Africa is ever so clear. Since the days when the British launched armed raids into Sierra Leone to capture men, women and children into slavery and throughout seven decades of coercing the country to succumb to British domination, the progress of Africans had been severely stunted. The combination of ideological bigotry and lethal weaponry have had a catastrophic and devastatingly destructive effect on African societies. Rampant abuses of humanity and the perpetration of appalling crimes pervades the continent. Widespread lynching, the use of Africans for target practices, raping of African women, young girls and boys, the pillaging of African societies and unconsented neutering of people were but a few of the violations of Africans.

These irrational behaviours were repeated throughout the continent by gun-toting bigoted imperialists.

The use of lethal weapons in Africa contributed significantly to the destruction and destabilisation of African societies. Weapons are often supplied to both sides that are in conflict by colonial masters to maximise the mutual destruction of Africans to the point of insolvency and economic vulnerability. These situations provide capitalists with imperial ambitions, relative advantage to dictate terms to battle weary Africans in order to exploit their resources.

Lethal weaponry is only one of an array of modern measures taken by colonialists to perpetuate their domination of Africans. Economic, social and technological tools are also part of the imperialists' armoury. A variety of economic and political sanctions are usually imposed on countries for noncompliance with economic conditions, particularly those imposed to facilitate exploitation. Social media is effectively used to influence the culture, behaviour and reactions of Africans towards authority and social order. Drone technology is widely used within the continent at will to illegally gather information or target and execute specified military activities. African leaders and governments are perniciously classified as terrorist if their political philosophies are perceived to be at variance with imperialist norms. A variety of measures are usually taken to thwart any form of deviation from imperial diktats.

Religion was also a powerful tool used to pacify and control Africans. Christianity and slavery had complemented each other effectively, especially during the transition from kidnappings and raids to colonisation and the domination of Africa. Christian missionaries operated alongside slavers and colonialists and usually not far behind when crimes and other abuses are meted out to Africans. It was clear that Christianity was integral in the process to enforce culture change. During the era of slavery and colonisation, Christian missionaries did not actively seek to stop the barbarism against Africans but instead, they participated in the abuse and succeeded in pacifying those who militate against subjugation.

Christian missionaries betrayed the trust of chiefs and other leaders by misleading them that they possessed moral values that distinguished them from their barbarous colonial accomplices. This was extremely deceptive as some of the missionaries went on to commit hideous and unpardonable crimes against Africans. During the ugly violent periods when treaties were obtained illegally with extreme brutality, Africans who were converted to Christianity were used in some cases to precede their rampaging colonial accomplices to engage with chiefs, convincing them to sign treaties that turned out to depose and disposes them of their authority and wealth.

Despite the influences and manipulations by colonial speculators, African missionaries, who were converted to Christianity prior to their return to Africa, were misguided and illusory about the relationship of religion on civilisation within the continent. They, like their Caucasian mentors, often referred to

Africa as the Dark Continent and that Christianity was the ultimate salvation for the people. A belief that was inculcated into them and their fore parents during the perilous period in servitude. They falsely believed that the Christian God had bestowed the power on their ruthless masters to enable them to dominate Africans as slaves. They, however, failed to understand that the immorality and savagery of slavery had no celestial fervour. Some of returnees who were Christian converts who thought they were bringing light to the Dark Continent were presumptuous and presupposes that they were better civilised than others in the continent. This mind set made it much easier for colonialists to surreptitiously use African missionaries to placate their kinfolks and exposed them to vicious exploitation and abuse.

In Sierra Leone, during the prolonged period of carnage, when the Temnes were fiercely resisting the aggression of British expeditionary forces from deposing their chiefs and expropriating land, following the signing of illegal Treaties, British missionaries made early contacts with the Mendes on the other side of the country, prior to the advancing militants. The role of the missionaries was to approach the Mendes seemingly unarmed, accompanied by a few Temnes who were not converted Christians themselves but coerced to become carriers and porters. With the knowledge of the fighting that was going on with the Temnes, the Mendes were themselves preparing for all-out war with British expeditionary forces. The missionaries placated and cajoled them to surrender in order to minimise material and human loses. British missionaries proselytised the Mendes and promised them that the expeditionary forces will bring with them salvation and hopes for a brighter future if they refrain from aggression.

Whilst the move to concede to the colonialists was considered strategic on the part of the Mendes, it was also mutually beneficial to the expeditionary forces who had taken a heavy toll during years fighting the ferocious Temnes.

However, when Mende chiefs were deposed and their land commandeered by the colonialists, they and their people saw things from a rather different perspective. Instead of blaming the missionaries, who had somehow ingratiated themselves to them, they immediately blamed the Temnes who had accompanied the missionaries and regarded them as traitors, for the second time in their troubled historical relationship.

It was the Christian missionaries who misled, pacified and created a false sense of security amongst the early settlers in Regent village, who rebelled against the payment of tax to the colonial administration. The settlers allowed their hopes and expectations for divine providence to distract them from the scrutiny and sincerity of the missionaries. They let their guard down exposing weaknesses that the administration capitalised on and proceeded to corral the recalcitrant leaders and their followers. The settlers were constrained within the confines of the Kings Yard, a purpose-built enclosure designed to exert control over their community. As a result of their devoutness, the settlers were unable to figure out that the missionaries shared the same philosophy and objectives of the colonial administration. The sponsorship of the construction of a church within the enclave by the then governor, Charles McCarthy, after whom the church was ironically named for his altruism and his presumed generosity was an indication of the co-ordination between the colonial administration and the missionaries. Charles McCarthy was subsequently killed in the Gold Coast after his miscalculation to confront the King of the Ashanti in his pursuit of land for the British Empire.

Christianity succeeded in effecting major cultural change within Africa. The construction of churches and schools brought people together seeking divine assistance in the pursuit of emancipation from repression. The strategic approach of Christianity was initially to engage adult Africans who were resisting subjugation by reducing their dependency and belief on traditional practices and rituals. Most were ultimately converted and convinced about the unseen power behind the abstractness of Christianity. They were taught the virtues of obeying their superiors who were the embodiment of the almighty in whom they should pin their hope and trust. Africans did invest a lot of trust and confidence on the missionaries who often betrayed them and referred to them as *blind heathens*. Despite the deviousness of the missionaries, Africans continued to display their unwavering loyalty to them and their religion.

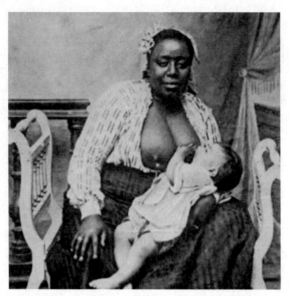

A converted slave mother nursing the child of her British masters

Portraits of *Jesus Christ,* the Christian redeemer, usually bore an uncanny resemblance to the British missionaries and colonialists were presented to the people for veneration and worship. This left an indelible impression on Africans who still believe that the British may have been appointed by divine providence, hence deserving of their respect and reverence. The people were transformed from working for the cohesion and sustainability of their communities to aspiring to be like the British, who they believed to be invincible after centuries of unrelenting violence against them. The settlers who held such belief found it incredible that a few gun-toting colonialists could exert such powers without divine assistance.

The paradox of such Christian beliefs is that a significant number of Africans were led to accept that salvation would come through British missionaries. Some do hope that their pain and suffering through hard unrewarded labour for the colonialists will all miraculously disappear and that through British Christianity, they will one day see the metaphorical *Promised Land.* No surprises, the British felt it appropriate to regard Africans as *"heathens in their blindness"* because of their unbridled loyalty, gullibility and subservience.

British missionaries believed Africans are devoid of religious faith and therefore in need of civilisation and culture according to their Bible. They believed that Africans were less adventurous and lacking natural intellect; that Africans were satanic and truly related to Judas Iscariot, who Christianity has strenuously tried to portray as African.

Missionaries and slavers would often quote passages from the Bible to justify their bigoted and depraved actions against Africans. The following are selected Bible passages that slavers and missionaries would read repeatedly to indoctrinate Africans in order to break down their resistance and to continue to dominate and control them:

Ephesians chapter six verse five to nine states: *"⁵ Slaves, obey your earthly masters with respect and fear, and with sincerity of heart, just as you would obey Christ. ⁶ Obey them not only to win their favour when their eye is on you, but as slaves of Christ, doing the will of God from your heart. ⁷ Serve wholeheartedly, as if you were serving the Lord, not people, ⁸ because you know that the Lord will reward each one for whatever good they do, whether they are slave or free".*

In the context of slavery, African imagination of Christ must resemble the physical appearances of the slavers, missionaries and subsequently, the colonialists who all held them in bondage. They are to be feared and revered in equal measure. The visible portraits of the Caucasian Christ that festooned all the places of worship serves as a permanent reminder to Africans of this resemblance, hence the spiritual obligation to serve their masters without reservation. The vivid portrayal of a Caucasian Christ hanging from the cross writhing in pain and agony was etched indelibly in the memories of Africans. The ancestor of the colonialists and missionaries, as embodied in the anointed Christ, had suffered on their behalf and the least that they as their servants could do is to return the favour in whatever way possible.

Interestingly, in the book of **Titus** chapter two, verses nine to ten, slaves were directed on how to behave to their superiors: *"Slaves are to be submissive to their own masters in everything; they are to be well-pleasing, not argumentative, not pilfering, but showing all good faith, so that in everything they may adorn the doctrine of God our Saviour".*

One, therefore, would tend to question who was pilfering from whom in the circumstance. Unconditional submission was expected from the people to their *colonial masters* at all times. Anything short of such behaviour was frowned upon by the masters and could invoke severe punishment and hardship. Africans fervently accepted such treatments and continued their obedience as the will of God. Abuse of Africans by colonialists and missionaries alike were widespread. The reverence with which they were held by the people prevented those who were abused from making official complaints through fear of retribution.

Luke, chapter twelve, verse forty-seven, instructed, *"And that servant who knew his master's will but did not get ready or act according to his will, will receive a severe beating"*.

Thus, if an African is aware of the lustful and perverse intentions of his superior towards him or her and refuses to prepare himself or herself for the pleasures of the master, he or she, according to divine providence, shall endure the wrath of the master.

On the other hand, schools were established and built across the continent not to turn Africans into a competitive intellectual force, but to influence their thought process, behaviour and psychology towards subjugation. Educational materials carried nothing about the savagery of slavery or the brutality of the process of colonisation. Children were taught values and ideals that created a utopian fantasy of the British colonial empire. The hope and belief that their association with the British colonialists and missionaries would bring them great fortunes rendered them extremely vulnerable to the depravity of the missionaries and colonialists alike.

Educational institutions were initially set up for the training of Africans in colonial theology to promote the values and ideals of colonial ideologies. Christian seminaries predominated colonial Africa and the curriculum and course structures were mainly based on the fair side of British society and culture, underpinned by fear, dedication and reverence.

Colossians 3:22: *"Slaves obey in everything those who are your earthly masters, not by way of eye service, as people-pleasers, but with sincerity of heart, fearing the Lord".*

Sierra Leoneans like other Africans were cynically taught to obey and revere colonialists with the respect and fear they reserved for God, as stated in the Holy Scriptures as presented to them. The use of the Bible by colonial missionaries to indoctrinate Africans was very effective. Africans believed that the colonialists were actually appointed by God and deserving of respect and adulation despite the immorality and depravity that characterised their religious and business conducts. Africans, on the cunning guidance and instructions of their *colonial masters*, would kill and maim each other demonstrating their "*sincerity of heart*" to their colonial master.

Through the teachings by missionaries, Africans romanticised the violence and sexual depravity that pervaded the society of the missionaries. These acts were aptly recorded in various popular series of colonial literatures. The purpose was to inculcate fear and respect for their tenacity and ruthlessness. The education curriculum was not designed to educate and equip Africans with skills to enable creative and strategic thinking. It was merely to enable Africans to understand and work within the constraints of the colonial structures.

Towards the emergence of the movement for independent rule by Africans, changes were made to aspects of education but without any material change in the political and economic structures. The consequences of such moves were to allow the flow of potential labour to Britain in the pursuit of British culture whilst undermining the impetus for local initiatives and developments.

Religion has had an overall negative impact on the continent. Societies that were already fractured through the antiques of colonisation and slavery became dangerously divided further into religious factions with the proliferation of various religious sects vying for influence and control. Africans have since been using religion in virtually the same way as colonial missionaries, in order to exploit each other.

Religion capitalises on the hopes of people with unrealistic expectations of extrication from the suffering and pain wrought upon them by the evils of colonial subjugation. Religion is always invoked by the powerful against the weak to facilitate exploitation and repression. Hope is the bedrock of religion but religion could not guarantee the emancipation of the people. There are natural characteristics that are common to Africans, that when pooled, produce synergies that will result in true salvation. These were values that were thoroughly denigrated by colonialism. The values, beliefs and culture that Africans share, that make them a race, are far stronger than the seeds of hate and division introduced by colonialism and religion.

The socio-economic and political situation have not been without the influence of religion. In many of the British colonies, churches all around continue to pray fervently and incessantly for the prosperity and wellbeing of the British Monarchy as their head of state. In Sierra Leone, such prayers of allegiance and dedication to the British Monarchy continued well into the first republic.

Political policies were influenced or frustrated by religious agencies. Such agencies were used in many cases to subsidise selected activities undertaken by African governments in order to create a situation of dependency. In others, oil is supplied at heavily-subsidised rates by Islamic countries in exchange for religious latitude. Religion has been used as an effective economic weapon to influence the socio-cultural direction in Africa.

Africa is a continent where untold crimes have been perpetrated, both political and religious. The people are remarkably resilient. How long and how much more they can continue to endure depends on how they perceive freedom and how they wish to govern and be governed.

Freedom is perceived by Africans in diverse ways. Some believe that the ability to vote in general political elections is empowering enough. The liberation from the shackles of slavery gave Africans a hope of total freedom; but hope without collaboration and mutual respect for each other as Africans will hardly achieve the freedom most dream of.

The brutality and subjugation of Africans by British and other Europeans during slavery and colonisation inculcated a pathological inferiority complex for Caucasians. Centuries of pent-up historical frustrations and anger by Africans are frequently let out against each other, often within the confines of meticulously socially-engineered societies they find themselves living in. This unusual and unnatural behaviour of modern Africans tend to obscure their focus and quest for total emancipation. The belief that slavery is a thing of the past by modern Africans as they have been led to believe is part of the continuing process of subjugation.

Slavery and colonial subjugation constitute the corruption and reprogramming of African minds, through religion, culture change and most potently, instilling the fear of Caucasians through extreme violence and torture. This concept is predicated on the destruction of the mentality of Africans whilst preserving their physical conditions to carry out laborious productive tasks. This is a dynamic process that will continue until Africans realise the need and urgency to regroup, rebuild their communities, uphold their cultures and re-educate themselves. The energies exerted by Africans in order to emulate Caucasians and the belief that by being proficient in their ways might prove that they are humans like them is totally flawed and absolutely futile. The African will always be a "*Nigger*" to the Caucasian, and a "*Nigger*" by their mentality is no more than a beast and an economic tool to be exploited.

The mental reconditioning of Africans through slavery, colonisation and present day manipulations have lasted for centuries. To copy this model and attempt to change the mentality of Caucasians would be utterly unproductive. Africans should not shy away from their history however brutal and dehumanising, as their ignorance of this significant past will continue to undermine their resilience, creativity and collective strength to determine their future prospects.

Chapter 16
Memories

Contrary to common views expressed in modern discourse about race relations and discrimination, the concept of slavery and all what it was about is still alive. To a large extent, the self-proclaimed *colonial masters* are motivated by their perceived success during slavery, colonisation and in their continued pursuit of imperialism and the subjugation of Africans. The democratic philosophy introduced by departing colonialists was accepted and adopted wholesomely by Africans. This has formed the basis of political governance which varies in its application across the continent and in many cases with predictably disastrous outcomes. When the alien system is combined with the avarice of capitalism and the unrealistic hope founded on religion, the results are complexities Africans struggle to contemplate. Capitalism has developed into an inextricable element of modern democracy, exploiting its weaknesses and moral deficiencies. Capitalism has taken hold in the wake of the introduction of democracy, influencing political ideologies and promoting further inequalities in Africa. The failure of democracy to produce governments of the people by the people, the world over has left Africa in particular dangerously unstable and less productive. The pursuit of an appropriate and ideal political system remains elusive.

The way Africans perceive themselves and behave towards one another and their inability to coordinate the way they govern, in order to achieve a goal common to all, have left the continent in serious socioeconomic disorder. A chaos that invidiously characterises and reflects colonial norms and aspirations. Sadly, Africa continues to fail to maximise its potential in a stable and sustainable manner.

The irrational compartmentalisation of Africa resulting from the Berlin Conference of 1886 has since left the continent in utter social and economic shambles. Africans had never contested the legitimacy and morality of such a conference by European bigots whose actions had had such seismic effect on an entire race. A conference that did not even once consider that Africa was the homeland of a people called Africans. The Berlin conference overtly and illegitimately sanctioned the private takeover of the Congo in particular by King Leopold II of Belgium who together with Britain went on to perpetrate crimes so revolting, their behaviours challenge human reasoning. In modern times, King Leopold II and his associates could well have been sectioned under the relevant mental Health Act. The scramble for the continent and the impact on its people is, however, one of the scarcely-explored and underreported historical events in Africa. The cultures of Africans were uprooted, decimated and replaced with hate and fear that caused utter confusion amongst the people. Communities were separated and surreptitiously pitched against each other. Gun violence was introduced into Africa to replace consensus, negotiation and diplomacy. Distinct features of African traditional societies before the savagery of slavery and the mayhem of colonialism were eradicated through intimidation and coercion.

The legacy of the Berlin conference and the impunity of colonialism in Africa were generally and undoubtedly what motivated the British to export tons of lethal weapons to Sierra Leone in order to perpetrate their imperial influence in a country that still carries the psychological scars of centuries of oppression.

The paternalism of Europeans as *colonial masters* towards Africans, absurd though it might appear, continues to wreak havoc and perpetrate the exploitation of the people and the continent. Governance within Africa will always be embroiled in controversy and turmoil depending on the intensity of the interest *colonial masters* wish to exert and their geopolitical and economic strategies.

Imperial interests and influences are imposed in many subtle and complex ways through the activities of corporations, religion, agencies and through forceful interventions, disguised in some cases in modern times as the "need to protect". The protection of who by whom is a perplexing phenomenon. The intervention in Libya in 2011 by European *colonial masters* on the pretext that the country's leader was about to kill his own people en masse was one such post-colonial gambit. The outcome of the intervention was near apocalypse with mass loss of lives of the people who were meant to be protected. The impunity of these actions remain unchallenged by Africans. The ever-present threat to the people and the prosperity of the continent as a whole is rather disconcerting. After the apparent conclusion of the British-led coalition to bomb Libya, the then British Prime Minister, David Cameron in the usual imperialist hubris, officially remarked *"People in Libya today have an even greater chance after this news, of building themselves a strong and democratic future. I am proud of the role that Britain has played in helping them to bring that about. And I pay tribute to the brave Libyans who helped to liberate their country"*. The news he referred to in his remark was the brutal murder of Col. Muammar Gadhafi the president of Libya and members of his family. David Cameron's actions and attitude towards Africans, similar to the actions of Tony Blair in Sierra Leone and the French actions in Ivory Coast, appear to be a developing trend of escalating imperialism within the continent. Hence the continuum from slavery to colonisation and to modern interventions, manipulations and the continued exploitation of Africa. During pre and post-colonial Africa, France in particular had continuously displayed strong paternalism and imperial influence within territories in Africa they once considered their property.

During the traumatic years of kidnaping and capturing Africans, France was also one of the main and active participants in the sale and exploitation of Africans. France fiercely competed with Britain over the extraction of Africans from the continent and in later years avidly engaged in the pursuit and control of territories, especially along the west coast. They managed to secure considerable swathes of the west coast which they held on to as various colonial outposts for centuries. Similar to Sierra Leone and other colonies dominated by Britain, France was extremely intolerant of any form of aspiration for independent rule by Africans under their command and control.

Surprisingly, in 2015, the president of France on a tour of some African countries went to Cameroon, an original German colony that was fought over with the British. Cameroon was subsequently divided between France and Britain after the First World War by the League of Nations with the northern territory allocated to France and the southern region allocated to the British. Such decisions had a severe impact on the culture of the country which was once a unified community. They were forced to adopt two languages and cultures alien to them. The visit of the French president was blighted by anti-French demonstrations over the continued meddling by France in the socio-political and economic affairs of Cameroon. Another contentious issue was that arms and ammunition seized from Muslim religious militants fighting in Nigeria turned out to be

French made. This was promptly interpreted as evidence of French imperialism in Africa and that riled the people intensely.

Within ten years of French rule of the northern region of Cameroon, a co-ordinated struggle for independence was initiated by the Union des Populations du Cameroun (UPC), a political party that was proscribed by the French colonial administration in 1955. A violent suppression of the struggles for independence by France ensued and lasted for years. An estimated four hundred thousand Africans were slaughtered by the repressive regime of France, including the assassination of Ruben Um Nyobe, leader of the UPC in 1958. Félix-Roland Moumié who bravely succeeded Ruben Um Nyobe in the continued struggle against the repressive colonial administration of his motherland did not escape the brutality of the French colonialists. In November 1960 he was killed by thallium poisoning in Geneva by the French Secret Service.

Many have risen to the challenge of confronting the collective and formidable forces of imperialism in Africa but few have survived the undertaking.

Although France like other European imperialists have never apologised for the senseless massacre of untold Africans, President Hollande of France in 2015 acknowledged the atrocities committed and indicated that, "*I recognise that there have been extremely traumatic and even tragic episodes,*" "*We are prepared, as we've always been, to open up the history books and search the archives,*" The president's comments were generally criticised by Africans as falling short of an apology for such heinous crimes against Africans during colonial repression within the continent.

In a rather strange turn of events during the same year 2015, Germany, a former colonial ruler of Namibia, finally recognised the brutality and mass slaughter of the Herero and Nama people during the infamous Herero Rebellion that lasted four years between 1904 and 1908 as "*Genocide*".

Similar to British Colonial Sierra Leone, Germany in a bid to establish an outpost for its own people following the Berlin Conference, obtained a signed Treaty purportedly being the purchase of a substantial piece of land within the Herero homeland of Damaraland. The acquisition which was facilitated by coercion was fiercely disputed by the Herero people but with colonial invasions, violence was the common currency used to conduct business. Within a couple of years from the dubious land take over, there was an upsurge in tribal skirmishes with the German invaders supplying lethal weapons to the tribes which exacerbated the conflicts. Amidst the sponsored tribal turmoil, by 1903, over a quarter of the Herero homeland had been confiscated by German settlers. Their livestock were taken away from them, and they were forced to provide unpaid labour as slaves to their unwelcomed occupiers. Women and children were repeatedly abused and summary killings for dissent were commonplace. The exploitation of the people was excessive and became unbearable. By the end of 1903, news broke out that the colonialists were proposing to construct a railway across their land and that a concentration camp was to be built to contain them. In early 1904, hostilities against the occupiers started by the unified tribes expressing their dissent to the invidious proposals of the Germans. The Germans sustained about a hundred casualties during the onslaught. Their administration unleashed ferocious reprisals, killing, raping and pillaging the communities of both the Hereros and Nama communities. Those who thought they had escaped the wrath of the Germans and made it into the desert for safety were subsequently corralled by the Germans and deliberately left to die of thirst, dehydration and starvation.

Hereros and Namas who surrendered or succumbed to the brutality of the German colonial administration were to suffer the gruelling hazards of the concentration camp. The Africans were forced to engage in excessive laborious tasks with little nutrition or sustenance. There were high percentages of deaths amongst the prisoners resulting from lynching, shootings and rampant corporal punishments. Prisoners in the concentration camps were also used as specimens for medical and other scientific experiments. Test on the Africans included toxic injections, dissections and retention of body parts. Some of those practices are covertly being carried out in some African countries in modern times.

Hundreds of thousands of Hereros and Namas were exterminated within their homeland by the Germans. The deaths of the people were so extensive, the population of these indigenous people was severely depleted. This dastardly act was one of the first recorded incidence of genocide in the modern world.

The following are quotes by the German supreme officer Lieutenant-General Lothar von Trotha who commanded the barbaric onslaught on the Africans:

"My intimate knowledge of many central African tribes (Bantu and others) has everywhere convinced me of the necessity that the Negro does not respect treaties but only brute force."

"I know enough of African tribes that they give way only to violence. To exercise this violence with crass terrorism and even with gruesomeness was and is my policy. I destroy the rebellious tribes with streams of blood and money. Only from this seed something new will emerge, which will remain." These statements encapsulate European attitudes and their deliberate intention to brutalise and coerce Africans into submission. The callousness of European savagery during slavery and colonialism in Africa is beyond modern comprehension.

African heroes who stood their grounds and challenged the absurdity of colonialism succeeded in many ways, despite the collaborative and highly motivated forces of European *colonial masters*. The conditions under which Africans were constrained were appalling and deplorable, smothering any prospect of progress, personal or national development. Needless to mention that the common feature of the necessary and prioritised measures taken by nearly all the revolutionaries were most importantly to recover land from foreign occupiers. The pursuit of education, healthcare, food production and the perennial struggle for total independent rule left countless Africans maimed or murdered by the avaricious and ruthlessness of their occupiers. They were men motivated and determined to explore alternative political systems as a variant of democracy that was thrust upon them by colonialists. The quest for an alternative by Africans purely stemmed from the fact that the colonialists who were tenacious about the implementation of democracy were themselves unfamiliar with the concept and never practiced it anywhere in the continent. African leaders were determined to formulate a system that would guarantee true egalitarianism amongst Africans within Africa following centuries of segregation, deprivation and repression. The incessant pressure exerted on them by colonialists denied them the flexibility to be creative and innovative. These constraints were what precipitated and gravitated them towards communism and socialism; systems that they felt were perceptibly closest to what Africans were familiar with. A system that predates colonialism. Communism was quite appealing to these heroes as a socio-political system that was being practiced in the Soviet Union and China. Their distrust for everything colonial led most of them to the former Soviet Union and China for inspiration and support. These moves put African leaders at odds with the disapproving European colonialists who were polar opposite to everything that communism espoused. Whilst some of the leaders survived the perils of pursuing independent rule, others became casualties of the cold war between the East and West following the Second World War.

These were men who through selflessness had given their lives for the honour and dignity of Africa and Africans by standing up to the pugnacity of colonial occupation, oppression, apartheid, exploitation and despotism. These intrepid Africans had all faded into history. A history that Africans were ironically taught to be ashamed of and a history that Africans should confine to the past.

The future success of Africans as a people and Africa as a respected continent free from the shackles of slavery and the vestiges of colonisation will only be achieved through understanding and recognising the pain, sacrifices and sufferings of their pioneers and heroes. Their successes and achievements must be celebrated in perpetuity. They must never be forgotten.

The memory of the following amongst many others who put their lives on the line in the quest of a political alternative free from the excesses and repression of colonialism must be cherished by Africans:

Bia Bureh

Chief Bia Bureh was one of the first Africans to stand against and confronted the belligerence and exploitations of British colonialism in the continent. When British colonialists decided to levy an illegal and unjustifiable tax, which was based on the number of bedrooms per household, Bia Bureh was incensed. His anger was borne out of the undue hardship and suffering his people had endured through slavery and the oppression of working in the labour camps. The natural resources from his land were exploited avariciously by the British without any form of compensation to his people. Women, children and young adults were abused with impunity to the disgust of the chief. The excesses of British colonialists were unbearable. When they decided to demand that the already impoverished people pay this unreasonable tax, which meant increasing labour hours committed to the construction of roads and rail tracks to facilitate the easy movement of goods for shipment, Bia Bureh had to act. Bia Bureh launched a robust resistance to the ferocious military machine of colonial Britain that was desperately committed to the enforcement of the infamous hut tax.

Bia Bureh was a legend who lived and died fighting for the liberation and rights of his people. He passed away at the age of sixty-eight years, August 1908.

Olayinka Herbert Macaulay

Olayinka Herbert Macaulay was the grandson of Rev. Ajayi Crowther, a returned slave and the first African bishop of the Niger Territory.

Herbert Macaulay was a nationalist who pioneered Nigerian nationalism. He was a staunch opponent of British domination of his country Nigeria. In 1908, he exposed British corruption in the handling of railway finances. In his assiduous drive for the liberation and respect for his people, he took on the colonial authorities in 1919 to reclaim land that the British had appropriated from the chiefs and local people. Olayinka Macaulay not only fought to reclaim land back from the British, he further demanded that compensation be paid to the people for loss of use of their land. Like many brave Africans who confronted the British hegemony, Olayinka Macaulay was arrested and detained several times for his indefatigable struggle against subjugation.

In 1944, Olayinka Macaulay co-founded the National Council of Nigeria and the Cameroons (NCNC) together with Namdi Azikwe, a patriotic organisation formed to pursue independence from European colonisation.

He eventually proceeded to form the first political party in Nigeria, the Nigerian National Democratic Party (NNDP).

After many tireless years of difficult and sometimes life-threatening struggle against British colonialism, Olayinka Macaulay fell ill and died in Lagos in 1946, at the age of eighty-one years old.

Patrice Lumumba

The first legitimately elected prime minister of the now Democratic Republic of Congo, who stood up for the dignity and respect of his people after years of heinous and brutal crimes committed by Belgium and Britain against them. Patrice Lumumba was an ardent advocate of pan Africanism as an essential for the prosperity of the continent. His detestation of the unprecedented evils meted against his people was undisguised. He had a vivid and optimistic vision for the progress of not only his country but the entire African continent. He was fervently against the uncontrolled exploitation of the resources the country possesses, whilst ordinary Congolese were starving to death.

Patrice Lumumba's unrelenting pursuit for a political system that would guarantee equality, fairness and humanity for his people, unfortunately, put him at odds with the collective and common interest of Belgium, Britain and subsequently the United States of America. An interest that was to relegate his people to perpetual oppression, exploitation and anarchy that satisfies colonial geopolitical desires. An interest that would extinguish Lumumba's emerging values, beliefs and principles for a fair society in Congo.

Patrice Lumumba was killed in the most gruesome, brutal and barbaric execution Africa had ever seen. The hate of the Belgians towards him for standing up for the rights, freedom and respect for his people was almost biblical. Simply taking his life was just not enough vengeance. His desecrated body was invidiously dissolved in concentrated sulphuric acid by his adversaries in order to obliterate all possible trace of him. The thought of his final place of interment becoming a possible shrine to his people propelled the colonialist to commit such a mindless and callous act. The people of Congo and Africa in general were deliberately denied a symbol of reverence and history.

Patrice Lumumba was slain and taken away from Africa in January 1961, at the prime age of thirty-five years.

Marcus Garvey

Born in the wake of the harsh conditions of slavery in Saint Ann's Bay in Jamaica, Marcus Garvey was strident in the pursuit of "Black Nationalism" and pioneered the "Pan-African" movement, promoting the return of liberated Africans in bondage back to Africa. He founded the *Black Star Line* in the United States supporting this enterprise for the economic empowerment of Africans and the transportation of Africans back home to Africa. His efforts were severely undermined, and the company became bankrupt. Despite his imprisonment and subsequent deportation to Jamaica from the United States, he became an inspiration to many. Marcus Garvey founded the Universal Negro Improvement Association and the African Communities League to promote the general uplift of people of African Ancestry within the Diaspora. He was a steadfast believer in the potential of the union of Africans.

Marcus Garvey delivered his philosophy of Black emancipation as eloquently as he was prolific in his writing. He remarked that, "*A people without the knowledge of their past history, origin and culture is like a tree without roots*".

Marcus Garvey was indefatigable in his fight for the dignity of Africans the world over, and despite the many obstacles he encountered in his struggles, he remained committed to his cause until his death in June 1940 at the age of fifty-two years.

Kwame Nkrumah

The first African to pursue and succeed in gaining independent rule for his people of Ghana in West Africa. Kwame Nkrumah was the first prime minister of Ghana formerly known as the Gold Coast under colonialism. He was a political activist with boundless energy and unrestrained ambitions for the emancipation of his people and Africa. He tenaciously pursued his dream for his country, taking on the vicious brutality and violence of British colonialism. Amidst the suspicions, conspiracies and threats from both the United States CIA and the British MI6, that Kwame Nkrumah was a communist with a proclivity to swing to the Soviet Union, he resolutely pursued his ambitions for his country. In his declaration of independence, he proclaimed:

'We are going to see that we create our own African personality and identity. We again rededicate ourselves in the struggle to emancipate other countries in Africa; for our independence is meaningless unless it is linked up with the total liberation of the African continent.'

Kwame Nkrumah was not only a patriot of Ghana but a pious believer of a united Africa, to which he also proclaimed that:

'Divided we are weak; united, Africa could become one of the greatest forces for good in the world.'

Kwame Nkrumah, unlike many of his peers at that time, recognised the deplorable state his country was left by the British. He embarked on the building of essential social and economic infrastructures that provided the foundation for future prosperity. He was committed to restoring Ghana's cultural identity and social justice after prolonged oppression by British colonialism.

Kwame Nkrumah passionately believed that the identity, dignity and potential of Africans can only be realised through unity. Through indefatigable verve and political vision he promoted the concept of Pan-Africanism. With the co-operation of other visionaries like him, he achieved the first step towards African unity by forming the Organisation of African Unity (OAU), presently the African Union (AU).

Kwame Nkrumah, like many other enlightened African visionaries of his time, continued to attract the malevolence of colonialists who loathed any form of development and equality for Africans. His subsequent overthrow from government was orchestrated by British and United States agents. He went into and remained in exile from his beloved country until his final days.

Kwame Nkrumah died in April 1972, after living a solitary life in perpetual fear for his safety, at the age of sixty-two years. A loss of immense magnitude to Africa.

Jomo Kenyatta

An erudite, astute and charismatic politician. Kenyatta worked assiduously, travelled and lived away from his homeland for a considerable number of years during the harsh days of colonialism. He acquired enormous knowledge and insight into European thinking and ideology. He firmly upheld the cultural identity and traditional principles of his beloved, Kenya.

Jomo Kenyatta, unlike some of his vibrant and zealous African compatriots, was largely considered to be a moderate politician who believed in reconciliation and peaceful cohabitation. He, however, was one of the founders of the Pan-African Congress. He became the president of the Kenya African Union and campaigned avidly for the return of land to Kenyans commandeered by the British. He also embarked on a movement advocating for independent rule for Kenya. His life was under constant threat from British colonialists who detested his quest to reclaim land that had been forcibly taken away from them. He was accused of managing the renowned Mau Mau rebellion against colonial rule and was later arrested and detained. After a show trial by the British colonialists, he was imprisoned for seven years with hard labour.

Jomo Kenyatta, without any bitterness for the injustice meted against him by the British colonial administration, assiduously pursued independent rule for Kenya and became the first prime minister of his country. His rule was dogged by British colonialists meddling and the promotion of tribal division and hate amongst Kenyans.

Jomo Kenyatta, an ardent Pan-Africanist, died free of hate for his British colonial oppressors in 1978. He was eighty-six years old.

Julius Nyerere

A beacon for enlightenment and vision to his people. His selflessness and benevolence made him one of Africa's genuine, honest and transparent leaders. His philosophy for social and economic development for Africa led to his *Arusha Declaration* that elucidated the concept of "Ujamaa"; socialism and familism as opposed to mass oppression by colonialism.

Julius Nyerere was one of the proponents of the Organisation of African Unity, and his belief in a liberated Africa was unflappable. He supported the removal of minority colonial domination across the continent with steely determination.

His political activism and movement to rid his country of colonialism did not escape the attention of the British colonial administration. Nyerere used his mild and affable personality to outflank the colonial benefactors and went on to achieve independent rule for Tanganyika, without the need for violent upheaval that characterised similar movements in other African states.

Julius Nyerere succeeded to become the first Prime Minister of Tanganyika and later the first elected president of Tanzania, the unified country of Tanganyika and Zanzibar.

Julius Nyerere remained politically active and exerted his influence in the transformation of Africa until his death in October 1999. He was seventy-seven years old.

Thomas Sankara

President of Burkina Faso and one of the youngest heroes of Africa. He was an avid proponent of Pan-Africanism and a strong advocate for social change and the elimination of colonial rule in his country and Africa. His passion for social, culture change and the fight against the legacy of the corrupt practices of colonialism motivated the renaming of his country to Burkina Faso, in place of the French Colonial name of Upper Volta. He was first appointed prime minister in 1983 in a government prior to his but was dismissed shortly afterwards and put under house arrest on the recommendation of the French colonialists.

Thomas Sankara was averse to the crippling fiscal conditions imposed by imperialism geared towards stifling the economic development and self-reliance of his country.

He remarked," *Our country produces enough to feed us all. Alas, for lack of organisation, we are forced to beg for food aid. It's this aid that instils in our spirits the attitude of beggars"*.

He proceeded to launch an admirable social, economic and cultural development for his country that he hoped could be replicated across the continent. Like many other former African colonies, he instituted land reforms to recover arable and productive land held by a few colonialists.

Thomas Sankara's revolution was underpinned by sound intellect and ideology that invariably put him in a head-on collision with the French colonialists. He was inevitably slaughtered in 1987 during a sponsored coup d'état. His policies were promptly reversed back to colonial diktats by his successor.

He was thirty-seven years of age.

Samora Machel

A genius and a patriotic African who passionately believed that Africa must be rid of the brutality of colonialism. Samora Machel was born into a family with a lineage and reputation of anti-colonial militancy. A family that rejected the dehumanising repression of colonialism. Samora Machel and his immediate family experienced the irrational and despotic bigotry of colonialism. His parents were instructed and forced to cultivate cotton on their farm for European markets instead of their staple food. Their land was subsequently confiscated and appropriated to Portuguese settlers who would produce cotton after their refusal to comply with colonial orders. In order to avoid starvation, his family migrated into South Africa to work for the apartheid regime in dreadful mining conditions where he lost one of his brothers.

Samora Machel's paternal instinct to fight back to regain their human dignity was ignited in his early adulthood. His remarks on the deplorable colonial medical situation for his people were "*the rich man's dog gets more in the way of vaccination, medicine and medical care than do the workers upon whom the rich man's wealth is built*". An epitaph that will resonate with Africans the world over.

Samora Machel became a member of the anti-colonial freedom movement *FRELEMO* which he was to command and became a true revolutionary. He fought several dangerous and ferocious bloody battles against the co-ordinated and resolute defence of Southern African colonial domination. He led his people to eventual victory and independent rule upon which he became the President of Mozambique in June 1975.

In one of his eloquent speeches, he espoused, "*of all the things we have done, the most important – the one that history will record as the principal contribution of our generation – is that we understand how to turn the armed struggle into a Revolution; that we realised that it was essential to create a new mentality to build a new society.*"

Samora Machel embarked on a drive to improve the social and economic conditions of his people and sternly pursued the recovery of confiscated land from the minority Portuguese colonialists. His rule was beset by co-ordinated and persistent hostility from the

Rhodesian oppressive government and the apartheid regime of South Africa.

Samora Machel was a shrewd politician and a brilliant military strategist, but in spite of his dedication and unrelenting vigour and drive to emancipate his people from centuries of the brutality and oppression of colonialism, he finally succumbed to the persistence of his adversaries, when a plane he was travelling in was brought down in 1986. Although the course of the crash remained a mystery, the suspicion was directed towards the apartheid regime of South Africa.

Samora Machel was cruelly snatched from his people of Mozambique and Africa at the age of fifty-three years.

Walter Sisulu

A mild-mannered gentleman, a Pan-Africanist with unparalleled commitment and determination to end oppression, racial discrimination and segregation in his homeland of South Africa. He was a traditionalist who upheld and promoted his cultural heritage in the midst of overwhelming colonial oppression.

Walter Sisulu, a strategist by nature, was a frontline member of various anti-colonial and antiapartheid movements. He campaigned vigorously against the unfair and unjust treatment of Africans, including the exploitation and abuse of Africans during the Second World War.

Walter Sisulu's rise within the African National Congress (ANC) was meteoric, attributable to his meticulous organisational skills, strategy and fearlessness. Despite several orders banning his participation in civil and other resistance to apartheid, he assiduously continued in the struggle for a liberated South Africa. After several arrests, detentions and escapes, Walter Sisulu was finally charged with treason and terrorism in the infamous Rivonia Trial and sentenced to life in prison in June 1964.

Walter Sisulu continued to pursue liberation indefatigably with the political organisation of the African National Congress (ANC), whilst being incarcerated in the notorious Robben Island prison.

His quest for education and enlightenment was boundless. In his book the *Long Walk to Freedom*, Nelson Mandela remarked,

'It was Walter's course that was at the heart of all our education. Many of the young ANC members who came to the island had no idea that the organisation had even been in existence in the 1920s and 1930s, through to the present day. For many of these young men, it was the only political education they ever received'.

After serving twenty-six gruelling years of hard labour in prison, he was released, and he immediately restarted his work to organise the ANC as a proper political party ready for participation in the formal transformational governance of South Africa.

Walter Sisulu was elected the Deputy President of the ANC in 1991. He remained dedicated and equally committed to the ANC until his death through failing health in May 2003 at the age of ninety-one years.

Govan Nbeki

A scholar and an astute political philosopher. He was a member of the editorial board of the *New Age*, a leftist newspaper in Johannesburg that promoted communist ideologies whilst denouncing the cruel and irrational apartheid regime. The paper and its editors were subsequently banned by the apartheid regime and colonial administration, a typical characteristic of the regime's repressive rule.

Govan Nbeki was a passionate believer in socialism as an alternative political system for Africa as opposed to the widespread authoritarian and divisive colonial rule. He proceeded to lead the African National Congress (ANC) and the South African Communist Party until his arrest and detention. He was charged with treason and imprisoned with other ANC colleagues for life.

Govan Nbeki was imprisoned at the Robben Island where he served twenty-four years with hard labour. After his release he served as Deputy President of the Senate of post-Apartheid South Africa and the National Council of Provinces.

Africa lost an eminent philosopher and astute politician in Govan Nbeki who passed away in August 2001 at the age of ninety-one years of age.

Stephen Biko

Steve Biko paid the ultimate price for Africa and the sterling struggle against the pathetic and hopeless apartheid regime that dominated his homeland, South Africa. He was popularly known to all as Steve Biko. A prominent leader and co-founder of the movement for the consciousness of Africans. He motivated, galvanised and transformed the dissatisfaction of students against apartheid into a formidable force in the political history of South Africa. In university, Steve Biko found himself in what was designated the "Non-European Section" by the bigoted regime. He became the first President of the South African Student Association (SASO) and chairperson of its literary publications.

Stephen Biko was a formidable orator, and the apartheid regime found it strenuous to ignore his appeal to young indigenous South Africans especially. He was expelled from the University because of his increasing political activities and was banned by the regime from speaking to more than one person at a time. This was amongst several restrictions placed on him. To even quote or refer to any of his speeches by the ordinary people was disallowed by the regime.

Despite the strangulating restrictions imposed on him, he went on to form a few organisations promoting the principle of self-reliance and social development. His influence and motivation through the consciousness movement resulted in the Soweto Uprising. Thousands of student demonstrated against Afrikaans, being the medium of instruction in schools. The response by the regime to the uprising was grotesque and disproportionately violent. Several hundreds of students were slaughtered and thousands sustained life threatening injuries.

Stephen Biko was a principal target of the apartheid regime following the Soweto Uprising. His arrest and detention was inevitable. He was detained under spurious charges of terrorism. He was brutally tortured during hours of interrogation by the apartheid regime, wherein he suffered severe injuries from blows to his head. He was transported naked and in shackles for over one thousand kilometres to a prison in Pretoria from Port Elizabeth.

Stephen Biko suffered severe brain damage and died from injuries inflicted on him by the savagery and brutality of the oppressive apartheid regime in 1977. Steve Biko was thirty years old. A tremendous loss to his people and a loss of an exemplary talent to the entire Africa.

Oliver Reginald Tambo

A Pan-Africanist, an intellectual and an adroit politician who played a pivotal role in the fight against apartheid and colonialism in South Africa. He was an active and influential member of the African National Congress (ANC), holding important positions including Secretary General, Deputy President and Acting President of the ANC. Oliver Tambo was a teacher and a professional and compassionate lawyer committed to pursuing justice and equality for his oppressed people.

He participated in numerous anti-apartheid movements and organised campaigns against the appalling apartheid regime. He was a perennial target of the apartheid regime and faced treason charges with a hundred and fifty-four others in the renowned 1956 Treason Trial from which he was subsequently acquitted.

Oliver Tambo went into exile after the dreadful Sharpeville Massacre and spent several years of hard and untiring work traversing the globe to gain support for the liberation of his country. Being a vital strategic member of the liberation movement, his life was never free from the threat of assassination.

After thirty years in exile, Oliver Tambo returned home to meet his compatriots with whom he had dedicated his entire life in the great struggle for the liberation of their homeland. Unable to undertake and play any further vigorous and active role, he was appointed Chairman of the ANC. He continued to interact with his people and exuded wisdom and advice despite his failing health.

Oliver Reginald Tambo, a colossus in the fight for the emancipation of Africa, passed away in April 1993 at the age of seventy-five years.

Nelson Rolihlahla Mandela

Nelson Mandela stared piercingly at the face of death and stoically pronounced the immortal words:

"I have cherished the ideal of a democratic and free society in which all persons will live together in harmony and with equal opportunities. It is an ideal for which I hope to live for and to see realised. But, My Lord, if it needs be, it is an ideal for which I am prepared to die."

An ideal that does not define humanity by skin colour; an ideal free from oppressive restrictions; an ideal that respects the life of Africans as humans; an ideal that allows Africans free access and ownership to their land; an ideal that Africans will be masters of their own destiny. Like Nelson Mandela, this is an ideal that the entire Africa should uphold and sustain in order to gain the respect and dignity of the race.

With those memorable words, Nelson Mandela, like a true African warrior, led his comrades on to Robben Island. An isolated prison where he spent eighteen years with hard labour out of his total twenty-seven years in custody, more than a quarter of his life. He and his colleagues were sentenced to life in prison where they were expected to perish.

Nelson Mandela and his co-accused were classified as terrorists and the African National Congress (ANC) was considered a terrorist and communist organisation by the United Kingdom and United States governments. A terrorist fighting for freedom from the brutal repressive regime of colonialism and apartheid; a terrorist fighting to reclaim his land from colonial occupation; a terrorist fighting for the respect and dignity of Africans.

The incarceration of Nelson Mandela and his colleagues did not stop the struggle for emancipation, rather, it provided fresh impetus to widespread political activism. Several Africans met their untimely death on the hands of the ruthless and mindless colonial bigots. During centuries of struggle for freedom from slavery, colonialism and apartheid, rivers of African blood have flown into the ocean of human indignity. The blood of Africans that must not be shed in vain, and the history of their struggles that must be kept alive.

On the 10th May 1994, Nelson Rolihlahla Mandela became the first African leader and President of the South Africa. On assuming office, President Mandela displayed unexpected humanity, dignity and respect for the sanctity of life. Vengeance, the watchword of oppressive colonialism, never once featured in his repertoire, much to the delight and relief of his erstwhile adversaries.

During his Presidency, Nelson Mandela showed the world over that supremacy is not derived from the complexion of one's skin, neither is it obtained from the shackles of slavery, nor from the brutality and coldness of colonial prisons, but from the ability to endure with humility and respect for humanity. After five years as president, he retired gracefully on the 14th June 1999 without hate or despise for anyone. Especially those who sort to destroy him, his family and his aspirations.

Nelson Rolihlahla Mandela, prisoner number 46664, lived the rest of his battle-weary life as a statesman and a father of Africa until he slipped away peacefully in December 2013 at the age of ninety-five.

It is a fervent hope that Africans can unite and recognise the need to establish and dedicate memorials across the continent to the evergreen memory of those mentioned here and other numerous men and women who in diverse ways resisted the enslavement and subjugation of their people but succumbed to the perils of their undertaking. The liberation and edification of Africans must continue.

****

There are countless number of Africans who through sweat, tears and blood made the ultimate sacrifice in the defence of their homeland and their human pride. They will always be remembered.

The heroism of Africans who resisted slavery from the mountains of Jamaica, those who forced their way out of the cotton fields of the Deep South in America and those whose unrelenting campaign precipitated the abolishing of the appalling trade in Africans must never be forgotten.

The certainty in this perennial struggle by Africans for dignity, freedom and respect is that bigotry and the ideology of supremacy defined by skin colour will not be eradicated through violence and endless marches alone but through unity, strategy, ideology and intellectualism amongst Africans.

The concept of *Black and White* colour coding developed from the scourge of slavery and invidiously labelling Africans as a pejoratively black race has been imprinted into the psyche of modern humanity. This concept has been systematically and methodically used to characterise Africans as villains and sub-human incapable of executing the simplest of tasks a less-than-average Caucasian (White) person would do. Africans (Blacks) have been made out to be unworthy of white compunction, and whites fervently believed that Africans (Blacks) were themselves responsible for their own capture and subjugation during slavery and colonisation.

Astonishingly, Africans have not been assertive enough to reject this characterisation but still allow themselves to be regarded as "*Black People*", "*Blackman*" or "*Black woman*" and "*Black Children*". This nomenclature has morphed into the generally accepted Blackman syndrome, cynically espoused by Caucasians to denigrate Africans. Africans are Africans and not Black people.

Over time, Africans have endured excruciating pain and suffering from deliberately-organised methods of subjugation inspired by hate. The insidiousness of this irrational hatred and unrelenting oppressive violence against an entire race, based on their skin complexion, defies the intelligence of ordinary human kind. The impunity of the perennial brutality against Africans by Caucasians tacitly legitimises centuries of subjugation and the brutal exploitation of a people. Astonishingly, those who perpetrated this horrendous suffering continue to exhibit and demonstrate unbelievable hate and prejudice against Africans the world over, with many honestly believing that such behaviour is ordained by God.

Africans should never forget their heroes who sacrificed their blood and paid the ultimate price in the pursuit of unrestrained freedom. The memory of the heinous savagery and barbarism of slavery must never be allowed to succumb to the effluxion of time. Africans should not be seduced by the culture of their oppressors and neglect what makes them a people.

Africans must initiate a cultural revolution that will motivate them towards achieving total mental liberation. Most importantly, Africans need to convert the fear and awe of colonialists inculcated in them through centuries of subjugation into individual self-esteem and a healthy respect for themselves and each other as Africans. Africans must recognise and uphold cultural values that differentiate them as a people and as a race from others. The inability of Africans to take this initiative has left generations vulnerable and susceptible to passive neo-colonialism and the continued mental conditioning of the people.

The horrendous criminal activities by the British and other European slavers in Bunce Island, "*the factory*", the labour camp in Namibia, Robben Island and throughout the continent must be preserved indelibly in history for the edification of future generations.

Whatever the socio-economic, political and religious circumstances are across Africa, one thing remains certain; the strategy to capture Africans into slavery that was modified to colonise the continent and subsequently to exert influences in post-colonial Africa will continue to morph and elude the ability of Africans to gravitate towards a unified force.

Will Africans within and away from Africa ever experience true freedom? That depends on how Africans the world over perceive themselves and recognise the unlimited potential that they can unleash through unity, community, collaboration and commitment.